Praise for *Man Overboard*

This engaging book is one that Bill Gates would be well-advised to read before he commits more money to fund programs designed by the educational establishment that has failed too many for too long. Gates won't be bored. Ric Klass is more than just a great teacher, he is also a great storyteller.

— Andrew Wolf,
Education Columnist,
the *New York Sun*

Ric Klass recounts his days as a math teacher in the Bronx with honesty and spunk. To watch him go from hoping to be a hero to just hoping to make it through the day is as humorous as it is heartbreaking. While irreverent at times, this page-turner of a memoir points to the pressing importance of finding solutions for our nation's struggling schools.

— Lauren McCollum,
TeachersCount.org

MAN OVERBOARD

Confessions of a
Novice Math Teacher
in the Bronx

Ric Klass

SEVEN LOCKS PRESS
Santa Ana, California

Seven Locks Press
P.O. Box 25689
Santa Ana, CA 92799
(800) 354-5348

Individual Sales. This book is available through most bookstores or can be ordered directly from Seven Locks Press at the address above.

Quantity Sales. Special discounts are available on quantity purchases by corporations, associations, and others. For details, contact the "Special Sales Department" at the publisher's address above.

Printed in the United States of America
Library of Congress Cataloging-in-Publication Data
is available from the publisher
ISBN 1-931643-86-5

Cover and content design by Heather Buchman
Author photo by João D. Andrade

All events described are true. The names of the high schools where the author taught—as well as the administrators, faculty and students—have been changed. The names of additional schools and administrators where he sought a teaching position have been changed as well.

DEDICATION

This book is dedicated to Joe and Hayley.

ACKNOWLEDGEMENTS

I am deeply indebted to many people for this book but especially to my wife and companion in my escapades, Anne, who has lovingly and unfailing supported my yen to live the life of a real Walter Mitty.

Many thanks:

To my publisher Jim Riordan for seeing the potential of my manuscript and to my editor Sharon Young, for her patience, sharp pen, and enthusiasm.

To Doyle Saez, whom I tutored and who first inspired me to teach in the Bronx and gave me permission to use his real name in this book. I learned more from his perseverance and courage to succeed than he ever learned from me.

To my brother, Jim, for his permission to use his teaching experiences and our times together in this book.

To my other brother, John Stadler, for his encouragement to write a diary of my misadventures and this book, and for his many insightful editorial comments.

To my students in the Bronx who suffered through my first year of teaching as much as I suffered teaching them. Although I didn't use their real names, they really wrote this book. I just typed it up.

To David Liebowitz for his expert advice.

And finally:

To my colleagues, the many inspiring and hardworking teachers who, thank goodness for such angels of mercy, stick through it year after year trying to help inner city kids who need our help the most.

INTRODUCTION

This story is a true tale of hubris and woe—mine. Many non-fiction accounts of inner-city teachers depict bright, young, enthusiastic college grads struggling against the hardships of their jobs and the difficulties of the children they're trying desperately to help; they overcome ignorance and prejudice by converting their young disciples into lovers of Shakespeare and Bach. That isn't my story.

Man Overboard chronicles the sad, comical, and even frightening daily routine of frustrations and pathos endured by a change-of-career liberal and would-be math teacher—me. Crash and burn summarizes my feeble attempts to help underprivileged high school kids—a tortuous and torturous trail inflicted by school administrators; the teachers' union; my own uncontrolled anger; and most of all, by the little darlings themselves. My former careers as aerospace engineer, market researcher, economic consultant, entrepreneur, university lecturer, filmmaker, and investment banker somehow led me down a terrifying path to that of an urban high school teacher. This is my actual journal—revealing both my pathetic setbacks and sporadic success.

On a splendid Sunday afternoon in the fall of 1992 at a Democratic booth in the Rye, New York, Village Green, I met the head of special education of a nearby high school. In passing, she told me that one of her students, a struggling junior from an immigrant Hispanic family, had just decided he wanted to go to college. Without giving it much thought, I volunteered to tutor him. Unknowingly, I had started my slow march off the plank—a new career. Beginning yet another plunge for me into the void of ignorance—traveling boldly where men had gone before—teaching high school mathematics to disadvantaged (can I say "ghetto"?) children in a public school. I think many of my predecessors knew what they were doing. I didn't.

Here's the thing. I had a victory with this boy and before long extrapolated it in my mind into changing the world. Perhaps show school administrators and teachers a thing or two about helping teenagers learn math. Maybe start my own student training programs. Yes, I could easily envision modest me humbly accepting accolades for changing the entire formerly intractable dilemma of instructing New York City's 1.1 million students. There's nothing like shooting a lucky basket that makes a man think he erred by not trying a little harder in high school to make the team and eventually going pro. It's easy—nay, nearly inevitable—to be a hero in your own mind. In other people's minds is a very different story—and by now it's clear that isn't my yarn. Before I started my journey in the Bronx, I didn't grasp the dramatic difference from helping my former disciple. Tutoring one highly motivated, exceptionally well-intentioned and polite boy was going to bear no resemblance to handling the disparate, untrained, unschooled, and unprepared freshmen thrust into my lap. This is a story prepackaged with schadenfreude that might make a reader very happy not to be there—except . . .

Except . . .

SEMESTER ONE

What You Doing Here, White Boy?

"Yeah. What's you doin' here in the Bronx?"

This from two black boys in the front row. I don't know their names. Leaning forward in their seats, they glare angrily at me as though they'd like to lunge up and punch me. The time is 4:20 P.M., September 8, 2003—my first day of teaching math at Central Bronx High School. Or at any other high school for that matter. This is the beginning of my final class of the day, a double period lasting until 5:46 P.M. . . . if I live that long. I'm a newborn high school teacher and this is my baptism of fire.

It gets worse. Room 213 has stadium seating so that a dozen of the thirty-three kids on my roster sit so far back they might as well be in Yankee Stadium, elsewhere in the Bronx. Now catcalls and wads of paper begin floating down to the front and land at my feet. The wide-open door leads to the deserted hallway. Most of the building has already emptied. The more than 3,000 children overcrowding CBHS have forced the administrators to create two shifts. Upperclassmen in the morning. Freshmen start around noon. Only a few classes remain in this huge, one city-block-wide, four-story edifice. This freshman algebra class sits toward the rear of the building. For all intents and purposes, I'm in this maelstrom alone with them—sink or swim.

"What now?" I ask myself. If these kids know I'm intimidated, they'll get really bold. I try to ignore the comments and start taking attendance.

Oh—and there are abandoned lockers in the back of the room. Loud, vibrating clangs bring them into focus. The kids there are walking around, vigorously opening and slamming them shut.

"Sit down and shut up or I'll call the police to do it for me," I scream red-faced at them.

This is a bluff. I know there's no help. I don't have the key yet to the emergency telephone and my cell phone battery is dead. I'm truly frightened that these kids will get so out of control they'll hurt each other and very likely me. But I am very angry besides being scared.

My rage exceeds their childish malice. Slowly and with a great show of disdain, the mischievous elves take their seats. The day has already been a nightmare. The kids resent coming back from summer vacation. And the last thing they want to hear about is anything to do with math. Every one of my four sections has been a struggle; the kids are barely willing to acknowledge their presence when I take roll call. It requires a continuous mixture of threats and pleadings to get them to fill out their names, addresses, telephone numbers, and school ID on the tiny Delaney cards, the official registry of attendance.

I fight every inch of the way for some quiet and a little cooperation. A pep rally and football game outside, below our windows, doesn't help a bit. I can't keep the kids from jumping up and craning wistfully at the freedom they desperately crave.

As the time crawls towards 6:00, I wonder whose bright idea it was to have the youngest children scheduled so late in the day. I'm knocked out and these little toughs are exhausted, too.

And get this: It wasn't even the bad luck of a short straw that I drew the late shift. I asked for it! The other teachers begged for the morning session. I told the head of the math department that I wanted an assignment that would assure me I could spend the entire year with my acolytes. I didn't want them to feel I had abandoned them after the first semester. In the movie *What About Bob?* Richard Dreyfuss, a psychiatrist, leaves his patient, Bill Murray, with disastrous consequences. I don't want my little ones to get a neurosis on my watch. From what I know of urban children, they might have had enough bad parenting already. Be careful of what you wish for . . .

When I arrive home, my wife says I'm ashen. I look and feel shaken. Today I dodged a knife or maybe a bullet. What about tomorrow? After my explanation, she's all for my throwing in the towel right now and moving my private equity firm back to Greenwich, Connecticut. A change of career can wait until I land a teaching assignment in cushy Westchester County or at a prep school.

Many of my friends congratulated me on my brave and noble decision to become a math teacher in the Bronx. I was sort of enjoying the kudos until this awakening. Decades ago, I taught Entrepreneurship to seniors in the business school at Georgetown University. Those undergrads were bright, energetic, and unstoppably on their way to the doors of financial and career success. That was the problem. I felt I wasn't making a big enough difference to them. They liked me just fine and I got high marks in student evaluations, but I was only whipped cream on the dessert of their education—not the main course. Not a big enough kick for me, I guess.

In contrast, over a decade ago I successfully tutored a disadvantaged Hispanic boy. I was a catalyst that helped him change his life. That's what I'm looking for now. You know, crescendo music at the end of the movie with yours truly humbly taking a bow—*Goodbye, Mr. Chips*, with a cooler guy like me.

A WEEK EARLIER—TUESDAY, SEPTEMBER 2

T Minus 5

As I enter CBHS, I walk by the principal's office my first day on the school payroll. On either side of his door hang large banners. On the left, a lemon yellow sign in red letters proclaims: "OUR GOAL . . . To empower all students to succeeding [sic] in a changing world." On the right, a red and white banner with blue letters: "Education is a team effort." Below it hangs a black flag with the gold lettering of the University of Vermont. I wonder why this particular college is singled out.

Before actually beginning classes, the powers that be of the New York City School Department of Education decide to give freshman teachers some introductory seminars on what we will face the following week. First, we have a greeting session in the auditorium led by the principal, George Gillman. Only he doesn't end the meeting as our principal. He's retiring and hands over the baton right then and there to Linda Fuego. Before taking a seat permanently, Gillman also mentions that several of last June's graduates now attend the University of Vermont. That's nice, I think. Good for them. Maybe they'll learn to ski. I also think, so what? CBHS has thousands of kids attending this tower of learning. Why is he talking about so few of them? What happened to the rest of our scholars?

Linda now takes charge and lets us know there's a new format for teaching this year called point-of-entry. With a humorless delivery and a pretty blank expression, she tells us it's "the latest push."

The Latest Push

Gone are the days when the teacher is expected to teach the students something—anything. No, very outdated. Our new breed of educators refers to this antiquated concept scornfully as "chalk and talk."

The major push by educators these days takes two forms: (a) student-centered teaching and (b) cooperative learning. Teachers must make the educational impetus come from the children. It's about the kids, stupid—not the teacher. Teachers should encourage the students to draw on their own experiences to discover math. Calculate square roots using what you've learned from rappers. Kind of like spawning little Isaac Newtons who discover gravity by apples dropping on their heads. Additionally, children can better learn from each other rather than have some has-been bore them to death. Instruction shall now be imparted in about ten minutes—at the outside—in what's called a "mini-lesson." The remainder of the period leaves the little philosopher kings to discover for

themselves, in groups of four or so, the joy of solving simul-
taneous equations—and better yet, instruct their slower,
albeit willing, peers. There you have it, Gilbert and Sullivan
classrooms: educational skim milk masquerading as cream.

Linda strikes me as what she has probably been for some years, an efficient paper pusher. Not at all a leader we want to follow into a pitched battle. I'm new here and don't know to what extent leadership will play a role in her also-new position. I'll find out soon enough.

Model Behavior

The point-of-entry model consists of an interactive mini-
lesson by the teacher, to be followed by independent and then
group work, preferably in herds of two to five kids. The more the
merrier, it seems. Then, in whole-class sharing, the groups
report to the class the results of their efforts. Meanwhile, the
teacher engages in individual child assessment and encourages
self-correction strategies. This pinnacle of pedagogy concludes
with the children summarizing the essential points that were
learned during the session. These points should be the objectives
the teacher has written on the blackboard before the class begins.
And, between us girls, Joel Klein, the Department of Education
Chancellor and notorious former anti-Microsoft gladiator, will
be sending spies to monitor us closely—to see that we don't
screw up. Or more likely, simply ignore his directive.

Simple, *n'est pas*? The tenured teachers express their reaction in loud groans. I don't know what to think. My singular exposure to group work only reinforced my prejudice against it. I only know I'm here to do a good job helping urban children. I want to resist my natural "I'll do it my way" mindset. I'll try to do whatever is expected. At the confab's conclusion, I try to congratulate Linda on her promotion, but get brushed off. I don't really care. I'm here to teach, not to socialize. Still, I wonder how she'll treat the teachers now that she's the top dog here.

I'd been advised by teachers in the know to corner a supply of lockers for my own use. So, after the welcome, but before the introductory seminars, I lose no time in staking out my territory. With my combination locks in hand, I snag one in each of the rooms I'll be using. By no means am I the first to claim real estate. Some lockers display bold signs, proclaiming title and warning against interlopers. Judging by the faded paper taped on them, the large coat lockers were no doubt appropriated in ancient times. Perhaps when Gaea still ruled and the Titans had not yet walked the earth, squatters seized this terra with:

"DO NOT CLIP. PROPERTY OF SO AND SO."

Goodness gracious, such possessiveness. I promptly post the same admonitions on my metal turf.

WEDNESDAY, SEPTEMBER 3

Taking Inventory

I size up the other math teachers as the seminars continue. I'm still operating under the misconception that a superior knowledge of mathematics will play a part in my role here. I wonder if the others really know the subject at all. One reads about the substandard teachers in the U.S. foisted upon our children, but to my pleasant surprise I find a strong math department.

Several very smart and successful change-of-career people hang their hats here. Rob Simmons, 6'2", lean and balding, whom I met at the faculty lunch last June, was a big-time Wall Street honcho for twenty years. He managed perhaps billions of dollars. Teaching is a significant cost to Rob whose investment career in asset management, I think, put him on par with The Street's elite. He's a quiet guy, the kind who, when he does talk, you want to listen. Rob's in his fourth year, and the more I know him, the more I feel he is the kind of guy I want in the foxhole with me.

Another of the faculty is a Ph.D. in pharmacology. Several others are former computer mavens who certainly must know their way around a math curriculum. The career teachers aren't chopped liver, either. They appear intelligent and hard-working, but gripes about the school system dominate their casual conversations.

Dear John

No bathroom key continues as a minor annoyance. The secretary for Mr. Santino, the new replacement as Assistant Principal of Organization, says that keys have to be cut for the new teachers. Would I fill out the proper application?

"Will hopping up and down on one leg hurry the process?" I think, but don't ask. I'm still the new duck on the pond here.

Mission Possible

I'm feeling upbeat. My immediate supervisor, Mr. Tqiqi, the Assistant Principal of Mathematics, oozes with the old-world grace, charm, and civility from his native Algeria. He gives me my class assignments. Not too shabby—only twenty-three periods a week. The usual number is twenty-five classes a week, or five per day. I'm assigned all freshmen. Good. I'm happy I won't have too great a load in my first semester, as I soon will begin my Mercy College courses. Maybe I'll get lucky and even be able to teach the same students as they progress to higher-level courses. I'd even volunteer to work the late (unpopular) shift if he can guarantee my request. I get the late shift, but no guarantee.

In my own high school days, I had the same elder, graying math teacher, John Schacht, for the last three years. All the students held him in awe. Misbehavior was unheard of in his class. His "harrumph" when kids were absent on field trips scared me from ever going on one. Although I went to a small Midwestern public school, every year many of his students went to the best colleges. What a great accomplishment if I could do the same for my own apprentices. And from the Bronx!

We also get into a discussion about the use of calculators in the classroom. Mr. T. claims even if the students have calculators, they won't know how to use them. I do a mental double-take. His candor takes me by surprise. Maybe I'm in for other surprises.

The Parking Game

may be my biggest headache. Around the corner, residents of several rent-subsidized, high-rise apartment buildings mop up most of the available spaces. No on-site spots at the school available, of course. In the opposite direction, other schools' employees snatch the spots. Competition also comes from office complexes across the street. I'm driving around and around the nearby blocks, scouting a legal void for my chariot. It's aggravating. Why can't they—whoever "they" are—provide us noble teachers with parking? Having my own space in Greenwich for the past few years has spoiled me. I know that, but my nose is out of joint anyway during my endless cruises around the block. So commences the first of many importunate episodes in my public school teaching career—insults to my still secretly inflated ego.

Book Deliveries

After the seminars end, I use my spare time delivering textbooks to my strategically located lockers. I spread them around on different floors and opposite sides of the building so that I'm not far from where I'll need to eventually deliver them. Mr. T. directs us not to distribute the books to the students for two weeks or so, which I find peculiar. I'm told there's considerable moving around of students in and out of courses, and the teachers are responsible for the books they've doled out. If I give books to students who migrate to other classes, I'll never have any leverage getting them returned. The freshman books are new and supposedly cost NYC sixty bucks a pop. When you multiply that by the number of freshmen and sophomores in New York City, it adds up to a lot of do-ray-me. The school is not kidding about salvaging these books.

Girding for Battle

What's the best way to prepare myself for next week? Watching old movies, of course. I rent three videos. It hasn't occurred to me before that Sidney Poitier played both sides of school's natural enemies: a teacher in *To Sir With Love* and a student in *Blackboard Jungle*. He was a bit long in the tooth for the latter, though. While the films all had upbeat endings, I hope my life in the Bronx won't mimic Glenn Ford's character in *Blackboard Jungle*. A knife fight with a troubled teenager isn't in my plans. Edward James Olmos' role in *Stand and Deliver*, as the real-life math teacher who inspired his young wards to excel at calculus, catches my fancy. As I watch the film, I envision myself leading my own students on the path of knowledge and all that good stuff against the odds and adversity. I'm a hero, too. I surge with emotion stemming from the gratitude of my scholars and peers. And then the credits roll, bringing me back to reality. But I'm pumped for Monday.

MONDAY, SEPTEMBER 8

Blast Off!

Surprise. All my classes are changed. Now, instead of a light load of twenty-three classes per week, I have twenty-seven. Two more than the standard, union-sanctioned twenty-five. I have the afternoon shift that lasts up until 5:50. Boy, I asked for the late shift and got it—and I got the early shaft as well. Mr. T. says not to worry. He'll make up for the extra classes in my schedule next term.

Well In Formed

We're handed the itsy bitsy Delaney cards, a legal document I'm told, for the attendance of each child. We must circle the kids' first day of attendance on its perpetual calendar. Victor, a veteran teacher and CBHS's resident quidnunc who seems to know all the ins and outs of the educational bureaucracy, gives me an example of the importance of these little dealies. If, say, a boy commits a crime and I mistakenly mark down that he's present, then maybe I'll be held responsible for his whereabouts at the time of the crime. I'm not sure if I buy all that, but I take his word that they need to be accurate. He gives me another tip. Be sure to get the kids to write down their telephone numbers on the cards. Catch the little devils off-guard. They'll never give it to you straight once they realize you'll use it to call their parents to complain about them. Am I going to be doing a lot of that?

Lots of busywork today. We also have multiple bubble attendance sheets to mark—both a daily and weekly, that will be collected by roving administration assistants interrupting the class, and a version for homeroom teachers (that's me). For one of my classes, that's four copies of attendance for each child. What time-and-motion expert dreamed this up? The fact that the other teachers don't consider it the burden I do doesn't ease the aggravation I feel. Nor do I stop to consider that maybe it's my own inflexibility that's to blame.

What I'm not told is that I'll have to keep repeating the procedure over the next several days, handling a steady stream of surly, tardy kids and late arrivals. I'll also be wasting class time to mark absent loads of kids who have already transferred out. The attendance sheets don't reflect these changes until weeks later. And then there are the many kids who show up only once or twice. It's not that they've transferred out (they stay on the roster). They simply never come again. Ever.

Keys

If I'm ever a supervisor again—and I hope that's never—my first item of business will be to fork over all the keys needed by hirees to get into the building, office, desk, filing cabinet, and water closet. These first few days have been difficult enough, but I can't get into the teachers' lounge, my classrooms, or the men's room. In the meantime, when nature calls, I either have to wait patiently for custodians wandering past, or flag down some harried male teacher.

TUESDAY, SEPTEMBER 9

Trouble in Paradise

While I don't have an out-and-out riot like yesterday's last class, the landscape's a lot different than I expected. I start to ease into the subject material, but new kids keep piling in and interrupting my train of thought. The children are mostly rude, unprepared for high school, and maybe worst of all, very easily distracted. I do have a few respectful children, but they say nothing to their peers about the disruptive behavior all around them. Just getting through the day seems a formidable task for me. Tate Hornsby and Peyton James—I know their names now—in my 14th period class spew out more "white boy" remarks that I ignore—for the last time.

Outreach

CBHS requires all teachers to regularly phone parents. Give them feedback on their child's behavior. The teachers, including me, already want and need the parents' help to bring the students under control. Others, again including me, and this time in spades, also see it as a kind of revenge on the little brigands. Another more touchy-feely theory floats around. Calling a kid's parents to complain lets the child know you have no ability to handle the situation yourself. Essentially, you're not there to help, but to spy—just another adult who's out to punish. Part of my brain buys that hypothesis, but since I'm required to call homes by the powers that be, I don't fret over it (the notorious "I was taking orders" defense). A few teachers warn me that I can expect some of the parents to be as hostile to me as their children are. Personally speaking, I never encounter any parent that isn't grateful for my call. Mr. T. also encourages us to make positive calls, praising offspring, when warranted.

I make my first outreach call today to Melinda Vasquez's home. A woman with a different last name than Melinda's says she's the mother. I soon learn this is the norm, not the exception. Melinda already stands out in my class as a championship pain in the rear. Refuses to stop talking. And when I describe her as "insubordinate" to her mother, it's only sugarcoating "crude" and "vulgar." The mother tells me Melinda had the same problem in junior high and says she will talk to her. When I hang up, I consider that if Melinda's behavior is nothing new, mom's one-on-one talking to her now probably won't do the trick. I make a bunch of other calls but don't get a hold of anyone.

The Faculty Men's Room

Any man will tell you the top priority for any new job is the answer to: "Where's the men's room?" Wisely, the faculty has a separate men's room from the boys', and it's keyed! Not a bad idea, but the assistant principal's office still has no keys and I have to fill out another application to get one. Misplaced the last one or something. In the air, I smell the beginning of a long series of bureaucratic obstacles to smooth sailing at CBHS.

The third-floor men's room seems particularly noxious. As one would guess, the two commodes, solitary urinal, and washbasin—all plumbed within a few square feet of each other—squeeze in more than full occupancy between class periods. However, the stench, unflushed toilets, and paper towels clogging the pissoir disturb me the most. Are students getting in here? I think not. In an emergency, without a key to the staff sanctum sanctorum, I use the boys' restroom. It's perfectly acceptable and in a decent sanitary condition. Is it possible that the teachers don't know to flush the john or dispose of hand towels?

Who's the culprit? I suspiciously eye the hall guards—"Deans" they're called here. I consider surreptitiously taping notes to the walls . . .

FLUSH THE TOILETS—YOU PIGS!
THROW THE TOWELS IN THE TRASH—DIMWITS!

. . . but reconsider. What if novice teacher me gets caught posting hate notes in the john? I'm also irritated that the towels run out by mid-day so that I must either: (a) not wash my hands—evidently a common practice here; (b) wipe my hands on my pants; or (c) use copious quantities of toilet paper. Typically, I choose the last resort.

I haven't spent much time on the first floor, but after a meeting there late in the day, I visit the faculty men's room. I'm immediately suspicious—clean, no odor, toilets flushed, no towels in the urinal or sink, and TWO (!!) dispensers of towels with lots left in both. This conspiracy doesn't elude my Hercule Poirot eye and nose. This *toilette* is down the hall from the assistant principal's office and, of course, he must have a decent restroom. In my mind, this inequity explains why teachers support a union—just to fight against such injustice. I now realize the men's room experience sinks decidedly with each floor I climb. I decide to never use the men's room on the fourth floor. I don't think I can take it. A creature of habit, I use the third-floor men's room anyway, despite the unpleasantness. Have I turned into a Ms. Priss?

WEDNESDAY, SEPTEMBER 10

Getting to Know You

I start to get to know more of the math faculty. The group as a whole is racially and culturally diverse. For example, Marisa. She's calm, pretty, blonde, and Russian. I love her accent. She surprises me when she says she's teaching thirty-five kids in bilingual Spanish class although she doesn't speak Spanish. She and her husband are observant Jews; she pays for Friday coverage of her late afternoon classes so she can be home for the Sabbath. Then there's Will Gerard, who seems severe but whom I think is a clandestine softie. He's another former computer expert who knows the ropes around CBHS. Another good source to learn the lay of the land.

Stand and Deliver Redux

I decide to lay a trap for the next kid who cracks some "white boy" comment. I'm going to imitate Edward James Olmos' speech in *Stand and Deliver*. Last summer in "Technology 609," at Mercy College, I created a neat little interactive PowerPoint presentation on the history of mathematics. It has an extra focus on math's origin in cultures of color. I patiently wait for my prey. Peyton is my first victim. On cue, at his first "white boy" sneer, I launch into my act.

Me, perfectly calm and upbeat, "I'm glad you said that, Peyton," I commence with a smile. His wide-eyed reaction whets my appetite for the upcoming, delicious treat. I inform them cultures from all over the world, encompassing more than thirty languages and representing Latin America, Asia, Africa, and Eastern Europe, comprise the Central Bronx High School student body. I emphasize that in my classes, regardless of a student's cultural heritage, his/her background includes a tradition in mathematics.

I won't let the kids get off easy after Peyton's unwise gibe. I continue. For the past 5,000 years, mathematics has been part of the history of all cultures. Mayans discovered the number zero. A small number of Mayan documents have survived destruction, including ones in major museums of the world.

I echo the dialogue from the movie, "If you're Hispanic, then mathematics is in your blood."

I'm not nearly done. Egyptians and other ancient cultures used advanced mathematics for the prediction of seasons, and solar and lunar events. Multiplication and division were invented for the extensive trade they conducted, I tell them.

Reiterating my theme, "If you're black, then mathematics is in your blood."

I go on to talk about Asia and Greece. I mention Kepler and Newton, but pretty much downplay Western Europe's role in math. It isn't the point I'm trying to make to these minority students.

"Mathematics knows no boundaries of race or color. It is an intellectual pursuit for all mankind. There is no race in my class, just students of mathematics," I emote in conclusion. The kids got the picture midway through my talk but I'm not going to show any mercy after Peyton's rudeness. And I want to make sure it won't happen again or they'll have to listen to the entire speech once more. I'm sure they hear what I'm saying, for a change. They might think the message is corny, but they don't show it. At the least, they know I believe in their ability to learn the subject. The day ends with my feeling quite pleased with myself. I need more of this. But I've got to change this room. The amphitheater seating and continuous noise outside is too disruptive.

Ms. Abrahamson

In every big organization, there's an obnoxious obstruction to progress—someone who's been a veteran too long to fire and too vital to the functioning of the organization to antagonize. Joyce Abrahamson, weighing in appropriately with the title Program Chair, plays this role at CBHS. I antagonize her anyway.

Ms. Abrahamson looks wide and formidable enough to have been placed in her swivel chair with the laying of the foundation of the building. She's queen of scheduling, programming, and classroom designations—and no one gets in her way. I'm getting nowhere with her changing my room. The auditorium seating of the 14th period class seems more hazardous every day. So far, the missiles from the back have been paper, but the near riot of the other day forebodes worse aerial attacks to come. My request for a new venue doesn't even deserve consideration. "Too busy . . . still scheduling . . . not possible . . . not now," quickly flows from her curled lips. I'm summarily dismissed. But not terminated. I'll be back.

The Little Darlings

Most of the freshmen who attend CBHS are incredibly difficult human beings. It's not that they're bad people. They are not. And they aren't hoodlums or bad seeds. What they are is a combination of all the usual tribulations of adolescence plus an immaturity that places them at kindergarten behavior. Right from the playground directly to high school. In one way or another, most of them were socially promoted to CBHS in the first place. Here, they hit a concrete wall of passing the Regents exams or not graduating. Add to all that a history of failure in school, a high proportion of dysfunctional families, and—I'll bet a donut and coffee to anyone's nickel—a high incidence of attention deficit disorders. What are these kids then? Big babies with lots of problems. I don't know if I'm up to the challenge.

Take, for instance, Alvin in my 14th period class. Many of my perpetual nuisances like to sit as far away from me as possible so that their antics can go mostly unnoticed or at least partially hidden. Not so with Alvin. He sits so close to me he's practically in my lap. But he's a nonstop buffoon anyway. I go to a student's desk to answer a question and when I get back, my grade book is missing from my desk. I'm riled. Alvin swears he has nothing to do with its loss. As the bell rings, Alvin asks me if that's the missing spoils on the floor next to my desk halfway between us. Just childish nonsense, but it's going on all the time in all my classes.

Demarco Boynton, Khalid Salmans, and Johnny Carton run neck to neck with Alvin for disruption prizewinners in my classes. But they're not easily categorized. To paraphrase Tolstoy, all good kids are alike but each problem child is a bête noir in his own way. Demarco, probably the smartest of the three, has the genius of perfect timing. This interloper has a penchant for pushing, shoving, and occasionally climbing on the tables. Mostly in fun. He knows exactly when I'm ready to bounce him from the class and call for military backup. He ceases his high jinks on a dime. He also hates my guts and makes it obvious to me and the rest of the class. I'm not sure why. I'm on his case, but not more than the other noisemakers. Khalid is sly. Tries unsuccessfully to hide his juvenile travesties of pestering the girls, throwing spitballs, nonstop gabbing, and general mischief making. At least Khalid does it all with a smile. Even his scowls when I try to put him in line somehow seem good-natured. As a teacher and an adult, it makes me feel bad to admit I plain don't like Carton. He strikes me as mean-spirited. He's fond of insulting his classmates, especially defenseless girls, and adds a continuous background rumble to the noise level.

THURSDAY, SEPTEMBER 11

Today I give my first quiz worth only three points to all my classes just to wake them up. What a jolt of reality for them. Now they know vacation really has ended.

End Run

I don't like taking no for an answer. I haven't yet shaken the misconception that I'm doing the world a big fat favor by teaching here. I used to earn an actual decent living and the $43,786 I'm making, from my point of view, constitutes a gift to NYC. I want to do good work here, but please allow me a decent chance to at least survive. At any rate, I form a new game plan. Go around Ms. Abrahamson by appealing directly to her supervisor, Mr. Rhoda.

I take matters into my own hands and tiptoe into Ms. Abrahamson's lair. As soon as I walk in, she glares at me. With some kind of animal instinct, she knows I spell trouble (i.e., a change in plans) for her and lets out an almost imperceptible grunt. A distinct grimace emerges on her expansive physiognomy in currents spreading from her squinty eyes and rippling across her fleshy jowls. She projects vehement rejection before I even cross the portcullis of her den.

Me, ignoring the corpulent bacchante, "I've got to change rooms, Mr. Rhoda. The kids are fifty yards from me, completely unmanageable, and the sounds of the football practice booming in at the end of the day drives them and me crazy."

Amiable Mr. Rhoda looks sheepishly at Ms. Abrahamson. Equal doses of fear and administrative respect manifest themselves in his tone and demeanor. She's acutely tuned into the fact I'm trying to end run her. She calls an ominous audible, "There are no available rooms. I'm busy with important scheduling that must get done," she signals.

Rhoda punts. "Ric, gee, I'm sorry. We're kind of fouled up. We'll see what we can do."

I'm still not out of the game as far as I'm concerned. Changing venues, I now decide to score a win with Mr. T.

I get my hands on a bathroom key today. Thank goodness for small favors. And a second small victory. Before the 14th period class, I ask Peyton and Tate if they want to hear my speech about the history of mathematics again. No. "OK then, enough with the 'white boy' jazz." Their nods of resignation tell me I'm done with that particular irritant.

FRIDAY, SEPTEMBER 12

The T-L

The teachers' lounge has quickly become my primary refuge. This aerie nests on the third floor, conveniently next to Mr. T.'s office. The marred, windowless door lacks any signage, making it an inconspicuous burrow for we downtrodden instructors. On its face, the approximate 15' by 20' dimensions make the T-L seem adequate, but certainly not luxurious. A black, battered couch rests under the windows opposite the entry door.

On the left, three different types of copying machines do heavy duty for the entire school. Actually, two of them have been reserved for the math department. I never found out how this feat was accomplished, though I suspect that Mr. Santino, the Administrative Assistant Principal who used to teach math, has a hand in it. Administrators, including Santino and Mr. T., have their own gear.

A tall, handsome cupboard—with two glass-paneled doors packed mostly with math books— occupies the near wall. On top, storage boxes bearing Will Gerard's name cram together with enough room for maybe one more box—mine. A few nondescript prints blight the three windowless walls in hopeless decoration. One homely copy of a copy even has a tag denoting that a former teacher—a lasting humiliation to him, in my opinion—donated it. Long tables facing each other pack the central area. All day long the staff comes by to grade papers, gossip, eat lunch, or just splash down and screen themselves from the kids. The microwave on the immediate right hums throughout the day from constant use. The odors of foreign cuisines wafting from it and the variety of languages, ethnicities, and cultures in the room remind me of the famous bar scene in *Star Wars*.

A water cooler sits tucked in the far right corner. One of the jug delivery guys tells me later that the dispenser has never been cleaned. An almost certain health hazard. And speaking of viruses . . . on the rest of the right wall, four out-of-date computers line up, all firmly bolted to the table—and rightfully so, I might add. They're networked to the far right by a solitary HP laser printer. Not a vast resource for so many teachers, but not the worst one could imagine. Except—two of the computers don't work at all (and never do for the whole year). Also—both mice on the hypothetically working PCs have gone kaflooey so that I can't get the arrow to go directly where I aim it—the pointers float all over the monitors. That's not the end of it. Of the two more-or-less working computers, one of them has a variety of digital diseases surging through its microprocessor veins and keeps slipping into a coma.

I'm not done complaining. My prima donna attitude still has far to go before it disembodies. The infected computer is the master PC that controls the printer. If the viral PC is down, the printer doesn't work either. One could easily spend all his free time finagling with these problems. That "one" is often me. I gradually discover the primary use of the PCs isn't creating lesson plans or preparing tests, anyhow. No, siree. The computers are jammed with letters to friends, principles of investing (not even remotely a school subject), and oodles of resumes.

The printer does make nice copies, though—when it works. It has its own shutting-down idiosyncrasy. Sometimes, for no apparent reason, it also refuses to work. Juanquier, one of the other math docents, shows me a trick. Take off the side panel and press the loose a/c wire connector back into place. Works like a charm. So, all in all, the T-L has one operational computer, a detail I consistently neglect to share with the computational *illiterati* among the faculty who occasionally drop in for a Microsoft Windows quickie. In the valley of the blind, the one-eyed geek reigns supreme.

Exceptions to the Rule

The headache coterie of classroom clowns has dominated my thinking for the past few days. But I'm trying to accentuate whatever positives I can find, as well. Thank God there are at least a few silver-plated linings in these turbulent clouds. The good news is that not all of the youthful multitude acts out on a regular basis. The bad news is that 80 percent of them do. Kenya Maftah comprises part of the exception. Judging from his accent, he might be from Africa. Not only does he pay attention, but he demands that I pay attention to him. All the time. When he has a question, he wants me to stop whatever I'm doing. Right then and there. Not in a minute or two. Kenya is vocal about his demands, as well. He shouts at me to halt and come over to his table. Now. So he's making himself a pest of a different kind. He's doing poorly in math but I respect the ferocity of his determination to succeed. Stella Vantino is another complainer, insisting on personal and instant tutoring during class. But to the poison pot she adds bitter complaints about my teaching and uninterrupted yakety-yaking with her girl-friends when not being personally catered to. If only all the kids had it in them to demand an education. Nevertheless, I wish those two would give me a break and pipe down a bit so I could at least try to teach the others.

The minority of students who are struggling to get an education just keep their heads down without complaints to their peers about the incessant misbehavior. There are other exceptions. Joselyn Bando sits in the front row, tunes out her classmates, and tries like the devil to take it all in. Not all that successfully, I'm afraid. She knows this and anxiety squeezes out of her every pore. But I think her efforts will pay off. The same goes for Brandi Ailey, notable for her friendly disposition.

Ms. Abrahamson–Last Round

Besides verbally badgering Mr. T. about my room change, I try to land an organizational uppercut by putting it in writing. Kind of a low blow, but I figure possibly effective.

Mr. Tqiqi,

I would like to request a room change from room 213—period 14, Math M#A1 Sect 11.

The reasons are as follows:
1. The large class size is not appropriate for stadium seating, especially for freshmen.
2. Guards are not present on this floor at that time, creating an unsafe environment for the students and me.
3. The room's large windows make for an unacceptably hot room in the late afternoon.
4. The room's windows face the football field, which at 5–6 pm presents an unacceptable distraction to the students due to the presence of sports practice at that time.

Respectfully submitted,
Ric Klass

By the time I hand it to Mr. T., I'm fairly sure he sweet talked Ms. Abrahamson into relenting, because at the end of the day I get a new room assignment. Leave it to him to gain an amazing knockout.

SATURDAY, SEPTEMBER 13

What TGIF Means

I never appreciated what a weekend meant before. When I had my own homebuilding company in Washington, D.C., I would sometimes notice my secretaries putting on their coats, and say, seriously, "Lunchtime, already?"

"Ric, it's 5:30." I'd lost all track of time. It became an almost standard joke at the office.

Nevertheless, I'm no workaholic and enjoy a day off. But today I'm recovering, as if from major surgery. I treasure every hour away from that chamber of mutual adult and child torture—school.

MONDAY, SEPTEMBER 15

On the Level

Before students enter high school, the New York City School system has already academically rated them in Levels. They are 1, 2, 3, and 4. The Level 4 child is blessed—strong academics, good in standardized testing, likely to go to college. And another thing, definitely not enrolled at CBHS. The Level 3 kid is your average hale-fellow, well met. Doing okay—not knocking your or his socks off, but probably will make it through high school. Maybe go on to college and even graduate school. We don't see much of her/him either in our neck of the woods. Now we come to our constituency, the 1s and 2s. The 2s aren't doing too well. Below average and struggling—it's going to be a challenge to get through high school. We've got plenty of them. The 1s? Need I say? They're everywhere at CBHS. And, don't you know, we're supposed to keep the rating secret from the kids if we teachers happen to uncover them from a guidance counselor or by some other miracle. But we don't really need to see the scores. The children broadcast their low ratings in every class with their inattention and lack of skills. CBHS in its entirety should be classified as a special education institution with all the attendant personnel required to help these children. Obviously, the school's not pigeonholed that way. Too expensive for the taxpayers. Anyhow, I'm filled with enthusiasm for the task at hand. Helping needy kids is why I took this voyage.

"Mr. T., you know why I'm here. I'm going to raise the kids one rank, maybe to a two," I exclaim breathlessly when he's laid out the level facts about CBHS to me. Mr. T., very polite and politic, "Well, that's good you want to do so well." His cautious reply reveals his courteous skepticism. I know I will prove him wrong. Really, on the level.

I score another small administrative victory. I get an elevator key. I need one to take the overhead projector floor to floor. My blackboard chalk writing is a joke. The kids can't read it, and neither can I.

MONDAY, SEPTEMBER 15

Judgment Day

I call Tate Hornsby's home and get his mother on the horn. Tate was one of the guys jumping up, running around the room, and slamming the lockers on the first day when I felt genuinely terrified. I read her a laundry list of infractions. Upon hearing the record, a fair person would rank Hornsby the #2 or maybe #3 U.S. public enemy. Refuses to stop talking, lies about his identity, disturbs other students, and *grimaces*. Yes, grimaces. He scrunches up his face, glowers, and shakes his head at me all through the period—when he's not otherwise acting out, that is. Am I toooo picayune? Maybe. But just try to teach a class with a laughing hyena doing its best to distract you. Mom is upset and will talk to her son.

And the identity fib? Here, I take part in the indictment. I still don't know the kids' names. I can partially excuse myself because I still have so many kids transferring in and out my classes. No matter, I've got to memorize the names, and fast. Anyhow, Tate tried to hide his name. Any kid anywhere, urban or not, has some initial fun when the teacher doesn't know who's who. So the rest of the kids in the class participate in deception. It's a hoot. They forget that sooner or later there's a day of reckoning. Tate's was today. I look up the schedule of Peyton James, which is the name Tate's been giving me, and I go to Peyton's phys. ed. class. I ask the coach if I can talk to him. The coach says sure and nods to the real Peyton James(!) the kid I thought was Tate—another even bigger troublemaker, by the way. In other words, Tate and Peyton switched names in my class for yucks to confuse me. Luckily, I don't flip out because the real Tate is shooting baskets on the other side of the gym. I confront both of them. They're sooooo sorry, even though it doesn't stop them from laughing in my face. My call today to Tate's mom is partial repayment. Peyton will get his, too.

More Parking

At first I was concerned about my car, a newish BMW convertible. Even considered buying an old jalopy to drive just for school. I could envision spending more bucks on repairing vandalism than I'll even make here the whole year. The first couple of times I park here I hang around the car to see whether kids passing by will pay attention to it. *Nada*. The plain white color with black top doesn't seem to attract notice. I think kids are more turned on by a flashy color or racing stripes. I'm hoping maybe the letters BMW aren't in their vocabulary at all. Maybe kids will be too scared off by the frequent police cars patrolling the area to make mischief on my ragtop. I hope all these things.

Flyers appear in my mailbox from the principal and the teachers' union claiming that they're collectively making every effort to create more spaces for the school staff. Veterans of CBHS assure me that won't happen in my lifetime. I should mention that there is a staff parking lot with some twenty spaces or so for the hundreds working there. A five to seven year waiting period tells me that I needn't bother to add my name to the list.

I arrive very early to park directly across the street from the school when the signs allow it. Street cleaning prohibits cars some days. The trash in the street doesn't reflect this loving care. Today, I think I find a "secret" place some blocks away on a well-groomed residential street. A solid steel phalanx blocks spots everywhere around the school. But here, I guess someone on this block vacated it on the way to work just before I arrived. I'm a little concerned about walking here at night, but grab the solitary spot anyway. I plan on keeping this hideaway secret.

Clothes

When I started at CBHS, I wasn't sure what to expect of the kiddies' couture. I knew I'd see the hideous overblown baggy slacks that make the boys walk like they have their pants full. I'm told the kids here are underprivileged—but they sure don't look it. Even the neediest appear urban chic. Would-be *fashionistas* dress even better.

The staff attire? Mr. T. himself always looks dapper in suit and tie, but the math teachers' dress ranges from lawn-mowing pants cum rumpled shirt and tie, to bowling jeans and a jersey shirt. Running the spectrum from A to B, so to speak. As for myself, I dress in shabby genteel. Pressed, worn, tan chinos; blue, button-down monogrammed shirt; red-striped power tie; and not-so-new white sneakers. Kind of '60's Harvard Yard where I've done time in fashion prison for decades. I want to appear neat, but not distance myself too much from the kids.

Copier Strategy

The demand for copying time is intense. Presumably, I could leave material to be copied at some office in the basement if I didn't need it until, say, retirement. So all teachers eventually make the pilgrimage to the T-L to do it themselves. Competition isn't the only problem. The copiers frequently get jammed or run out of toner. For days maybe. Then you're SOL. But I get there early in the morning. Not only do I do the copying for today, but for the next few weeks. It's dog eat dog in this Xerox wilderness.

TUESDAY, SEPTEMBER 16

Kobe

continues to give me the most trouble in my 14th period class. He's another of the "white boy" catcallers. He's an athlete, fine-looking, clearly popular, and an opinion leader. He's also a smart aleck. Standing up, throwing things, playfully tugging at the hair of pretty girls, occasionally shoving other guys. Sometimes even a near fistfight—in short, a math teacher's nightmare. Yet. Yet. He answers questions, raises his hand, does problems on the board in a breeze. Besides all the qualities that are driving me crazy, he's got the talent and brains to be somebody.

Most of these kids could do the work if they wanted to, but they're so easily distracted, so easily led astray by the few incorrigible kids who desperately want company in their misery. If I can get a few opinion leaders in each class—a solid center—the majority might swerve to the opposite direction, towards an education and prospects after high school. Yes, if I can get Kobe on my side, I've got a chance in this class.

Graduation Time

In my 14th period class, I ask Peyton to stop with the gabbing. "Don't get crazy on me, nigger."

I guffaw so hard that the kids think there's something wrong with me. Tears of laughter come to my eyes and it takes a couple of minutes for me to recover.

"I've graduated!" I think. "No more 'white boy.' I'm going to reach these kids." I smile for the rest of the period. It's late but I stop into Mr. T.'s office to repeat my new moniker. He tells me to take it as a compliment. It means you're a friend.

WEDNESDAY, SEPTEMBER 17

The Staff Cafeteria

lies buried in the basement floor. The dimensions measure roughly 20' by 60'. Depressing yellow bulbs cast dimly on the few industrial-type tables and the five-foot-long serving table. A United Federation of Teachers-sponsored microwave sits against the wall. It's never plugged in for some reason. From a bird's eye view, this cafeteria lies adjacent to the student's own feedbag, but thankfully with no direct passage. To get here, one can walk down the stairs or take forever on the elevator. I take the stairs. I note that the maintenance people never use the stairwell—maybe it's against their union rules. The entrance to our dining hall opens off a side hall, so I never see students in this cafeteria—the driving reason this room's my morning sanctuary. Here, I can gird my mental loins to prepare myself for the culture shock of facing my classes.

I'm not entirely welcome here. I'm a brown bagger, mostly because I'm a vegetarian but also to save a little dough.

Now then, the chatelaine of this gourmet's paradise is a thin, graying, black woman who eyes me suspiciously. I'm not a customer and I think she wants to be sure I don't poach on any of the worn-out looking delicacies sweltering on the steam table. Though I'm completely innocent, perhaps she thinks that I want to filch *en prise* a bagel or English muffin laying next to the register. I can tell she's on alert when she sees me use the toaster for my own home-purchased rye bread. She knows darn well she didn't sell the goods to me. Furthermore, she coldly watches me nuke my coffee in a giant styrofoam Dunkin' Donuts cup. No doubt, I've confirmed a cheapskate welsher status. Noting her vigilance, I politely ask if I could buy some butter for my toast. She looks relieved that I'm not ripping off the DOE and, even better, showing respect for her command over the culinary court.

"Oh, I suppose we can spare a little butter," she demurely answers with a kind of combination Southern drawl and Bronx accent one can only find here in the Big Apple. I respect her wanting to protect her terrain and the school's money. From now on I'll be sure to greet her courteously so I can continue to peacefully hide here.

THURSDAY, SEPTEMBER 18

Settling In

The public may complain about teachers, but here in the T-L only shoptalk is heard. Everyone's focused on doing the best job possible. The teachers are dedicated in a way I wouldn't have expected before coming here.

I shoot the bull with an amiable Hispanic teacher, Cortez Amigas. Although a native of Puerto Rico, he grew up in the Bronx. He's now in his ninth year with the NYC school system, including six at CBHS. In his former life, he was a process server at a law firm and then went into computer programming. After college, he couldn't find a programming job and so landed in teaching.

"Over the last six years, the school has gone down. We didn't always get the rejections and the kids thrown out from other schools. Now the skills are much lower," Cortez sadly tells me.

Only the principals have their own desks or even cubbyholes in this school. My own office consists of a discarded box for copying paper in the T-L. I retrieved the lid, too. Will Gerard, whose seniority affords him space for four—count 'em—four boxes on top of the tall bookcase, offers to slide one over a bit so I can stuff mine in. His gracious hospitality isn't lost on me. I'm deeply indebted to him. No joking, though, getting to be friends with the pros here will pay off. I'm gaining respect for what it means to be an experienced teacher. I'm becoming friendly with the others here, too. Lindsey Holden, a psychology grad just two years out of Case Western Reserve, looks young enough to be one of the students. She chats happily with another young recruit, Amber Firenzi, a cheeky Smith grad and former actuary. Together, they fill the T-L with their daily exuberance. I need any updraft I can get to sail through the day.

FRIDAY, SEPTEMBER 19

A Note in My Mailbox

advertises a series of ten professional development seminars to be held in the UFT Center starting next week. I want to be a better teacher, although the discussion group sounds like it might be a waste of time. The extra two classes a week, frequent staff meetings, having my own kids at home, plus my Mercy College homework, makes time a premium. I decide I'll go anyway.

Bad Actor

I find myself dazed during the 12th period class. The session progresses eerily in a stream of consciousness. Kids are mumbling. I'm talking, now writing on the blackboard. Suddenly I wake up. "What am I saying?" It's the Ric-y Horror Show and I'm performing a most disagreeable number for my disinterested and hostile audience. It's Friday and they can't wait for the curtain to fall. I feel the same way. But I still have two more performances before I seek the weekend entr'acte.

SATURDAY, SEPTEMBER 20

Email to a Chum

Dear Gary,

Overall, it's been a difficult time, both in the discipline and bookkeeping arenas. I guess because of funding and political issues, NYC schools make teachers do an inordinate amount of paperwork and that's been getting to me. Some of the kids are fine, but I've had a hard time balancing teaching with dealing with the problem kids. I'm working on some ideas that I hope will improve the classroom environment. NYC schools are also implementing a new educational program emphasizing group learning. That's hard to do when I already have so many students wanting to do anything but focus on the topic and would be most pleased to just gambol in groups.

I can't get into ichess, either. (our online chess game)

Best,
Ric

MONDAY, SEPTEMBER 22

Harriet

Klugman, a sweet, matronly woman of a certain age, has become my mentor and tormentor, simultaneously. The deal is this: I get my temporary license to teach in NYC because Mercy College evidently has struck a Faustian bargain to educate novitiates in the arcane and black art of teaching. NYC, therefore, will allow (!) me to teach and earn a living (or unreasonable facsimile thereof) doing so while I'm in the Mercy program. I'm in a catch-22. I already have two master's degrees and plenty of math credits to be eligible for a license. I even suffered through a summer of education courses to fulfill that requirement. Except, and this is a bigee, I don't have one year's teaching experience in a secondary school. *Entendido*? I can't teach school unless I've already taught school. This is true, believe me.

Sooooo, I have to keep taking classes—not for my enlightenment—but to keep me eligible to work. Consequently, my Mercy College internship program substitutes for the student teaching aide work I would do if I were twenty years old and enrolled in a teachers' college. Dealing with these kids drains me by the end of the day. And the Mercy College mentoring consists of unremitting busy work at night—weekly assignments, answering questions on required reading. Well, I suppose I have to learn the educational jargon somewhere. Take "Gardiner's Eight Intelligences" and all that rot. Comes in handy in conversational gamesmanship with one's cohorts or in occupational self-defense. Occasionally, I learn something pretty interesting or even useful, maybe.

I'm not alone in the adult paper chase. Most of the new teachers here are change-of-career recruits. Many were lured in by the NYC Teaching Fellows program—which was created to make a dent in the annual teacher deficits. Those teachers actually have it worse. At least in the Mercy College program, I can go home and read the textbooks on my own. The others have to go to night school. Well, better them than me. Somehow, their programs drag on until December of the next school year. Mercy on me, Mercy College lets me graduate from their program at next summer's end. Here, I'm a little bit of a hypocrite. Actually, I could stop at the end of the school year after getting my required teaching experience, but I've decided that I'll be only a few credits shy of a master's degree at that point. I might as well complete it. I secretly hope that my teenage son will take due note that his old man isn't too old to go to school himself.

Observations

mean performance reviews in plain talk. Mr. T. gives notice that I will have my first official observation this Friday. Several of the teachers have been visibly upset by the prospect of their observations, especially since Linda, the new CBHS top nabob, might attend as well. My attitude? If I'm not doing a good job, fire me—a sentiment I repeat to my colleagues that in retrospect sounds (and was!) snooty. Nevertheless, I don't want to make Mr. T. look bad. I'm expected to prepare a lesson plan that includes the point-of-entry model. No problem, I do that every day when I get to school at sunrise. And I should identify relevant "MST standards," whatever that is. Mr. T. schedules a pre-observation conference the day before so as not to freak out the teachers.

Liberal without a Pause

Although I consider myself a social liberal, in truth I've had little contact with blacks or Hispanics. My own high school in Bexley, Ohio, had only one or two black kids and I didn't know them. In college, I was friendly with only one of the small number of blacks, a fraternity guy like me. But I never particularly gave much thought to my preppy pool-playing pal's color. Same kind of thing when I was in grad schools at USC and Harvard Business School. Color was never an issue that thrust itself into my own daily life. And in my varied careers of engineering, real estate development, and investment banking, I almost never even met blacks or Hispanics in these professions. The one exception was a black partner I took into my Greenwich firm, a highly educated Yankee living in Scandinavia. I'm still getting used to being in an environment where almost everyone, including the teachers, is a person of color. I like that I'm getting a taste of what it must feel like the other way around. Part of my own education.

Kobe—Part 2

I wish I could take the credit, but I can't. I've told Kobe privately on several occasions that I believed in his ability to excel and could he, pretty please, stop aggravating me in class. Sure, he says; he'll cut out the slapstick—but they all say that in private. Now, all of a sudden, he's great, not perfect mind you, but a definite asset. This 13th–14th period class has become mind-numbing. Maybe I've got a chance now.

Mr. T. finally gives the go-ahead for the teachers to hand out textbooks. So far, I've been copying pages in them for handouts. Distributing the books means more paperwork. Each kid has to sign for the book, a very heavy sucker intended for the first two years of math. The book blotter lists the kids' names, addresses, book serial numbers—everything but hat size in this yet another unending record keeping. It's like traveling in Switzerland where they hole punch everything in sight. I instruct the kids to keep their books at home—a practice followed by most of the freshmen teachers. Maybe this way they'll do the reading. No way are they going to schlep them back and forth from home. Besides, I'm responsible for retrieving them. They're sure to lose them if they tote them around.

Mr. T. considers me something of a crank for my continual questions and requests. Time to spread the wealth around. I write a letter to Linda's replacement as Assistant Principal of Organization. I guess it's the stepping-stone to becoming a principal. I'm bothered by the isolation of working in this mostly empty, humongous cavern until dark. I want some kind of connection with civilization.

Dear Mr. Santino:

I would like to request phones for Rooms 313 and 250. There is only a cord there now. I feel a phone is essential for maintaining security and safety for the students and me.

Respectfully submitted,
Ric Klass
Math Dept
cc: Mr. Tqiqi, A.P.

I think my innocuous letter added me to the administrative foe list.

TUESDAY, SEPTEMBER 23

Dialing for Dads

Tried to reach the homes of twenty or so students in the past several days but only got through to ten of them. Lots of bad numbers—a common phenomenon, evidently. Many of the kids move from apartment to apartment. I'm told many families get evicted and others can't afford a telephone. I try to reach Alvin's home. He's a fixture on my incurable disease list. Alvin's mother refers me to his father who lives separately from her—another familiar story. I call Mr. Torento. He's upset with my report but appreciative to get the lowdown on his boy. Alvin visits him on weekends. Mr. Torento asks me to tell his son that he's "not a happy camper" to hear reports of misbehavior and ceaseless talking. In the 14th period, I tell Alvin about my conversation and repeat verbatim his father's camper status. Alvin's distressed that I ratted on him and begs me not to do it again. He promises to reform and not to misbehave anymore. And, in fact, Alvin's now an attentive, model student . . . for this class, anyway.

WEDNESDAY, SEPTEMBER 24

Prestidigitation and Pugilism

An effective inner-city teacher can be likened to a magician or, perhaps, a boxer. A never-ending bag of tricks to keep the kids entertained and engaged becomes a necessity. A bunny out of the hat with visual aids and a couple of jokes one day. Pigeons out of the sleeves with reading aloud and individual instruction the next. Just as necessary, the scamps need to be controlled or even intimidated. A jab with a threat of suspension on Tuesday followed by an uppercut with a call home to the parents on Thursday. Here's the story: Everything works once. Calling the parents, asking politely for some consideration, exiling them to the Deans' office. You name it. The problem is nothing works twice or certainly not twice in a row. And no solution a teacher dreams up works for more than a day. We're all in a sustained state of reinventing our approach every day for these kids.

Alvin's bad boy behavior in my 14th period section proves the rule that solutions last a day. If that. Yesterday, he swore eternal good-boy behavior. Today, bad boy as usual—angry dad or not.

CYA

We new teachers assemble for a staff meeting, somewhat belatedly in my opinion, to learn the nitty-gritty about staying alive here. I learn right away, any illusions that teachers are "professionals" should be left at the door. We're given a pep talk plus a warning. The theme is: Do what the administrators want, "cover yourself." I was never much for kissing up. I'm unlikely to start now.

Then we move into a little professional development time. We're a captive audience, after all. These sessions come right out of "Conducting Meetings for Dummies" urging the scoutmaster to make the troops work a little. We won't know it's been good for us, otherwise. I'm asked to write about one thing that has gone well, what one challenge have I met and overcome, and what is the greatest challenge facing me now? I write that Kobe has gone from being the worst student to being the best, I'm trying to manage my anger, and my greatest challenge is classroom management—reaching as many congregants as possible, not just the choir.

Another topic sprouts up: "They (who is 'they,' anyway?) don't want to see rows. They like the double horseshoe setup." And so on. Seating of the kids is a big issue here. So . . .

What is the Seating Thing?

Unless you're a teacher, the classroom seating arrangement probably doesn't strike you as a big deal. But it's a very big deal. For one thing, THE LATEST PUSH is cooperative learning. Now how can these kids cooperate with each other (read "twaddle") unless they're seated facing one another or grouped closely? Sitting in rows as I used to do in elementary, junior high, high school, college, and three graduate schools doesn't seem to cut it anymore. At least with the educational theorists who apparently have the school administrators by the jugular vein these days.

Seating arrangements in vogue now include horseshoe, double horseshoe, and pairing of desks in twos, threes, and fours. Classes need to be student-centered. Central to the concept is placing the stronger kids next to the weaker ones. In itself, not a bad idea. But what if there are no stronger kids? Or what if there are a couple of kids who can do the work but they like to work by themselves and not be dragged down by the nitwits? Or what if the stronger kids make a bigger pest of themselves than the others? Not theory for me, but the way it is.

I'm not comfortable with nouveau seating and neither are my change-of-career cohorts. Amazingly, not everyone agrees with me, especially those who had once taught tots. Putting little toddlers close together on a big mat and reading to them worked for many elementary school teachers. Why not here? Why not, indeed.

I have to keep in mind that I'm teaching freshmen in the Bronx. A flock of birds flying by—no, three birds will do it—creates a sufficient disturbance to rouse an entire class to rush to the window to see the amazing spectacle (and hope to stall until the bell rings). In my novice opinion, seating my own flock in a perfect goof-off array is teacher suicide. Mr. T., savvy to this possibility, cautions us to go easy on pairing kids up right away, even in groups of two. "Give it a couple of weeks," he warns. He knows very well that if we put kids together before they've gotten used to being back from the playground, it will be bedlam. If that's not the case already. In my own education and in my previous teaching, we cut the horse manure and got to work. Now, every little thing has to be tweaked *ad nauseum*. But, maybe they're right and I'm wrong.

T-L Chitchat

Pension benefits get top billing in the gab here. A sufficient-size audience motivates Victor to pontificate on the subject, concluding that making life difficult for us is part of the administration's plan. NYC hopes teachers will die before collecting their pensions.

When I complain about my kids, Victor volunteers that I haven't seen anything yet. The really bad kids don't bother to come to school for the first few weeks and when they do show up, all hell breaks loose. I hope he's kidding me since I'm a rookie teacher and all. Friendly harassment. But his expression says he's dead serious.

Glenn, a teacher that I thought I'd become pretty friendly with, tells me I'm arrogant. Too aloof in the T-L. In God's plan for me here, it's evidently not enough that I've got testy kids to deal with. All the same, maybe it wouldn't kill me to alight from my lofty, imagined heights.

And the printer's not working as usual. *Wunderbar.*

Letting It All Hang Out

Today I decide, "Yes, I'm going to spend some of my precious midday free hours in professional development." I guess it's the right thing to do. Katherine, a Brit who runs the sessions in the UFT lounge, has a low-key but slyly engaging manner.

"What would we like to learn about in the series?" she asks. But I know she knows darn well what we'll be doing in these sessions—learn a little, laugh a little, cry a little. Mostly, we new teachers turn the hour into a koffee klatch gripe session: the late afternoon classes; the lack of preparedness of the students; and jee-zus, their insolence. We let our hair down and it feels great. I'm going to keep coming. Ditto for the others.

Standing and Sitting

Every day has its own little stories. Today, I ban afternoon ambles around the classrooms. The kids like to get up and take paper wads to the trashcan. It's a favorite pastime that includes high fives with buddies to and fro their seats. And doing it several times a class is more fun than just once.

In three of my classrooms, the kids sit at tables instead of individual seats. Probably useful for the biology and chemistry lab classes they were intended for, but in mine merely opportunities for note passing, pushing, hair pulling, and other nonsense. To make it worse, the teachers in the classes before mine arrange the tables facing each other. They want to ensure the administrative spies don't catch them teaching kids in groups of less than four. As a result, I have to race to class to move all the tables into rows before my kids get there. I've been in an invisible tug of war with the previous teachers. After changing the décor, I then hustle to get the objectives of the day written. Today, I'm beat and resolve to call the shuffling quits. But first the teacher greets me at the door.

"You win," she says. "We're too pooped to switch them anymore." Amen to that.

I don't quite finish the lesson in my 14th period class and offer to keep on going for whomever wants to stay. To my surprise, several kids stay seated and ask me to keep going. Even Alvin sticks around, although he still fools around a bit. I give them my pitch about how life is a race and they must run like crazy even though they can't see anyone running next to them. It seems like every time I feel that I'm wasting my time on these children, I'm encouraged to hang in there.

THURSDAY, SEPTEMBER 25

APB for Teachers

At the faculty lunch, we welcome a new math department hire from Belfast, Ireland. I know that New York City is hard up for teachers, but I didn't know they advertised as far away as the Philippines and the isle of Erin Go Braugh to attract math talent here. Casey had been laid off from his teaching job in Ireland. He turned down an offer from London for tax reasons and thought it might be a good idea to come teach in New York City. His brogue is so thick I don't always understand him. When I can interpret his comments, they're pretty witty. I can't imagine what the kids must think. They can barely speak English themselves. As he walks into the T-L, he's pulling chewing gum off the back of his pants. He turns around and asks if it's all gone, but it isn't. There are still great big green spots right in the middle where some kid has planted it as a gag. And it's not a four-leaf clover.

Today, I have a pre-observation conference. I feel miserable. I had leg cramps last night from running up and down the stairs here, and have a headache now.

Behind the Iron Curtain

Overall, I'm a washout in the first three teaching periods this afternoon. The kids are wild. I send three to the Deans' office in 10th period class. For some reason, a long lost friend of Melinda's, one of my unrelenting banshees, had disappeared from class during the first two weeks of school. Suddenly she's back. The sisters-in-mischief become witches on wheels, standing, laughing, talking, loud and boisterous. I finally order Melinda to leave and report to the Deans' office. She just laughs in my face. She knows that teachers are essentially powerless. I peek outside the door for a guard to bodily remove her, but the hall is deserted. The phone still isn't repaired.

Afterwards, I feel like going to confession. I limp to Mr. T. and tell him I have good news and bad news. The bad news is that I haven't done my job and completely miscarried in teaching the little scamps anything in my first three periods. The good news, he inquires? The good news is I'm feeling upbeat and happy. I'm not really all that worked up about it. I conclude I'm going to keep cool from now on. I've been ineffective today but didn't get bent out of shape over it. I'm ready to keep pushing on with the day.

Absenteeism has decimated my next class to only fifteen students. In this small class, I now rule with an iron will. The slightest hint of commotion from these lowly comrades receives an uplifted eyebrow. Unwanted laughing brings a cruel smirk, creating instant fear and obedience in my politburo of education. My apparatchiks goose step to the blackboard where they actually get some math done this period. For me, it equals a week's vacation at a commissar's dacha.

I march with confidence into the 14th period class. I already have some of the usual troublemaking cubs in this class by the short hairs. I called their parents the previous night. All said I would find a different child the following day. This gives me exactly one day's cooperation from the most disobedient and unruly children. I don't need to say a word to the usual poltergeists. This is the kind of victory that I've been hoping for. Nothing's perfect, because now I have to pounce on one of the better students who starts acting up. I finally order him to the Deans' office. "Goodbye, Leo. So long, and please write." My sendoff amuses everyone but Leo. I don't actually want the good students to get into trouble. Other teachers tell me many kids are afraid of their parents and that a call from me could result in their getting a beating. But my main mission is to defend the class as a whole by bringing it under control.

In the T-L, Ms. Tottle, a senior teacher here, volunteers her opinion. "Kids are like rodents, vultures. They keep springing up. What's America coming to?" On the other hand, someone mentions that Tony Curtis as a kid had been a gang member in the Bronx. Perhaps these kids will make it somehow, too.

FRIDAY, SEPTEMBER 26

Pandemonium

literally means exactly what I deal with today—all demons. I discipline twelve baby ogres. The worst incident makes me physically sick. I'm writing on the blackboard when a fistfight breaks out between Ricardo Juarez and Antwan Halter. Against school rules, I step in between them to stop the fight and take an unintended glancing blow on the shoulder myself. The DOE stipulation that I can't step in myself when two kids punch each other seemed irrelevant until I got hurt.

Also, I'm not insured if I interfere. I can't seem to learn the trick of keeping my antennae alert at all times. I should have been able to see the battle coming, but I didn't have a clue. Antwan gets a purpling, but not bloody, blow on the cheek and refuses to go to the nurse's office. I feel personally responsible. I'm so upset, I want to vomit. And these two aren't even nearly my worst kids!

Melinda gives another Academy Award-winning performance by braying at the top of her lungs at one point in the 10th period. Really. I kick her out several times but the Dean keeps recycling her back into the classroom. HDPE #2 plastic bottles should only have it so good in this city. Can I survive with this havoc every day? Another downside to all this commotion. I leave the classroom feeling disappointed. At Georgetown University, where I had been a lecturer, I had a rapport with the students—not here.

Pacing Guide

Mr. T. observes my 12th period class on evaluating and comparing real numbers. In our post-observation conference, he comments that the kids were all answering at once in a choral response without being called upon. I didn't even notice it, to tell the truth. For that matter, it could be worse. Usually, I can't get the kids to participate at all. If they all want to answer, it sure beats the alternative. In any event, I'm grateful Mr. T. unfailingly makes positive and helpful suggestions. From kibitzers, "constructive criticism" never intends to be anything but a dig.

He also tells me I don't give the kids a chance to do the explaining. It's true. I'm afraid of losing too much time. One mandated department task I take very seriously is plowing through the material. We're even provided a daily pacing guide for the freshmen and sophomores to tell us what page and exercises we should be covering. And I pretty much do it. Many of the other teachers are already way behind.

Math Potpourri

In the required textbook that we must cover in the first two years, there's tons of material in varied subjects, unlike what I had as a kid. The rainbow of colors and the excess of fonts splashed in it don't help. Evidently, some poohbah thinks eye candy makes for a good math text. Luckily, we can't get visual diabetes. Just looking at the book makes me a little nauseous. To keep my lunch down, I make black-and-white copies of today's material. The freshman curriculum is a mishmash of algebra, geometry, and probability.[1] They arrive here from eighth grade without the basic skills anyway, and so immediately become confused by the variety of disparate topics without mastering any of them. I don't want to overstate the textbook problems, though. Most of the kids won't do any work, regardless of presentation or subject matter.

Cursing

The prevailing wisdom in the T-L conjectures that the relatively small size of the girls compels them psychologically to out-profane the boys in self-defense. I'm not so sure. First of all, some of the girls overshadow and outweigh me by two to four inches and twenty-five to fifty pounds, respectively. I've seen big teenage boys back off from picking on the fair sex when confronted by a female onslaught of physical advance and verbal assault. There's more than one of our CBHS sweeties who could force my retreat in a different setting. I'm more inclined to believe survival of the fittest reigns here, regardless of gender.

---

[1] In March 2005, the New York State Regents Board announced that the high school math curriculum would switch back in 2005–06 to the traditional algebra I, geometry, algebra II, and trigonometry, pre-calculus sequence.

MONDAY, SEPTEMBER 29

The Longest Day

A phony iconoclast, I sometimes dupe myself into thinking I'm not like everybody else—but I am. At CBHS, I've quickly fallen into a rut:

5:15 A.M. Get up. Take my wide variety of vitamins. I truly need them now. For a while, I tried getting up even earlier to go to the Y and work out when it opens at 5:30 A.M. But I found I had to go to bed at 8:00 P.M. to get enough sleep, and had no time with my family.

5:55 A.M. Buy vanilla-flavored coffee at Dunkin' Donuts (decidedly not decaffeinated). I practice my Spanish with the Hispanic manager who tells me he works seven days a week. It's killing him and the pay is terrible. I'm sympathetic because I can see myself saying the same thing some time soon.

6:20 A.M. Arrive in time to get a close (and safe) parking space.

6:30 A.M. Let myself into the dim T-L. It's dark now and will stay that way until spring. I prepare lesson plans and grade papers until my first class. Although my first period isn't until 12:30 P.M., I refuse to do CBHS work at home.

12:00 noon Before my first class, I eat one sandwich (vegetarian), some pretzels, a diet-whatever, and one tangerine. Sometimes I go crazy and have two.

12:30–1:11 P.M. 8th period. First semester algebra.

1:15–1:56 P.M. 9th period. A double period with either the 8th or 10th.

2:00–2:46 P.M. 10th period. First semester algebra.

2:50–3:31 P.M. 11th period. Gather my courage in the T-L for my next class.

3:35–4:16 P.M. 12th period. First semester algebra for repeaters. In other words, these kids aren't freshman! They're mostly notional sophomores who flunked the course last year.

4:20–5:01 P.M. 13th period. On Tuesdays and Thursdays, a double period of the 12th or 14th.

5:05–5:46 P.M. 14th period.

5:46 P.M. and 30 seconds Bolt to my car.

6:15 P.M. Arrive home and thank heaven above every time I make it in one piece, physically. But I haven't yet made it home safe, mentally. I love my golden retriever Hunter too much to kick him, so I take my frustrations out on my wife and kids instead. CBHS is beginning to ruin my life.

7:00 P.M. Do my seemingly interminable and useless make-work assignments for Mercy College.

9:00 P.M. An end of endless thoughts about quitting teaching before merciful sleep.

It's a long day.

Although prior to CBHS I had taught and tutored, my career mostly has been as an entrepreneur of various sorts without the confines of a tight schedule. When you teach, you've got to be there—five perform-ances a day. Now, I'm a tiny cog in the DOE wheel. I haven't been a minuscule component since I worked in an aerospace factory in Southern California. That was after college, where we were busy putting men on the moon. And the job was fun! I'm invisible here, decidedly not in control of my own time. My habits become my refuge. I always sit in the same place in the T-L. If someone's in my preferred seat, my rhythm is interrupted. My ability to get through the day after accomplishing so little becomes compromised. I'm slowly transmogrifying into an insect. I'm Jeff Goldblum in *The Fly*, but instead of killing my victims, I'm teaching them mathematics.

Calculators

I bring a host of prejudices about teaching high schoolers to my work here. I plead guilty to the charge of "It wasn't done that way when I was a kid" syndrome. I'm aware of my psychological limitations and try to curb them. Calculators figure to be one of my hang-ups. When I was a kid and walked to school through three feet of snow every day—year round—we didn't have calculators and didn't need them, by golly. Teachers of a certain age don't like calculators in class. Don't need them. Makes you dependent on them like spell check on the computer. With a calculator, you don't learn basic arithmetic skills—they promote mental laziness, most problems don't require it, interferes with conceptually understanding the material, and so on.

I would think math teachers, who actually know some math (i.e., studied a fair amount in college as opposed to learning it in schools of education) would tend to feel this way. But my hauteur is wrongheaded once more. Because here it is again: CBHS is a public urban school. We debate the issue here in the T-L. Many of the seasoned teachers argue that the kids feel empowered when they have a calculator in hand—a little edge on their side. Other pro-calc teachers point out many kids are visual learners. And with calcs, like the universally used TI-83, one can draw instructive graphs. Our charges like pictures and find the calcs fun. Besides, they can now be used on SATs and other standardized tests. I'm definitely softening from my hard stance—maybe learning something.

Go Forward or Back?

Forget the arcane uses of logarithms, arcsines, permutations, et. al., integrated in a $10 scientific calculator these days—our kids don't even know how to multiply and add. This indubitable fact generates an ancillary debate among my peers in the T-L. Should we go back and teach them elementary school nuts and bolts? There's no unanimity among us on this topic. For one thing, to get a Regents high school diploma, the kids have to pass the Math A exam. Going backwards at this point in their education will be time-consuming. Moreover, if the kids don't know the tables by now, regressing that far will probably permanently turn them off to math. We'd just be adding insult to injury for trying to teach them baby stuff. It's good to know the basics, but does one really need to add or multiply anymore? Practically speaking, any workplace that requires it has a cash register, adding machine, or a calculator. But our debate doesn't go far. The math teachers are king of their classes—only to a point. We all must cover the required materials of whatever course we're instructing and that doesn't leave time for going back to the ABCs. But maybe that's a big mistake for our kids. Maybe hustling them in and out the door without more tender care cheats them out of catching up. I don't know for sure.

Open Door Policy

My 10th period serves as a repeater class for upperclassmen who scrubbed it before. While in my other sections there are some on the register who don't show up, in this class one would have to say that there are only some kids who do show up. Take Elaine Reydando, a soft-spoken Hispanic girl. She's polite, does some homework, and passes the tests—albeit, barely so. I can't figure out why a nice girl like her failed in the past. So I ask her and she tells me a familiar story. She was a diehard truant but she's grown up now and wants to graduate. Lately, she's been showing up at lunchtime asking me for one of my tangerines. Last Friday, she actually seemed angry when I told her I didn't have any for her that day.

After she arrives today, for a long time past the late bell, no one else appears. So I start to tutor her. Then she stands up and looks deeply into my eyes. Too deeply.

"You know I'm trying extra hard to do well in your class."

"That's great, Elaine."

"I love you, Mr. Klass."

Looking down at my papers and starting to perspire, "Uh, huh. Well, yeah, it's good to like your teachers."

"No, Mr. Klass. I don't *like* you. I *love* you."

Through the window, one of the teachers walking by sees us by ourselves and without saying a word, opens the door. I thank him profusely. I forgot I can't be in a closed classroom alone with a student. With all the to-do one reads about teachers getting sued or put in jail for big and little crimes and misdemeanors, I don't want to take any chances. I won't leave the door closed again with a solitary child—especially Elaine.

Today, I send this love letter to the Deans' Office:

Written Statement
September 29, 2003

Last Friday Sept 26, 03 in front of the class Nasir Handy threatened to follow me and pop my tires. His threat was a result of repeated attempts to quiet him and his refusal to go to the Deans' office.

Sincerely,
Ric Klass

TUESDAY, SEPTEMBER 30

The CBHS Diary

On Mondays, the *New York Times* "Metropolitan Diary" column prints anecdotes—slices of life in NYC. Here's mine: I am a bona fide coffee-o-holic. Two weeks ago, I went to the coffee shop around the corner from CBHS to try out the java. In earnest concern, I asked the proprietor, "How's the coffee?"

Of course, "It's the best." He watched me carefully as I gingerly took the hot paper cup from his hands. Inconsiderate me, I walked out without first tasting it. So I return for the first time since then. The owner instantly says to me, "So, you liked the coffee?"

Lucky Them

I decide to let the kids know exactly how lucky they are to have me as their teacher.

"You know, kiddies, I don't *have* to be here. Some teachers teach to earn a living, but I'm 135 years old and this is my retirement. I'm here because I want to be."

I feel a little guilty saying all this since some kids might interpret my self-congratulations to mean the other teachers don't want to be at CBHS. Nevertheless, one boy actually thanks me! I look carefully at him for any trace of sarcasm or wisenheimer—but there is none. I actually get through to one of them. The day isn't a complete loss.

WEDNESDAY, OCTOBER I

Makeup Test

Today is test day for all my classes. Consequently, a day of relative relaxation as far as I'm concerned. Some of my students feel the same way. Instead of charging into the test, one girl checks herself out in her compact mirror, then slowly puts on her lipstick, mascara, and eyeliner. I can hardly believe my eyes. Finally, she does get around to looking at the test minutes before the bell rings. Flunked beyond an eye shadow of a doubt.

On My Soapbox

I recently visited my son's public high school during "Back to School Night." The halls were sparkling, the walls freshly painted, and the large classroom floors were covered with attractive carpeting to reduce the noise. The principal addressed the parents via a connection to a TV monitor in each classroom. My son's math teacher told me he had twenty-two students in the class (considered large for this school). Only one hour earlier I had come home consumed from CBHS with classes of up to thirty-two students. There, the noise from even a pencil tapping echoes on the dingy unpainted walls and marred, bare, wooden floors.

Is it any wonder that children from underprivileged homes have such a low success rate in school? The overcrowding alone is sufficient to make it nearly impossible to reach most of the children. In my repeater class where I have relatively few students, I'm able to answer individual questions in

*detail. True classroom management, even with difficult chil-
dren, is possible. Only two or three misbehaving students in
a classroom of twenty-five or more already undisciplined students make teaching nearly impossible. It's an environment
more analogous to managing a prison ward. Conservatives
might castigate the children or their parents, but in my not-
all-that humble opinion it is the role of society to find a
solution to cure or alleviate an existing difficulty—not to
ineffectually point a finger. Smaller and better-appointed
classrooms and school facilities in lower income neighborhoods would go a long way towards creating a better educated
next generation.*

THURSDAY, OCTOBER 2

Lesson Design Review

Another professional development meeting today. Katherine, our
leader, is a great listener and to my surprise I learn something. A group
of four new teachers talk about lesson design. Somewhere in my head I
still think being a good teacher should be automatic, something natural.
But I'm finding there's substance to correctly formatting a class, considering the learning styles of the students, varying the activities, and
reinforcing previous lessons. Even more. The group enjoys sharing the
school gossip.

Charter a Path to Success?

Read an article today in the *NY Times* about a successful charter
school where one of the teachers calls every child's home on Sunday.
This story only convinces me that charter schools can't be the answer.
Can we hope to institutionalize passion? Yes, there are a few schools
nationwide that have formed a core corps. Their rarity is proof that it

can't be standardized. Fervor can't be institutionalized *en masse*. Schools need dedicated teachers, but how are we going to find and keep eternally young and single zealots who devote not only their working time but their home life to reach NYC's 1.5 million kids—and pay them next to nothing as reward?

FRIDAY, OCTOBER 3

Billingsgate

I'm having a hard time being spoken to in a disrespectful manner by my students. Very disquieting and insulting. I've never in my life encountered anything remotely like it. More importantly, these kids don't realize the extent to which it reflects so poorly on themselves and their parents/legal guardians. These downtrodden kids can't bring me down a fraction of how they lower themselves. During the Watergate days when I was living in D.C., an elderly, black taxi driver once told me how sorry he felt for Richard Nixon.

"Why's that?" I asked.

"Because he doesn't realize he has sinned and so he can't ever be forgiven by God," the religious cabbie replied. My students don't even know how bad their manners are. How will they ever repent?

Lately, Joselyn and Tiqnaz, a demure girl from India, have been coming to me at lunchtime for help. Joselyn's tightly knotted, beaded hair seems to emphasize for me the intensity of her desire to do well. Without the din of her compatriots, she learns more in fifteen to twenty minutes one-on-one than in a week of classes. I'm impressed by her tenacity. I hope like hell she makes it. I'm still too tightly drawn myself to even consider passing her if she can't prove herself on the tests. Tiqnaz aspires to become an M.D. Her English language skills prevent her from grasping much of the class work and she's been wiped out by the quizzes. Very distressed about it, too. I'd like nothing better than for the two of them to do well, but I don't have that much confidence that the small time we spend in tutoring will overcome their problems.

MONDAY, OCTOBER 6

Home Work—Not

A simple fact surfaces—these adolescents just won't do homework. I'm worn out thinking through the reasons. Many of them simply can't. To begin with, almost all the freshmen are unprepared for high school in any subject area. They haven't tested out as Level 1 and 2 for no reason. Their math skills are incredibly weak. In each of my classes, more than a few of the children can't tell you how much six times seven is. Really. Then why are they here? Where else would they go? is the answer. Studies show keeping children back doesn't help them. And so these sad little boys and girls just get pushed along until...? Until they plummet off the face of the planet and smack adulthood hard and fast in the face.

I would say a majority of my students truly can't focus on much of anything for more than moments. *Can't*, not won't! I know that some of these statements may seem like exaggeration. They're not. The consensus of the chitchat in the T-L maintains it's a certainty that many of the kids were born to mothers who were under the influence of crack, drugs, alcohol, or some other substance abuse. I know that lots of kids don't like math, but our students' inability to concentrate or even sit quietly for a short while must also be physiological. In my layman's opinion, it's a solid bet that we have a very big population of undiagnosed ADD or ADHD kids here.

A zero work ethic pervades the kids as well. And "work" is part and parcel of the word "homework." Excessive TV watching plays a role in this. I know how TV enervates all our children; but these kids have no motivation and for many of them, no role models at home to guide them on a productive working path. One girl told me I couldn't call her dad because he's in jail.

In my classes covering elementary statistics, I ask each child how many hours of TV they watch on school nights. The bulk of the answers range from two to as much as eight hours per night, and average about four and a half. Astonishing.

Finally, many of the kids don't have a quiet space at home to work, read, or think. Math requires practice to achieve any kind of proficiency. What's the answer? Do the "homework" at school. We should provide tutored study halls midday and at the end of each school day to see that at least some independent work gets accomplished. That's if I were emperor.

PDA

I find myself asking the same question as the chain-smoking, nervous Martin Short used to do in a bit on *Saturday Night Live*: "Is it me, or is it him? It's him, isn't it?" The public display of affection seems way over the top here. In the halls, these kids don't stop hugging, kissing, or touching each other. And it's not just the boys with the girls. The girls kiss and hug each other, too. When PDA erupts in my classroom, I firmly put a stop to it with a finger-wagging, "No huggy-bear, kids." Usually, this gets enough of a laugh to fluster the two amorous octopi to halt the embrace. But I'm leery of taking on the whole student body's groping in the corridors. I go to my resource of first and usually last resort, the teachers' lounge, to seek the answer to my queries: When did this start? Does it go on every-where? To the teachers with teenage children of their own, "Does it go on in your kids' high school?" No definitive answer. No one is really sure what the story is. We all *do* know, however, that sexual harassment is a big, huge, and gigantic no-no for us teachers, the kids, and for nor-mal people, too. But is it sexual harassment when the kids engage in PDA? Could a teacher get in trouble if he sees it and doesn't report it?

At the end of the day, Mr. Short and I haven't made progress in our search for truth. It is them, isn't it?

TUESDAY, OCTOBER 7

Low Marks for Me and Them

I give a quiz today. Despite my urging that they bring calculators for the exam, most don't. The high score from all sections is 55 percent. Everyone sank. CBHS has a couple of Eastern Bloc teachers. In the T-L, I discuss the kids and my failure with Lila Korkna, a math teacher from Albania. She's empathetic. As for her own personal education, she learned what I'm teaching in second grade.

I may have successfully proselytized three converts today. Natalie, José, and Keanu, three of my interminable obstructionists, all took the oath to reform. Talking to me on the way out of school, Keanu explains that he's become a Catechumen because his friend who does drugs, dropped out. He doesn't want to join him.

Spoiling an uplifting moment, a kid calls out to me, "Hey, man, pull up your pants."

Me, "Keep a civil tongue in your head," hoping I wouldn't get beat up. But I err. I should have said, "I am not the enemy. You are your own enemy."

WEDNESDAY, OCTOBER 8

Dean Aid

I've made friends with one or two of the Deans. I give Dean Candie a list of thirteen troublemakers from two of my classes. I want to give him more from the other two sections but he thinks that's all he can handle. Getting rid of the agitators would solve most of my problems. I'm hoping that working directly with Dean Candie will give me better results than my letters to the office.

Curses

I'm such a misfit here. Every day consists of uninterrupted f _ _ k, m-f _ _ k, kiss my _ _ _, and s _ _ t, just for openers. When I ask the girls in my class not to talk that way, they look at me as if I were a Martian. Maybe they're right. I'm thinking: Teachers from the Bronx—bred in the bone with low talk and impervious to it—are the right ones to teach these kids. It's not that the Bronx or ghetto-born teachers here are uncouth, not at all. Maybe the foul language just rolls off their backs, is ignored, or perhaps laughed at. I don't know. And yet, when I've tutored disadvantaged kids one-on-one they keep it clean. I always tried to keep my language with them at an elevated level as a model, and they often asked me about the words I used.

THURSDAY, OCTOBER 9

My file at the Deans' office must be getting fairly thick by now. Here's today missal:

Written Statement
October 9, 2003
Ric Klass
Math Dept
Central Bronx High School

After class had started, I approached Quinton Franklin who was standing at the window and told him to sit down, whereupon he started screaming at me in a very threatening manner and told me to stay out of his space. A few minutes later while I was teaching, he said, "Shut the fuck up, bitch," disrupting the class and encouraging others to be disrespectful. It took several minutes to regain some semblance of order in the classroom after that outburst. Quinton later told me he could do the work but won't and would instead try next term. He added that he answers the phone at his home and that if I tried to call his family he would just hang up. During a group activity portion of the class, he made no effort to work. I offered to tutor him and told him that it is not my job to hurt students. Later on he was standing again, this time at the door. I tried to talk to him after class but he waved me off and wouldn't talk to me. I cannot allow students to think they can threaten and insult me, thereby not only hurting themselves, but making it very difficult to control the class.

Sincerely,
Ric Klass

To my knowledge, despite my letter, Quinton is never disciplined for his behavior today. I find out in the T-L that this fatherless child works after school every day to support his deserted mother, a crack addict.

Dean Candie tells me he's been too overloaded to get busy on the troublemaker list I gave him so I decide to enlist the help of another Dean in my purge. I give Dean Parsons a list of six unleashed pups from period 14. Collar them, please!

FRIDAY, OCTOBER 10

What Misery Loves

The T-L provides not only an asylum for the teachers, but also a convenient gripe arena. Teachers who've worked in Westchester County tell me that the assistant principals discourage new hires from even setting foot in their lounges. They even make it forbidden territory—or else. They know the salons nurture seeds of unrest. I complain a little about my kids to the sympathetic ears of Ms. Dantillo, an experienced and seemingly calm pro. She tells me she has her problem kids, too. And she teaches in one of the new small schools also jam-packed in this building! It's a relief to hear, even though I know she just might be trying to make me feel better.

Hustling

Ms. Abrahamson does her scheduling job well. Every sequential class I teach lies on a different floor on the opposite side of the building. Almost in a different galaxy far, far away. I assume that's the school policy—giving teachers plenty of exercise between classes. Getting the old heart pumping has much to recommend it. Although I'm getting more paranoid by the day, I'm not alone scuttling like a mouse in a whirling cage. Some teachers have to race from the basement to the fourth floor. Using the slow, and only occasionally working, elevator doesn't cut it.

What's the matter? Isn't a little hustling good for me? Well, yes—except consider this: The periods are forty-one minutes long. The four-minute breaks are the only time to go to the john. And I like to pass out calculators to the kids who must sign for them (or without doubt will get stolen). Then there's putting my name, date, aim, to-do problem, and homework assignment on the board. If I'm even a bit late to class, the period is over before it's begun. It could take five minutes to use the elevator to reach another floor—a near necessity if I'm carting an overhead projector.

With an overhead, I can cover twice as much material and, most importantly, keep my back turned to the blackboard. Why don't they teach that life-saving rule in my education classes?—never turn your back on THEM. Did I mention that my chalk handwriting is illegible unless I write v-e-r-y s-l-o-w-l-y? I've given up on using the overhead projector—no time to get it to class. Now I need to learn to write on the blackboard while facing the students. No kidding—some teachers are experts at it. Last weekend I discovered that big variety stores sell chalk holders. Seeing the doohickeys, I immediately realized that I'm the last one on earth to find this out. My blackboard handwriting improves today but still is pretty rotten.

And lastly, I bump into Quinton in the halls. I tell him I think he's intelligent and want him to do well. I hope to break the ice with him if I can.

"Mr. Klass," he looks at me helplessly.

"Yes?"

"You don't know what life is like for a nigger like me," and runs off down the hall.

At day's end I'm shattered.

TUESDAY, OCTOBER 14

Deans

The Deans' role at CBHS combines that of military police, KGB spy network, and ineffectual hallway gumshoes. Some of the shamuses are teachers doing deansmanship part-time. Others are hulking guys barely older than the students and none too-civilized looking themselves— basically just bigger and meaner versions of the kids. Frankly, it's fine by me if the Deans occasionally intimidate the kids. Something/some- one needs to keep them in line some of the time, even if it's our own dementors.

The problem, it seems to me, is that the set rules get fitfully enforced. Posted signs all over the place prohibit do-rags, for example. But all the boys wear them and the Deans usually say nothing. Why don't the monitors at the front door make the kids take them off? It's intuitively obvious to the most casual observer (as technophiles are fond of saying): When some rules are not executed, all the rest go down the tubes as well. CBHS would be better off without the do-rag prohibition than not making it stick. Our Supreme Kahuna is new at the job, but she's been around long enough to know that.

The Deans become crucial to late-working teachers when this mammoth school empties out. You can forget the police munching donuts at the front door (I kid you not). Bellowing for help wouldn't be heard—and if heard, would be ignored by them. The Deans also like to congregate and banter, but they spread their own sports and sex conversations a little more evenly around the long cavernous floors.

Even though I've convinced myself that the kids pose more of a physical danger to each other than to me, I'm jumpy when it's dark outside, the halls are vacant, and I'm alone with twenty-five kids who would like to kick my ass for keeping them here. And under mathematical torture to boot. The few Deans still wandering the halls are my thin blue line—may heaven protect them.

Elaine, from my repeater class, hands in seven better-late-than-never homeworks. May her tribe increase. I tell my kids it's never too late to hand them in.

WEDNESDAY, OCTOBER 15

First Grading Period

Pretty dismal—seventy-four out of 104 students failed. Just thirty-two passed. Melinda missed fifteen classes. This equals three weeks of the six possible and was reflected in a grade of 45, meaning she didn't just fail, she didn't show up. In fact, she shows up only sporadically for the rest of the semester and then only for a few minutes before she wanders out again during class. To where? I wonder.

All but eleven of my passing students just squeaked by with marks of 65. And the eleven best kids all scored only a 70. I might have plenty of complaints to make about CBHS, but pressure on me to pump up the grades isn't one of them. Mr. T. allows his math staff to call it as they see it. Nevertheless, consistently marginal results will reflect badly on him, too. What's happening to my goal of moving 80 percent of the kids to Level 3 or better?

In the 10th period, Quinton won't take out a pencil, despite the fact we've developed somewhat of a rapport. It's also the last time I see him. Probably in this incarnation. Same silent pencil protest with Lilian. She walks out of class. I'm so frustrated. Why is it so damn hard to bring or even ask for a pencil? They're so very troubled here. So many just can't get out of their own way.

I need to count my blessings. I pat myself on the back just a little for a small dose of evenhandedness. Archenemy Demarco, blabbermouth Stella, and even the prankster Alvin sneak by with 65s. The grading is entirely in my hands. I could have weighted their peevish, green-eyed malice so heavily that they would have failed. But they got the test scores, albeit narrowly, I required to pass on my overly complex rating scale. Joselyn's hard work scored one of the 70s. So did Kobe and Brandi. I feel good about this. Here's what these diverse personalities have in common. If you collectively tallied all their days missed from absences this grading period, you would get the number zero.

Do Nows

serve as the teachers' opening salvos—a hallowed tradition posted prominently on the blackboard for the kids to see when they manage to wander in. It instructs them to promptly take their seats and get to work on either a short spiral assignment or an introduction to the day's lesson. "Spiral," by the way, is educationese for reviewing past work. Apparently, while the word "review" works fine and is universally understood, "spiral" stands a good chance of not being immediately intelligible to non-teachers. Thereby making it preferred usage. One must, however, give some grudging appreciation for the word's added visual connotation, a hopeful image of a child looking back in his/her notebook—an entirely non-existent occurrence at CBHS.

At any rate, the idea is to warm up the little angels to actually being in math class—kind of like stretching exercises before they pump iron. In reality, the Do Now gives the teacher (who has just sprinted the maximum number of floors that can be programmed for him) time to get his brain organized and in working condition. Corralling the colts into their stalls takes top priority. Next, badger them to: take off their do-rags, stop yakking, take out a pencil, take out a notebook, take their heads off their desks, put away the cell phones and CD players, and get to work on the Do Now. Many will do none of these things except under maximum duress and interminable repetition by the enforcer—me. Then I take attendance.

Mr. T.'s rule of thumb postulates that this entire process should take less than five minutes. I'm sure it does for him, but sure as hell not for me. Herding the students and taking attendance alone takes more than five minutes and by the time all the aforementioned is over, I'm a solid ten to fifteen minutes into the period, and I haven't begun my mini-lesson. Worse. Ninety-eight percent of the kids blow off even trying the Do Now to begin with. For openers, no pencils. We could teach M.S. Escher a thing or two here at CBHS about patterns with no beginning and no end. Nothing like starting each and every class with a double dose of frustration. The Do Nows for most students are Do Nevers. Veteran teachers do a much better job getting into gear at the beginning of class than I do. I'm gaining respect for the know-how to accomplish this formidable job. I want to do better.

THURSDAY, OCTOBER 16

More on Co-op

Katherine tells us we're going to discuss cooperative group learning today. I brace myself. She assures me it can work. Pair the weak with the strong, give bonus points, don't let friends sit together, give each person a task, give time parameters. All right already. I respect Katherine's judgment. I'll try it some more.

FRIDAY, OCTOBER 17

On Schedule

The extra sixth class on Tuesdays and Thursdays strains me considerably. You wouldn't think so. But it does. Just like all non-educators, I had imagined that from a time perspective, teachers have it pretty good. Leave at 3:30 or 4:00 P.M. Only teach a few hours a day—nothing like a real job. Lots of time off and vacation. Doesn't pay that well, but on balance, pretty cushy. An entrepreneur, even the owner of a hot-dog stand, rules in his domain. Here I'm at the lowest rung, filling in a slot as nursemaid and intermittent instructor for overgrown babies. And I have to do it right on schedule!

One odor definitely not a hot dog wafts in the halls today. The aroma of pot's bouquet has its epicenter just outside the math department headquarters. Kids smile as they walk by. The teachers frown in consternation.

MONDAY, OCTOBER 20

Success Stories

Newspapers love to tell stories of the sublime and the ridiculous. Education is one of those subjects like movies in which everyone has an opinion and, therefore, qualifies as an expert. The sublime stories are the ones where selfless, intelligent people—mostly youngish women—struggle to create a special school where the formerly unwashed ghetto children are bathed in Shakespeare, classical music, and endless love. It's not that I doubt the veracity of these urban legends, I just don't believe that these true-to-life fairy tales have much applicability to the vast, troubled educational system we have in major cities.

When I taught Georgetown I stayed away from the success fables that often populate entrepreneurship programs. How Bill Gates created Microsoft in a garage may excite students, but has little relevance to the hard work and long hours awaiting 99.99 percent of future self-employed workers (a more accurate and less glamorous phrase than "entrepreneurs"). My own favorite case spins on a former government employee I knew who had turned in his retirement fund and mortgaged his house to start a doorjamb company. He finally succumbed to a myriad of problems and lost everything, including his pension. When he visited my class and told his tale, the kids were speechless—flabbergasted that someone actually came into the class and openly recounted his failure. Afterwards, one student followed me for four blocks to my car, exclaiming in dismay, "How could he do that? How could he lose his pension? Hurt his whole family?" For me, that's the reality of the *entrepreneurship game. Success in educating the Bronx children will come no easier.*

I had no success today. This is becoming my daily reality.

TUESDAY, OCTOBER 21

Nothing Works

Katherine suggests that I let the kids know more about myself to develop a closer-knit group. All right, let's run it up the flagpole—so later in class I venture that I was once in the movie business. Totally bored and uninterested. What dunderheads! What can I do to get them interested?

Nonplussed

Alvin found another way to give me ulcers. Whenever I correct him, his reply, "Cause I'm black," reverberates around the room. I dismiss the accusation, of course, but every evil lie, if repeated enough, has its believers. From the expression of some of the kids in the class, this awful canard has found a home.

Because of the ethnic and racial diversity, I imagine CBHS must have enough cultural issues without outright lies. Judging from my own classes, the mix is about 45 percent black, 40 percent Hispanic, 5 percent Asian, and 10 percent Eastern European, mostly Albanian.

WEDNESDAY, OCTOBER 22

Distracted

Among my numerous frailties, absent-mindedness looms right up there. I daily forget staff meetings, papers I need—you name it. Forget the Freudian analysis—I've always been this way. The kids' incessant commotion in the classroom yanks me off track. The little ones often ask why I get so upset with their endless chatter. It's not only the lack of respect for me as their teacher and wasting time. It's also the distraction of their easily diverted compatriots. And as for me? Their feeble-minded teacher loses his own path in the perpetual hum of the little dumplings' idle gossip. Endless avid inanities paint the room with white noise—a verbal street fugue musically progressing through sex, clothes, and sports, and back again to sex. The topics aren't unusual for adolescents, I suppose—it's just the manifest hostility I encounter when I have the nerve to suggest that the conversations be conducted outside the classroom.

THURSDAY, OCTOBER 23—FRIDAY, OCTOBER 24

Parent-Teacher Conferences

preside today. I decide to write a note to the parents:

Central Bronx High School
Ms. Linda Fuego, Principal
Math Department Mr. Tqiqi, A.P.

October 23, 2003
Comments to Parents/Legal Guardians
by Mr. Klass, Math Department

1. I truly like all the children I teach at CBHS. They are nice people.
2. I teach math to freshmen because I feel that math is the stepping-stone for opportunities in higher edu-cation, regardless of the specific interest or future occupation of the child. In addition to the math skills themselves, math teaches an ability to analyze and a discipline in thinking that benefits children in

all their school studies and will help them in their future life in the real world.

3. It's my observation that all of the children I teach could at a minimum pass Math A if they had the needed desire, attitude, and study habits. Beyond merely passing, many of them could do quite well if they choose to apply themselves.

4. To ensure success, the children need to apply themselves in the following ways: They must attend class on time every day, illness and family emergencies excepted. Many children fail to attend with regularity or come to class late. Math is not difficult, but it does require building on each day's new topic. Missing or being late to class puts the child in the position of falling behind, creating a difficult catch-up situation.

   a. They must sit quietly and take notes. Many children, even the better students, talk and misbehave in class. Kids love to talk with their friends. They should do so outside of class. Many children are surprised that I'm unhappy with them just because I've had to ask them three times to stop talking. Besides hurting themselves, children who talk out of turn create a disruption for the entire class.

   b. They must do their homework. I give about thirty minutes of homework each day, including weekends. Their textbooks should be at home and are not used in class so there should be no reason why they can't do the work.

   c. I recommend that all the children in my classes go to the free Saturday math tutoring classes from 9:00 A.M. to noon starting this Saturday. Children can come and go at any time and do not need to register. They do not need to stay the entire time nor come necessarily at 9:00 A.M. Children who are in sports programs can come after practice.

5. To help ensure a future success for your child, I ask for your help.

a. Please see that your child does his/her homework. This does not mean doing the work for them. Ask to see their class notes and the homework assignments I put on the blackboard every day. It usually involves reading a few pages of the textbook plus ten to twenty questions. I usually assign questions for which the answers are at the back of the textbook. I do this so that the children can monitor their progress and determine for themselves if they are on the right track. Ask to look at the work. You do not need to know math to see if the assignments are being completed neatly and the questions are being answered.

b. Please see that your child takes a scientific calculator, graph paper, pen/pencil to class every day. Many children arrive every day at class without these needed items, which I've begged them to bring from day one.

c. At this conference, I've told you if your child has been a discipline problem. If this is the case, please do what you can to convince your child of the necessity of good classroom habits. They will like the class better and do better as well.

An important part of their grade is classroom participation and behavior. They will not do well in my class if they misbehave.

d. Please have your child attend the Saturday math tutoring classes. I will give extra credit to the students that attend and work during the sessions. I will be checking attendance and discussing results with the Saturday math tutor.

These comments are mine alone and do not necessarily reflect the official position of Central Bronx High School."

A good letter, even if I say so myself. Except that I never send it. I show it to Victor and others in the T-L.

"What? Are you crazy? Never put something like this in writing. You'll get fired just like that." What's the big deal? But I'm learning that this school is a far more political animal than it might seem on the surface. I decide to communicate my letter directly to the parents that attend today's function.

Laughing Best

Not many parents show up. One habitual class annoyance comes with his mother and soon breaks out in tears. He confesses he doesn't know his math tables. To see this great big boy cry almost brings me to tears as well. I advise flash cards and a calculator and to come to me for help. None of these suggestions are ever followed.

Stella arrives with her mother. This student is a never-ending conversationalist who evidently has just complained to mom about my not helping her. Her mom indignantly confronts me, launching into her daughter's grievances. When I explain that her daughter spawns half of my class problems, the meeting takes on a different complexion.

The last visitor caps off the day brilliantly—Alvin's older sister. I explain her brother has smarts and could do much better but acts out to beat the band.

"And his accusation that I pick on him because he's black has no foundation whatsoever," I add defensively.

"Black? We're not black, we're Puerto Rican," says she. *Formidable.* What a gift from above this *belle* has brought me! He who laughs last . . .

FRIDAY, OCTOBER 24

Cooperative Learning Revisited

Skeptics of a student-centered approach, like me, are mollified somewhat by the fact that children nowadays just can't sit still and focus on anything, let alone Pythagoras. Ten minutes of instruction is probably past the breaking point for most of our pupils anyway. I'm warming up to the idea of a short lecture and then breaking up the kids into small groups. I approach the groups one at a time and coerce the vacant minds into learning some math by instruction a gaggle at a time. You can't teach them as a class, but in small groups some knowledge can be stuffed down their throats—something like concocting math pâté in these unwilling urban geese. If I can teach some kids, some math, some of the time, in small groups—it's been a helluva productive day. Theorists extol the virtues of students teaching each other. I'm not going along with that conjecture—the blind leading the blind. For me, cooperative learning means individual teaching.

A Weekender Gift

They also serve who wait—or something like that. Anyhow, I spin a web in the 14th period. Spider-like, I wait for Alvin's nightly *J'accuse*. He's ensnared on cue. After some typical monkey business and a remonstration from me:

"Oh, yeah. Cause I'm black, huh?" pops out.

"According to your sister, you're Puerto Rican. Not black."

Howls of laughter from his classmates must still reverberate in his ears. Case closed.

MONDAY, OCTOBER 27

Someone to Teach

I drum out thirteen kids in my classes. I'm somewhat heartened that a few of the pack hand in late homework. Gerald Peron forks over five. Even spastic-acting Stone Gotlins proffers one. Shaneika in the 14th period antes up seven. I had been after Noki about his homework. He's clearly doing well, but I want him to do better. He shells out five overdue.

Oh, yes. Noki. A new arrival in CBHS and the U.S., for that matter. Having this boy in my repeater class almost makes up for whatever else goes wrong in the day. Noki's from Pakistan. His parents sent him here to get a better education. To the Bronx? To CBHS? If this is an improvement for the boy, I can only guess what it must be like in the schools there. Well, anyway he lives here with his relatives. His uncle, I think. He can answer nearly all the questions in class and scores 90 plus on the quizzes. He's invariably well-mannered and prepared. A good sense of humor, too, and doesn't mind much helping the other kids in the class if I'm instructing a particularly lost child. I wish all—no, only 10 percent—of the kids were like him. Why be greedy?

And why is this standout in a repeater class? Scheduling problems. Coming from overseas, he arrived late to CBHS. Of all the kids I have, maybe I'm on his case the most. He's good in math, but in my life I've known better. And ones who work much harder, too. I'm deathly afraid that his relative excellence over his peers will put him to sleep. I even advise him to leave CBHS and apply to one of the new small schools where many of the better students have already fled. I don't think I'm getting through to him on the urgency, though.

Lights Out

Axiomatic among math teachers with problem (read: infuriating or delinquent) children:

The glee of a difficult child = (teacher's anger)^{nth} as n approaches infinity.

In other words, the angrier a kid can make the teacher, the happier he is. Creating a disturbance in class brings a halt to the teacher's lecture about some boring algebra. It also has the added benefit of preventing his peers from learning, too.

As winter approaches, evening arrives ever earlier in my afternoon sessions. Alvin, that overgrown baby, finds other ways to tweak me. He unleashes a particularly active hot button—turn out the lights on his way out the door, preferably with as many students left in the room as possible. By the end of the 14th period, the kids are ready to riot and run amok. My own flash point diminishes daily so that mentally I'm not far behind them. It's night outside and our courtyard windows face the opposite side of the building, adding to the dreariness. So when Alvin turns out the lights, it's totally dark in this interior classroom. I shout at Alvin who high tails it into the corridor and down the stairwell, making his getaway. It's become a nightly ritual and my only option is to stand at the door with my hand over the light switch. Even this maneuver doesn't always do the trick. Alvin sometimes rushes into the hallway, pressing his body, scorpion-like, on the opposite hall wall. Then pounces. He quickly pushes away my hand and then turns the light off anyway. I end these classes in a nightly rage.

TUESDAY, OCTOBER 28

From Here to There

For most of the kids, math is a bugbear to be avoided—a meaningless, incoherent, useless jumble of numbers and symbols with its major purpose to interfere with their preoccupations of dating, fashion, and music.

I decide to bring a little relevance into the classroom by asking students what they see themselves doing in five years (asking what they want to be when they grow up seems too juvenile and condescending). I've asked this question casually before but now I seek an answer from each child. The idea is to ambush them by pointing out the importance of math in whatever career they pick. The kids and I are both in for some surprises. Interestingly enough, surviving in a rough neighborhood, and perhaps even living in an unstable home, doesn't necessarily change a child's aspirations.

To my astonishment, they want to be doctors, lawyers, engineers— the kind of responses you'd expect in the burbs. Brandi Ailey wants to be both a doctor and a lawyer. One of the boys specifically aspires to be a chemical engineer. I'm shocked that the young man even knows the term "chemical engineer." Almost all of the children share two common elements:

#1: they have high hopes;

#2: none of them are passing my tests, paying attention, turning in any homework, or taking notes in class.

What gives?

I make my pitch for relevancy. Doctors obviously have to know math for the required science and chemistry courses and for dispensing correct medicine dosages. Lawyers use math for business reasons in real estate, wills, and commerce. Actors and professional athletes need to know how to manage their assets or their managers can filch their cash. I inform the wise guy who responded "drug dealer" that crime is a big business. Even though drug dealing would hurt him and others, top drug lords are expert in cash flows. Overall—mission accomplished, but the reality gap between their goals and what it takes to attain them strikes me hard.

In well-heeled suburbia, the kids, for the most part, pay attention, do the homework, and relentlessly troop toward their dreams. How can these kids think they will obtain heights with no effort, no focus, no work ethic, and no skills in math, English, science, or history? It seems impossible that they could even think of achievement with absolutely no effort on their part. Has the unreality of music videos or media's focus on millionaire athletes so clouded their minds that they live in some dream world? A few of them will survive. But the others march relentlessly toward and then off a cliff at the bottom of which lies a cruel, uncaring world that will swallow them up. I look at the children—and that's what they are, just little boys and girls and not young adults—and I shudder.

In the T-L, I share the experience and my concerns with the other teachers. The old-timers show no surprise.

"How can we get them from here to there?" My question is met dispassionately.

"They will never get from here to there," Victor answers. "Most of them are already goners." The question will now haunt me daily. How can we get the kids from where they are to where they dream of going?

WEDNESDAY, OCTOBER 29

The Candy Man

I go to Plan B. I'll engage at least some of the kids by bribing them. At least I know where I'll stand with them. My kickback is candy— Tootsie Roll Pops, peppermints, and flavored balls—all individually wrapped. I want to make sure the bribees don't suspect poisoning. I buy on the cheap from a discount odd-lot store in a mall near my home. I use the calculator on my nerdy black, plastic Casio watch to optimize the per piece price—2.8¢ is my max for the little beggars. I'm not a math teacher for nothing.

My idea works this way—payment for work only. So I begin my sales program: Answer my question, read aloud when asked, volunteer to go to the board, or—God forbid—hand in homework and get paid a treat. Candy for homework rarely gets any takers but miraculously the other offers seem to work a charm—for some of the kids. It amazes me that bored teenagers will actually do some work for a couple of cents of peppermints, but several of them even become anxious for it.

I routinely blow off shirkers during class who ask for freebies, but I generally cave in at the end of class after a sufficient amount of supplication. The word evidently is out. I talk tough in class, but I'm slowly gaining the reputation as a pussycat in private—which I am. Now occasionally, kids whom I've never seen wander in and beg for sweets. My carrot has me a little concerned. What if the little suckers (the kids I mean) are diabetic? What if they choke? To tell the truth, I'm not big on asking permission—for anything. I was pampered by my doting parents (may they rest in peace, even if they know I work in the Bronx) and spent the last two and a half decades being my own boss. If I had always asked for permission, what would I be now?—a schoolteacher maybe. I ventured into my own businesses mostly to avoid the words, "May I . . . " But these days, I'm a little litigation conscious, so I play it safe.

"Mr. T., may I give my students candy?"

"You're the teacher," thus spake our Assistant Principal of Mathematics with a smile. We were both satisfied with his Delphic reply. He won't interfere with me but won't sanction it, either. For my part, I gave notice that I dispense possibly prohibited goodies. Nevertheless, I still run the risk of interference from on high.

While the kids sure do talk dirty, they're unbelievably fastidious about their sweets. "Hey, mistah, this one's unwrapped," says

Shaneika, evidently a juvenile gourmet. I look at the ever-so-slightly unraveled end of a cherry ball. Shaneika took the bait in my 14th period class and answered a question.

I examine the allegedly damaged goods closely. "Looks fine to me," I reply unconvincingly.

Shaneika leaves no room for argument. "Well, it ain't." I always relent and replace any rejects. What's the use of a bribe if they won't take it? The candy routine has gotten a little out of hand. Naturally, they've come to expect treats for just anything—taking a seat, having a pencil on hand for a change—breathing comes next, I suppose. I sometimes balk at outright swindling, but mostly I give in. Like I say, I'm a closet pussycat.

THURSDAY, OCTOBER 30

Vicious Attack

Today, kids from outside CBHS attacked a young, female gym teacher. She's taken to the hospital. According to the newspaper, she suffered two hemorrhages in her left temple and a fracture to the right side of her skull. She's in a coma. Although we all hear the rumor of the incident, the administration says nothing about it.

FRIDAY, OCTOBER 31

Tonight's Halloween. Very few of my kids attend classes. Result: The students that show up learn more than they had in the entire prior week. I have no management control problems and can individually help the ones that need it. Other teachers report the same phenomenon. Small classes are where it's at.

MONDAY, NOVEMBER 3

Teacher Alarm

The school is buzzing with the reports of the attack on the gym teacher. What's responsible? everyone asks. The school's overcrowded. Many kids act hostile. Security is all but non-existent. All this makes the teachers, especially those on the late shift, very concerned.

Mr. T. gives us the go-ahead to finally hand out the textbooks to the repeater classes. My concern over this issue proves unnecessary: The kids still have theirs from last year—they never turned them in. Excepting only Noki.

I eject five kids in 8th period class. During my breaks in the last few days, I've tried to call eleven different homes about problem children but only got through to three of them. The point of the calls isn't only to get some help on the misbehavior, but also to let the parents know that their kids are failing. Two moms make appointments to see me but, as in the past with other such meetings, they never show up. Four urgent messages I leave for return calls are never returned and two numbers are wrong.

What a terrible day. More transferees pile into my sections. The administration calls the new students "over the counter." Sounds like drugs or low-priced stock. They aren't from the neighborhood necessarily. OTC means that the kids just walk in from anywhere in the city and get placed here. Some kids travel long distances to get here. The even more overcrowded or more troubled schools are exempted from OTCs, so CBHS gets a boatload. And they never stop arriving. It feels more like Ellis Island than a high school. It's not the children's fault. Many have migrant parents, go through endless evictions, or come from broken homes.

TUESDAY, NOVEMBER 4

Our Leader Speaks

Today's Election Day. No school, just professional development programs and opening remarks in the auditorium from Linda, our principal. The subject is school security. With a blank expression and in matter-of-fact monotone, our stolid matriarch tells us not to worry. Everything's under control. This doesn't cut it by a mile with the teachers. One of us in the audience comes on very angry with her. He must be tenured, I think, to take this attack-dog posture with her. Our saturnine sachem counters with her own complaint that the teachers aren't keeping the doors on the phone cabinets locked. That's why many of the tellies are out of order.

I see. No wonder security stinks here. It's the teachers' fault! This blame-the-victim posture couldn't be lamer. Don't they give new principals "How to Talk to the Faculty" lessons? Her knuckleheadedosityness keeps me muttering to myself throughout the day.

No *Noblesse Oblige*

The experienced teachers conduct the programs for today and some are pretty interesting—even helpful. Ms. Toni Harmony, who's retiring soon, exhibits a large white plastic or vinyl-something sheet. She writes the class objectives on it. Instead of rewriting the info on the blackboard in each classroom, she just carries it around with her, saving valuable time. Good idea. I ask to borrow it for a minute to measure it. I return it and put it next to her while she's yakking with another teacher. Later, she sees me and screeches that I've stolen her precious *objet d'art*. Normally, I'm a peaceful dog, at least with colleagues, anyway. But, I'm violently awakened and yap back at her. I enlighten her that I gave it back. So abashed to be rude to another teacher. I'm humiliated. Later Mr. T. questions me about the incident. He asks me to apologize to her, regardless of who's at fault. She's a senior teacher with many friends and connections. Not a good person to antagonize. I would comply if Mr. T.'s request were based upon *noblesse oblige* or merely being a gentleman. I don't know why for sure, but I don't seek a truce with her.

WEDNESDAY, NOVEMBER 5

A Harpy Revisited

Ms. Harmony isn't through with her dementia. She spots me in the hall and starts in again with the screaming maenad business. I tell her once more, this time calmly, that I put her laminated Hope Diamond right next to her yesterday. For proof, we troop off together to the scene of the crime, and there it is. I'm thinking I should apologize for being rude to her even if she started the skirmish. But before I do, she huffs, puffs, and prances out of the room with it. I proved her wrong and got no sorry-about-that from her. But yet, I spoke harshly to a lady and here I am complaining about the kids' behavior. I'm not happy with myself.

Sex Talk

Khalid knows no shame. He makes a sexually explicit comment to Shreya Newman and I pounce on him. I threaten to have him suspended if I hear any more loose talk again. Besides wanting to protect the female students from harassment, I'm concerned that if I don't take a strong stance I could be accused of complicity. At this age, both the boys and girls engage in all kinds of innuendo with heavy doses of touching, grabbing, and hair pulling. Mostly they like it, so enforcing a no-sex talk rule to the nth degree becomes nigh impossible.

Close Encounters of the Unwanted Kind

CBHS, a 3,000+ student, four-story building, one-block wide and a half-block long, doesn't have elevators—it has *an* elevator. It works only sporadically and then carts, for the most part, perfectly healthy-looking kids one floor up or down. Today, one strapping youth on the lift looks like he can bench press the math department. And another thing—kids aren't even supposed to use the elevator unless they have an elevator pass, are accompanied by a parent or teacher, or are obviously infirm. There are many in the last category. But mostly it's packed with plain lazy bambinos who don't want to walk, whatever the rules are.

Once or twice I did see a Dean throw an ineligible kid off the elevator, so I begin to do the same thing. But the thing is this—whenever you're not forced to be in the company of the cursing, squirming, do-ragged kids, you avoid it. I don't want to be congealed into a mote by them, or even see them for the precious few moments of a ride from the basement to the third floor. My brief experience in kicking these seditionists out is this: If you ask to see a pass, they're insulted—and won't get out. Except that I hold the door open until they finally leave. My strong-arming leaves the remaining adults and authorized kids fuming. I'm not so pleased myself. After a few of these identical episodes, I decide to use the stairs unless I'm weighted down or schlepping an overhead projector. Anyway, I can't take a complete day of moment-to-moment confrontation with the denizens here. Luckily, I'm on a weight-loss campaign anyhow and scampering up and down the stairs has melted a few pounds off. Also, I no longer need an oxygen tank after climbing up to the T-L in the morning. Maybe the brats have done me a favor.

The stairwells themselves prove to be ongoing, empty soft-drink and fast-food-garbage obstacle courses. The narrow trash-littered concourses also provide an opportune hiding place for cutting classes. For truants, a giant school like CBHS affords them a playground. The Deans rarely ask for hall passes and when they do, the kids just keep walking, pretending they don't hear them or maybe flip off, "Late for class, dude. Can't stop," then laughingly duck into the stairwell and disappear. Occasionally, the principal organizes a battalion to ambush the wandering vagabonds in a "sweep," but as the saying goes at CBHS—if it works today, it won't work tomorrow. Consequently, there's no lasting effect of a sudden truant raid. Rules not persistently and consistently enforced from Day 1 just get ignored.

Chatting Up the Deans

After hearing about the seriously injured coworker, making friends with the official goon squad takes on high priority. I get into a long discussion about security problems with two of the hall Deans in the T-L. Neither sees any light in the tunnel.

THURSDAY, NOVEMBER 6

A Sinking Feeling

slithers through me today. My students are slipping through my fingers. They're drowning. I throw out a life preserver but haul in very few.

We Have a Deans' List

here but it's not the usual one. I'm referring to a Deans' Referral Form for reporting student infractions to the Deans' office—in triplicate no less. I accidentally find out about the form in the T-L and immediately grab a fistful from the Deans' office. The idea is the teacher writes up the kid on the form, gives a copy to the Deans' office for follow-up, and maybe uses the last copy to send to the parents. So I go into action and start to write up all my problem kids—the foolery, habitual talking, disrespect, vulgarities, and other multivarious plagues *ad nauseum*. Very happy to have the Deans' Office (i.e., our internal military police) engaged in correcting all this mischief.

Except they're not very happy to hear from me. Via written edict, security lays down the law to Mr. T.: Tell Klass to quit bothering them with his petty problems. He passes it on to me. The decree comes from Mr. Santino who I think has correctly identified me as a teacher who doesn't like the status quo much. "Enough with the infraction reports" comes through loud and clear.

Nevertheless, I'm not one to throw away perfectly good triplicate forms that can still be used for intimidation against the enemy. I devise an alternative strategy that works perfectly in my 14th period class. One of my better students, Edwarto Mardija, decides to be disruptive today. After a couple of warning shots by me, I pull the form out of my briefcase and make a big point of writing his name down. I announce that I'm sending one of the copies to the Deans' Office—a complete lie as my missals are verboten, and I am now *persona non grata* there—and one home to his parents. Now Edwarto's parents hail from Eastern Europe. Romania I think. I've found that Eastern bloc moms and dads take a dim view of their children not behaving. And math, in particular, is taken seriously in those countries. I wish the native U.S. parents felt the same way. So Edwarto starts to visibly sweat. Begs me not to turn him in and quiets down. Keanu Shields, another jokester on my case today, couldn't care less if I took his Deans' Referral and broadcast it on the network news. Parental attitude counts plenty.

FRIDAY, NOVEMBER 7

Moments of Sobriety

occasionally land with a thud upon my students. They occur most frequently the day before or the day of a test. Today, mercy bestows some semblance of a day that could be categorized as "normal." I'm giving tests Monday and hand out sample versions that have precisely the same questions only with the numbers changed. I even supply the answers so that they'll know if they did the problems correctly. I'm concerned that I'm teaching so directly to my tests. None of my teachers in high school ever did that.

MONDAY, NOVEMBER 10

Never Easy Enough

Exams conclude. I'll probably pay for my relaxing Monday tests by the kids' acting out for the rest of the week. A quick look at them tells me my worries about making the tests too easy are unfounded. Despite presenting the same questions in the same order on the sample, many kids complain that they have never seen the material before. I'm vexed. All they had to do was spend an hour or so over the weekend to get a perfect score. The way I teach is an outright gift to any student who takes half a stab at it.

I Want to Love It

here. In the past, I've tutored children whom I think benefited from my help. In deciding to turn my life upside down by going to Mercy College for education courses, taking teacher qualification tests, and attending the required seminars, I sought to capture more of the same pleasure in helping kids be somebody. I see myself as a do-gooder. I can live with that. And these youngsters need my help badly.

I'm having problems dealing with the ungodly resistance I meet daily from these gremlins. My inability to connect with them disappoints and overwhelms me. This thought intrudes in almost every class. The Dean of the business school at Georgetown once told me that at the luncheon for graduating seniors, the boys on either side of him said that my class was the best course they had in their years at GU. What's happened? All the kids I taught then wanted to learn! I've badly miscalculated (not good for a math teacher). Before, I was always a demanding and tough instructor, but the kids liked me anyway—and worked hard. I've been caught completely off-guard. The kids here don't like my offerings and definitively don't want them. Aieeeeee! Now what do I do?

Being Watched

I'm staying ahead of schedule on the copying machine. Almost daily I hand out assignments to the kids. When the copier breaks down, and it does with regularity, I won't be caught with my pants down. Victor closely eyes me using the copier. I'm informed the official office in the basement should do big copying jobs. I make a mental note not to copy in front of him again. I don't like interference.

TUESDAY, NOVEMBER 11

I'm a Stiff

—at least to these kids. I'm always complaining about their incessant talking and horsing around, and lecturing them on the need to study, do homework, and the like. Pretty humorless. On the other hand, my compatriots tell me that being too buddy-buddy with the kids makes your job of creating class discipline impossible. In a work setting, I'm pretty private about my life anyhow and normally inclined to just get to work. But is that the right way to engage the kids? The literature on classroom management advises an even keel—not tough, not too friendly.

I try a new variation—add some relevancy about math and tell a little about myself as well. Warm things up a bit and get a little chummy. Maybe it's time for a little good-cop action. I stretch the day's topic on basic algebra to boast a bit about how I worked on the NASA Apollo Project in a computer simulation lab in Southern California. No response. Even rubbed elbows with the astronauts. No response. A little miffed on my part: "You kids *do know* that we went to the moon, don't you?" Massive shrugging of shoulders. OK. I just break off with the pals bit and get into the lesson. I'm disappointed. Thought the tykes would be interested in some real-life space-cadet stuff. What's it going to take to wake them up?

WEDNESDAY, NOVEMBER 12

Walking

Incessant talking and horseplay rule the day, Demarco being one of the most aggravating offenders. I discipline fifteen provocateurs for a multitude of misdemeanors or worse. Most of these children just don't get the fact that they're not on the elementary school playground any more and that high school really counts. When I consider that I gave each one of them two or more warnings and ended up booting six of them out of class, there goes the day.

It's not just the immaturity of the children that feeds the misbehavior. Stone Gotlins just can't sit down for more than a few minutes. He's forever getting up and walking around. I know I probably should just ignore him and get on with the lesson. But I lose my own focus with tomfoolery going on. My instinct, right or wrong: Put an end to it. I'm not a physician, but I feel Steve has some kind of undiagnosed attention deficit problem. Even when I see him in the halls, he's dancing in place, kicking his legs up high, and swinging his arms to some interior music in his head. I'd feel more sympathy if he were even somewhat polite. But he's not. Like many of the others, he's continually disrespectful and arrogant.

A Slap on the Wrist

One of the teachers I enjoy talking to the most in the T-L is Darwin Kerlak. I feel a guilty pleasure hearing his kids are worse than mine. Shame on me, but I also casually drop the fact that my student Joselyn continues to come to me for tutoring at lunch. Do you know that sweet Brandi Ailey who has such a delightful personality? And for the *coup de grâce*, oh, and my prodigal disciple Noki just broke the sound barrier with another sonic booming ace on an exam. His eyes flush with envy.

"My students suck. I hate them," says Darwin.

I utter appropriately sympathetic tsk, tsks. I'm careful not to agree with his sentiments. I'm scared that I'll sink into a state of hopelessness with my students, too, and then just blow off this whole urban teaching gig. Mr. T. interrupts us. Can I come into his office?

He hands me a complaint note from Mr. Santino, the A.P. of Organization. I had gotten tired of getting back torn, wet, and folded bathroom passes from my students. Frequently, they lose them anyway. Some kids never return from the bathroom or wherever they go. No problem. I just created my own with a rubber stamp I had made at Staples. I sign and date them and off the kiddies go to the potty or play hooky for the rest of the day. But good old-fashioned American ingenuity isn't all that appreciated here. I'm handed yet another official hall pass and told to use it. No more counterfeit ones, if you please. I'm pleased to comply, I tell Mr. T. Except that this time I simply make multiple Xerox copies of the real McCoy and use those. I don't hear any more about it, but I know I'm on Santino's "Can we get rid of this troublemaker?" list.

THURSDAY, NOVEMBER 13

Suddenly There Came a Tapping

On the plus side, some tots wake up. Shaneika Wilton hands in seven past homeworks. Celia hands in four. But twelve other students sprinkled throughout the day give me headaches. I give walking papers to eleven of them. If I wanted to write up all the troublemakers, I'd need a stenographer to teach here. All this is nothing by comparison to the outbreak between the 9th and 10th periods.

Okay. OOOO. KAAAA. I'm new to handling difficult kids and let my temper get away from me with the following result: Every day for the past week, a gang hangs around in the hall outside my 9th and 10th period classes, making catcalls to students they know in my classroom and knocking on the door. So, daily, I do the exact wrong thing. I go out in the hall and shout at them to be quiet. Get away from my classroom. Naturally, as soon I go back inside, the little weasels start to pound on the door even harder. Despite my room's location at the intersection of two long corridors, there are zilch guards around. Outraged, I repeat my over-the-top performance, but one of the troglotytes gets even angrier. He gapes menacingly at me through the classroom window. Then starts to batter it. Hard. He's breaking into the room to do God-knows-what to me with his buddies standing by. For a minute, I gaze at him, twelve inches from his face on the other side of the window. I look him directly in the eye to stare him down. It's not working. Maybe I should try something else. I get on the horn with Security. Mayday. One lucky thing—the window is plastic and not glass. It takes this delinquent about two minutes to punch out the entire window and the trim-work keeping it in place. In about thirty seconds, he's going to reach in and open the door. Now I'm scared. Maybe this kid or his accomplices have a knife. Finally, one of his buddies shouts that a guard is coming and they hightail it down the stairwell. A minute later one of the guards strolls in and asks what's the problem? I'm not all that gratified to see him. The marines showed up in time, all right. In time to carry out my lifeless body.

Love Letter to a Lackey

I've had enough and write the following letter. My understanding is that Linda has no clout to get better security at this school. Maybe this note will give her more ammo:

November 13, 2003
To: Ms. Linda Fuego, Principal
Central Bronx High School
Re: Incidents 11/13/03 and 11/03/03 and previously

Dear Ms. Fuego:

I want to bring to your attention two of many incidents regularly occurring in an [sic] around my classroom #313 between the 9th and 10th periods.

As I'm sure you know, classroom #313 is located at the intersection of the middle hallway and the main west hallway on the third floor. Three days a week I have a double 9th–10th period in that classroom. Between both periods, dozens of students regularly congregate with no security in sight. They pound on the doors of the classroom and make catcalls to the students inside.

Today, students pounded on my door and broke the window in the rear of the classroom. After a phone call, Security came too late to catch the students, although I did give a description of one of them. I felt physically threatened since they were looking straight at me as they pounded on the window.

On 11/03/03, approximately six of them forced their way into my classroom, running around, creating havoc while my class was in session. I yelled in the halls for several minutes for guards and help, to no avail. There were no guards then, and in general there are no or few guards on the entire floor. I was genuinely concerned for the safety of my students and me, not to mention that total loss of classroom control, which took me fifteen minutes to even partially regain.

Similar incidents happen to me regularly in room #250, including last night when a student tried to force his way into my room at the beginning of the 14th period.

This is a nearly nightly occurrence at this time and room where there is rarely any security to be seen on the entire floor after 5:00 P.M. As previously reported, the telephone does not work in room #250. Neither students nor teachers should be faced with this daily menace.

It is my understanding that for budgetary reasons the level of security in the halls has been reduced. If this is the case, I wish to express my strong disagreement with such decrease and in fact security must be significantly increased to protect the students and the faculty.

Sincerely,
Ric Klass
cc: Mr. T.

FRIDAY, NOVEMBER 14

Another Performance

Mr. T. conducts another observation. Linda doesn't show again, although I'm told she's supposed to sit in on a new teacher's class at least once a term. Mr. T. gives me a satisfactory rating on my "simple interest" lesson but I know I don't deserve it. His post-observation comments are right on the mark. I went too fast over the material, didn't give the kids a chance to summarize the day's lesson, didn't make kids sign a late log, and so on. I also distributed a handout without the school logo on it. No big deal there. Mr. T.'s attitude is absolutely supportive and positive. How did this terrific administrator end up here?

So This is Eden

The T-L chitchat centers on the new small schools sharing the same building as CBHS. A few call themselves an "Academy." But the name change isn't a panacea. For budgetary reasons they're crowded, too, with thirty-plus pupils per class. It's a simple equation: Kids = $. Funding comes on a daily per capita basis. So far, the small schools have an educational advantage: The students consist of kids who wanted a better school and applied to get in. They were interviewed along with their parents to gain acceptance. Filtering in aspiring students with supportive parents naturally makes the small schools successful, to some degree. Maybe even to a large degree. At first. Before the big schools are shut down and they have to take in my kids.

The new school experiment dictates that the teens all take the same classes together in every subject. Creating school spirit is the rationale. But it also means more trouble and rivalry among the schools clumped together in such a small space. I hear that gang fights are starting to break out among the new schools.

MONDAY, NOVEMBER 17

A New Direction

I try a new tack. I call it "Fail Quietly." I desperately need to bring down my own level of daily anger. It doesn't help them or me. Today I'm Very Low Key.

I use my most deferential and friendly tone and say to the big-mouths, "Look, guys, if you don't want to pass this course, all I ask is that you fail quietly. I won't bother you if you don't interfere with the kids that want to pass. Just sit in the back of the room and fail. Talk even. No problem."

Now this tactic has a positive effect. Temporarily. The ball's in their court. They look at me quizzically. I can almost hear them thinking: "Can I really not pay attention and he won't bother me?" But they also wonder: "Do I really want to fail?" The lion's share stay seated where they are and pay attention for a change.

The device produces mostly manageable classes today. But I know this strategy will not work two days in a row. No matter. The important thing right now is to gain my own self-control. Without it, there can be no lasting solution. My morale sinks a bit, though, after I learn in a staff meeting that a boy was caught with a knife today. I wonder what teacher will be faulted. It's certainly not going to be Admiral Girano, the Security fleet's commander, or that chipmunk-faced administratrix.

TUESDAY, NOVEMBER 18

All Other Issues Aside

"Can I keep doing this?" The difficulty of teaching here withstanding, I don't know if even in the best of circumstances I would enjoy teaching the same classes over and over. The repetition is boring. Yes, I do get better each time I teach a particular subject. That's good. Sometimes I even feel bad for the kids who have to suffer through my bungling first attempt. I ask around in the T-L. "Do you get bored?" The career teachers seem to find real satisfaction in continual improvement. Most of the new teachers are too busy coping with the same discipline problems I have to think about it. What Rob Simmons does tell me is that a guard removed a student who threatened him. Rob's a pretty tough nut. A former championship athlete. So if he felt threatened, I can only envision how I would've felt.

My apex for the day arrives when Kobe stays focused and asks questions while others play around in the last period. He's going to be somebody. But I'm no longer sure that the entire class will follow his lead.

WEDNESDAY, NOVEMBER 19

Hate Mail

My letter of November 13th to Linda was not well received, to say the least. Maybe I should have corrected all the typos. Anyway, our corpulent cobra lost no time in handing the letter over to Security.

Consequently, instead of a reply to my letter expressing a little sympathy, for crying-out-loud, from our titular leader and addressee, I get the following hate mail:

November 19, 2003
To: Mr. Klass, Mr. Tqiqi, Ms. Fuego
From: Freddy Girano, A.P. Security
Re: Third Floor Security

On November 19, 2003 at 1:15 pm, you called me to say that there was no security on the third floor. There, I observed two Deans, Mr. Mosconi and Mr. Manserd, as well as two SSAs (Note: I have no idea what an "SSA" is.), Agent Cross, and Agent Rance standing in front of your classroom 313. They explained to me that you called down despite the fact they were standing right there.

In the future, please be accurate in your verbal and written reports and responsible in your use of the Deans' office and security.

(and in handwriting at the bottom)
Also, 10th period you allowed your class to leave early.

It's suddenly clear to me. I'm the security problem. Life here would be hunky-dory if only Mr. Klass weren't terrorizing this blissful ivy-walled tower of academia. Forget the fact that my letter was about events on November 13, not on November 19 when I made another of my almost daily calls for help.

Other matters become clear as well. I've made a habit of ignoring the UFT as not relevant to a guy like me. Linda has made it clear that a mere teacher's call for help doesn't even merit a reply. She's going to play hardball with anyone who calls attention to problems here. More importantly, I've made an enemy of Security. This is serious. I have a frightening . . .

Daymare

The malevolent, young brood has gone over the top. This time they've rioted and there's no stopping them. One wild-eyed rabble-rouser takes out a switchblade—another, brass knuckles. The frenzied hoydens pound on the table, clamoring for my spilled blood. I streak to the phone and call Security. Luckily, I've left the phone cabinet unlocked against Linda's rules. The hallway goblin on the other end of the receiver hears my terrified voice and chuckles. It's too late to save me anyway. The school cops wait a good long time to show up and find my bludgeoned corpse. The hallucination ends with the evil baby sprites and school police alike exchanging high-fives all around.

Upon this reflection, I decide to take the adult and professional high road. I immediately scamper down to Mr. Girano, the Security chief, and beg forgiveness.

"I was trying to help by getting our security budget up," I plead with some sincerity.

Girano looks at me skeptically.

"I also think Security has a difficult mission but is doing a great job," I go on.

He deigns to forgive me—I hope—and he smiles a little. Bless him. I leave with some hope Security won't leave me hanging if I'm ever in true distress. As for her, our dear principal, she can take this job and stick it . . .

Up in Arms

The faculty continues to be upset over the unprovoked attack of the gym teacher. The unfortunate woman still can't work. The UFT calls a huddle about what to do. I decide to take a peek. I arrive late because it's held in the lunchroom, although the flyers say it's supposed to be somewhere else. We're told that charges are being pressed against the attacker. The union leaders remind us, "Custer was management." I take this to be standard union fire-breathing. From my point of view, the meeting serves primarily to let the staff vent its concerns. And they're plenty of them. We're scared of being vulnerable to physical attack because of inadequate security. Another concern voiced: Why can't we permanently get rid of troublemaking kids? They keep coming back to cause trouble after suspension or temporary relocation in another school. The meeting ends with no action plan. Mostly double-talk and slogans about union members sticking together.

THURSDAY, NOVEMBER 20

The Sweet Smell of No Success

greets me in the hallway going up the stairs today. Weed. If these kids are so stoned, why aren't they mellower?

Midterms today. Goodie. The kids usually don't cause as many problems.

FRIDAY, NOVEMBER 21

Kenya

While seeking refuge in the cafeteria this morning, I shoot the breeze with Kenya's history teacher. He tells me Kenya excels in history and writes brilliant poetry. I reconsider my view of Kenya. My thinking about him has definitely been lazy. He's one of the few demanding an education. But because he's so weak in math, I didn't give him credit for his innate intelligence and abilities. I hope not to repeat my error with other students.

Today I blissfully give more midterm exams. My witty remark, "It's better to give a test than to receive one," falls on unappreciative ears.

MONDAY, NOVEMBER 24

Thanksgiving starts Thursday. I bounce four kids in 8th period.

Hall Passes

I find this note in my mailbox today:

> Mr. Klass (I don't why she's so formal in this note since I know Janet, but maybe because she thinks I'll use it as evidence or something),
>
> I happened to see Khalid with your pass, had a tug-o-war with him over it, and won.
>
> Janet Mentari
> S.S. (social studies) Dept.

Janet attached one of my hall passes to the note. Well now. Although I'm sure many of the kids consider me an ogre on petty things like homework and keeping their yaps shut when not called on, there is some small stuff that I will not sweat. One element of that stuff is letting kids go to the bathroom. I'm sure girl problems cow all the male teachers into instant hall passes. Or at least that's what I tell myself. And if there's more than one or two needy ones, so be it. Still, I totally agree with the principal that we can't have kids abusing the passes to just wander the halls, and that's just what they do. Here's another take on it, too. If a kid wants out enough to lie about needing to go to the john, let him/her. One less distraction for the others. I'm already getting jaded about saving the world. Now I'm as happy as any other teacher to have kids who don't want to learn to just not be there. But Khalid has gone too far this time.

Khalid

I should dislike Khalid. He's a consummate pain in the neck. When he's not prattling to the girls next to him, he dares moving around the room to babble with a cohort. Whenever I call him on one of his misdemeanors, he indignantly denies any misdeed. Always. Even the other kids find him obnoxious and make fun of him. Now that I think of it, I should really, *really* dislike this pudgy hobbit. But I don't. I like him.

I'm something of a movie buff. A drama must have a good story. An action film must have action and a good story. But a comedy only needs to be funny, and Khalid is a funny boy.

His big, round, smiling face tells me endless lies: why his homework isn't done; why he shouldn't be punished for pulling Beth's hair; why he's forever coming late; or why he needs to bring huge, aromatic takeout Chinese lunches into class. I laugh just thinking about him.

His spunky demeanor is a holler for the other kids. They call him Snookie for a nickname and laugh when they say it. I don't know why. He hasn't caught on to how entertained I am, too. But yesterday I caught him with three of my hall passes. He's been collecting them by not turning them in when he gets back from the loo—taking advantage of my not-with-it-ness. I know he uses them to dodge the hall guards. Today Janet catches him with one more pass. Time to bring down the hammer.

Mouse to Mouse

La Capitaine strolls in unannounced and unexpected into one of my classes today. Minutes earlier, I was in the UFT lounge and jumped ten feet straight up when a mouse hopped next to my foot. I'm more stunned by Linda's appearance.

As our Supreme Chief enters, two of my rowdiest girls are in the midst of creating havoc. Linda's embodiment doesn't slow their mayhem a bit. Now Linda's no retiring flower and tells the girls with considerable sangfroid to quiet down right now. In turn, they call her a bitch and other niceties and demand Linda mind her own damn busi-ness. Meanwhile, I'm a deer caught in the headlights. I don't intervene. Linda apparently has the same protection as a head of state: At a nod from her, two guards whom I hadn't seen standing in the hall rush in and bodily remove the young harpies. I feel guilty all day. Mostly about letting a woman be insulted without taking any action on my own. Less so because she is our dour principal. I figure she has more experience than I and is entirely capable of handling the situation, which was cer-tainly the case. Still . . . did I do the right thing by remaining silent?

TUESDAY, NOVEMBER 25

Complainers

I sack five kids out of my 10th period class. Lately, a singular plague springs up. Her name is Stella Vantino. And she's cursing at me again. Akin to Kenya, she demands uninterrupted attention. No, I can't sim-ply answer the question she blurts out. I must stop my instruction, go to her table, and help her individually. Otherwise, I'm public enemy number one—and worthy of pretty low invective. But unlike Kenya, when I'm not at her elbow, she's busy gabbing away with any classmate within shouting distance. Stella's a caterwauling minx except when she's being tutored—an extraordinary genetic morph to the plain vanilla mischief-makers.

Losing Sleep—Losing Weight

I've always had a bit of a weight problem so when I start to lose a few pounds, "It's a good thing," I think. But when I realize I'm losing almost a pound a day, I'm not so sure. I quickly drop nearly fifteen pounds. Losing even one pound used to take a monumental effort on my part. I don't think even running up and down the stairs instead of taking the elevator would be enough exercise to account for the loss. What I am sure of is that my nightly insomnia isn't a good thing. I'm tossing and turning. How can I make this new career work? Can I help these kids? Is this a mistake? Should I focus on just helping a few and let the rest fall off the edge of the earth? Not exactly counting sheep before drifting off in reverie. My anger problem and my fatigue from lack of sleep add to my anxiety, big time. I find I'm even getting testy with Mr. T. And I still have regrets about not stepping in when Linda was insulted. What can I do?

I give a short quiz today. But before it starts, I try to show the classes how to do the problems. But they won't stop the bantering and childish diversions. In every class during the test, I have some kids ask me how to do the exact problem I just solved on the board. They tell me they have never seen any problems like the ones on the test. I want to howl. And the kids literally bounce up and down in their seats during the tests.

WEDNESDAY, NOVEMBER 26

Second Round

Today is the last day of the second marking period. Here's the score-board:

Period 8: one 70, one 65, and twenty-seven others fail.

Period 10: two 70s, three 65s, and twenty-three others fail.

Period 12: one 90, one 70, and fourteen others fail. This is my repeater class and really only four of the fourteen ever come to class anyway.

Period 14: one 80, four 70s, one 65, and twenty-three others fail. Nearly 21 percent of this class gloms a passing grade this marking period. I hereby dub them my genius section.

Unfortunately, Kenya and Demarco can't seem to get out of the 65 cellar, and I think the attention from boys yanked Brandi's grade this time down to a failing 60. Nevertheless, on balance, it's been marginally better this grading period. Several students upped their grade from 65 to 70, including the wicked witch of the Bronx, Stella. Kobe floated upwards to 80. But, despite the fact that Noki pulled down a 90, I'm disappointed. He still doesn't get it. The competition for excellence isn't here, but in the monied hinterlands, and private and magnet schools where frantic parents send their children for tutoring if their cherubs score below 96. The lack of co-stars at CBHS makes him lazy.

Absenteeism ranks as a major problem here at CBHS. The kids do poorly because they don't come to school and vice versa. Take Kobe as an instance. Despite the fact he can be a jumbo noodge, he's here. Every day. The net effect is if he only pays attention some of the time, my repetition of the basics can get through. And it does. Same for Brandi Ailey, Joselyn Bando, and even Klass-hater Demarco Boynton. They're unfailingly present in class. While many of the kids have every kind of personal problem pentimentoed by poor study habits, if they're here they've got a shot at getting through the system. While it seems to me that 80 percent of the kids can be classified as problem children, by no means does that signify that this same seismic quantity doesn't have the gray matter to cut the mustard. Take Lilian as an example. She's angry, hotheaded, boisterous, rude, and profane. To put it mildly. Still, she's no dummy. But she missed seventeen classes this grading period alone. She doesn't give herself half a chance to pass.

All courses give exams this week. Today, the day before Thanksgiving, I bribe my kids with math puzzles to do, accompanied by candy for all. Nevertheless, the children can't wait for the four-day vacation and still carry on anyway except in the 12th period.

Kristina, a sweet girl, but a tireless truant nonetheless, wants to go into fashion design. She sports a long, black, velvet coat; a handmade, chocolate brown leather bag; and intricately stitched designer jeans. I forget to ask her if she made her own stylish garments.

THURSDAY, NOVEMBER 27

Thanksgiving Vacation Prayer

I pray God is kind to those with good intentions—regardless of outcome—or else I'm in big trouble.

MONDAY, DECEMBER 1

Triage

The older, tenured teachers often have only upper-level courses. In effect, they work in an entirely different school—or maybe on a different planet. The kids taking pre-calculus and advanced algebra are the survivors of the system, the ones who have a guiding adult or their own internal gyroscope that propels them onward—only a small percentage of the 3,000+ kids here. They listen to the teacher, take notes, do the homework, and don't fight learning. They're still young and not perfect, but on the whole are manageable. These kids are the success stories from the ghetto one reads about in the newspapers. Their teachers are relaxed, calm, confident. They're doing good by helping kids who already know they want to be somebody and are willing to work for it—at least sometimes.

The rest of us humble slobs trying to teach the other juvenile aliens, slog away in a far different solar system. Almost daily I'm engaged in an ongoing debate with these other math teachers:

Which of two distinct approaches should we choose if we're going to do a good job and still keep our sanity in an inner city school?

Door #1: Cooperative learning—pair the best students in each class with lower-performing students. The theory is the heart of the cooperative learning push. Kids like to learn from other kids and teaching a subject is the best way to learn it yourself. Voilà. We've helped both the good and not-so-good kids at the same time. The younger teachers, especially the indoctrinated ones just out of teachers' college, embrace this line of attack.

Door #2: Triage—save the survivors. Let most of the kids who act out and fool around fail. They're going to anyway so we might as well help the kids who really could make a life for themselves. The others will just have to wait to grow up and maybe get a GED degree or go to a community college. Or maybe not. Some teachers, mostly the older ones, take this approach to an extreme. They put the "bad" kids at the back of the room and just ignore them. Let them talk, play games, and fail. The "good" kids sit close to the blackboard, next to the instructor and try, along with the teacher, to turn their back on the others. I was sickened when I first heard this description of a classroom setting. It's not why I came here. "I'm here to save all mankind," noble me used to think. I wonder if I can hold out and find a third way to reach these young folk before I surrender and walk through Door #2.

Neither Door #1, Nor Door #2

appeals to me. Whether I'm just not a practiced enough teacher to make a go of cooperative learning, or whether that line of pedagogy is a crock, doesn't make any difference. I can't make it work that way. I won't sacrifice 80 percent of my covey to the wolves.

I need a core of kids in each class whom I can connect to learning math. Maybe just four or five in each. My strategy is to engage a few opinion leaders, create centers of influence, and *sprinkle them in the classroom seating. All of us can be led by the nose—and most easily, kids without their own compass.*

Many of our children can be categorized as visual learners. In other words, you gotta draw 'em a picture. Okay. So today I take a stab at creating a graphic organizer. GOs come in different variations but the main idea is to pictorially present the information. It took about two hours last night to create my handout for today's lesson. The kids seem to like it but I made mistakes in its visual presentation. I can never make the lesson simple enough for them. For example, the kids don't know that 8/3 means 8 divided by 3. Who knew? They're high schoolers.

Blame the Victim

Marisa Fanto, the Russian teacher, enters the T-L, visibly upset—almost crying. One of her female students slapped her and then turned the facts on their head and accused Marisa of assault. The informed teachers in the T-L advise Marisa to immediately file a written report on the incident. The pros tell her that turning the accusation on the teacher is standard operating procedure for miscreants. They know that judges and public sympathy rests most heavily on the children's side.

TUESDAY, DECEMBER 2

Good Cop, Bad Cop

I chuck out Tyson Sumners, one of my better students. Ordinarily, I don't exile kids unless it's their third offense. It only takes a few misbehaving kids to ruin an entire session. Say, if three kids are fooling around and I have to address their misadventures three times each, I've not only used up half of my teaching time for that period but I've also turned off the kids who want to learn.

One of the hall guards peeks through the classroom window and sees Derek passing a note. The guard rushes in and yanks the boy out of class. Now Derek is one of the few kids who openly despises me. He's disruptive, too, but akin to his evil doppelganger, Demarco, leaves off when he knows I've had enough of his high-jinks. But he does his homework and occasionally answers problems. Guards go AWOL when I need them. But now, class stops unnecessarily for ham-fisted police action. Security can't seem to get it straight.

Who's to Blame?

Whatever goes awry in the class is my fault as far as the adolescents are concerned. If several wise guys interrupt the lesson, the students fault me. Not the troublemakers. I've tried to cop a plea by bidding the class to protest directly to the perpetrators. No soap. They don't buy it. Unfair—but there it is. My cohorts report the same phenomenon. In the classroom, I'm the daddy, the leader, the enforcer. The buck stops here whether I like it or not.

WEDNESDAY, DECEMBER 3

I drum out Kelsie Pines for her shenanigans and Stella Vantino stomps out swearing a blue streak after I warn her twice. Suddenly, a vision of *The Shawshank Redemption* appears to me. A jailbreak. Only this time, the warden breaks out. Me.

Intervisitations

sounds like a séance or Celtic rite, but it's only educationese for visiting another teacher's class. Mr. T., and I suppose school rules, mandates the staff to visit each other's sessions. It shouldn't need to be a requirement. It's a good idea, even though we have to do it. We also need to write up the expedition on a form. Here it is:

Name of visiting teacher: (i.e., me)
Date of visit:
Teacher visited:
Class visited:
Brief summary of lesson observed: (In other words, was I paying attention?)
Items to be incorporated by observing teacher: (What wonderful new ideas move me?)

And here's the kicker: The form has to be signed by me and the teacher I'm visiting. So much for any analysis. One consideration, though: It's only fair to be nice on these forms; otherwise, we'd have our own internal spy memos floating around.

I intervisit a special education class during a break. Because I have a few special resource kids, I'm curious about what goes on in this other teaching world. The small SPED room, as the kids call it, has a nifty wood, hexagonal table in the middle. Very personal and intimate. Ms. Grainger reviews a Regency Competency Test (RCT) in English with five twitchy students who squirm nonstop. Ms. Grainger explores their prior knowledge of the test paragraph and examines reading clues for answers to questions. Then she and the children take turns reading the paragraph, followed by answering the test. Some special ed children have the legal right to have the questions read to them by the teacher according to their own specific Individualized Education Plan (IEP). I watch a professionally taught lesson right out of the education college textbooks. Despite jokes about schools of education, in my mind, they serve a valuable purpose.

I create another graphic organizer to use in my classes, but it doesn't help with the lesson much. I have an ongoing difficulty. No matter how simple I think I've made the subject material, it's still too difficult for the kids. Every single topic I find too trivial to even discuss goes over their heads.

THURSDAY, DECEMBER 4

Under the Microscope

Mr. Tqiqi observes me again. This time, Mr. T. wants me to try group work. Mr. T. and other docents may believe in this bit of pedagogy but I'm still an agnostic. Mr. T. grants me another gift of a satisfactory rating but, in fact, I do terribly. The groups don't share their answers with the rest of the class and I do a pitiable job of giving instructions on how to work together in teams. The formal evaluation letter I get from Mr. T. has Linda's signature on it, saying she and Mr. T. enjoyed the session. She wasn't there. I still consider myself a businessman as well as a teacher and wonder if it's standard practice for the principal to sign an official document saying she was somewhere she wasn't.

FRIDAY, DECEMBER 5

Weekend Roundup

In my 8th period class this week, I drummed out fifteen kids after two warnings each. On the teensy weensy plus side, exactly one kid got one star, Alfredo Contero. In 14th period class this week, I show the door to three kids and give out fourteen warnings.

Thank you, patron saint of blackboard chalk. Not all kids beg for punishment every day. Jared Thompson snags two stars for the day. I make a big deal about it before he leaves the classroom. He's making a sincere effort to do well. Four others in the same class get two warnings each. Kobe comes to me midday in the library for tutoring. Nice to have a little positive reinforcement for my weekend sendoff.

Or is it? Maybe I'd be better off if I couldn't find a trace of deliverance in this undisciplined multitude. I could quit with a clear conscience. As it is, I'm bathed in just enough light to see shadows of possible redemption for them and me.

Snow Day

and early dismissal at 3:30. I'm happier than the children. Until I started teaching, I never took into account that the teachers love school closings, too. Students think teachers are robots that never even leave the school grounds. The kids outside act normal for a change, chasing each other around in snowball fights. As for me, I'm downright concerned. I'm blocks away from my secret parking space. Meanwhile, dozens of these masked and gloved demons try their utmost to do in anyone within firing range. The snow warriors supplement their ice-balls with rocks for an added lump on the head. If one of them gets the bright idea that a teacher has just become fair game, I'll be lucky to get to my car without a brain concussion.

My tired-looking, faded, and not-fashionable-even-when-new, stained ski jacket from years ago saves my derrière. Slouched over, with the hood covering my face, I creep past the imps lest, Thor forbid, I'm unmasked and snowballed to death with white bolts. Out of range, I sneak hurriedly beyond the ice-and-stone missiles to safety.

MONDAY, DECEMBER 8

More Than Welcome

describes my feelings for the Dean who yanks Lilian from my class today. She curses at him even more profusely than she usually directs my way. She's one sweet kid. The Dean should only enjoy the pleasure of her company.

Xmas Cooking

Prof. Richard Bucy, my advisor for my master's degree in engineering at USC, once told me, "Intuition is full of s _ _ t," (i.e., one's unproven assumptions can be decidedly wrong). And he should know. Together with another genius, he invented the "Kalman-Bucy Filtering Theorem," a mathematical technique for optimizing data. Used, I think, in every space, missile, and rocket program in the world, if not much more widely in other applications. His equation is non-intuitive in that by using apparently lousy info, one can improve on even better data. *Ja*?

Well, anyway, the point is that what seems obviously wrong can be very right and vice versa. Christmas draws nearer in this paper missile and spit-ball rocket factory. It's clear to me that in anticipation of the big holiday of presents and cheer, the kids will be a happy horde of hooligans. Obvious—and wrong. At the faculty meeting today, we're warned of the coming depression, increased hostility, and general malaise of the students as the holidays approach. Many students come from broken homes, without a mom or a dad—or both. For them, presents will be few and far between. Christmas just puts their unhappy circumstance in their faces. Despite their lack of academic efforts here, for many kids school *is* home—a place where their precious friends understand and share the same plight.

In class, Mikel chatters on about how his mom is going to cook a special Christmas dinner for him, complete with turkey, sweet potatoes, and gravy. The others, listening quietly for a change, gaze at him longingly. He will get a present—a mouth-watering and unforgettable meal prepared by his mother—just for him. My heart is in my throat. At this moment, they don't seem to me like my daily adversaries, just the vulnerable children they really are.

At a staff meeting, the special education teachers hold out a bright light. They tell us that all children can be helped. Don't give up. Find the needs and the positive and negative motivations to learn. The students' needs are tactile, auditory, and visual in nature. I come away from the meeting feeling that the special ed teachers are real-life angels who walk among us.

TUESDAY, DECEMBER 9

Jared continues to do well. I happily call his mom.
"Jared's doing well and trying hard in my math class," I tell her.
Somewhat disbelieving, "No *'buts'*?"
"No buts."
It feels good to make a parent happy for a change.
Coming back to earth, I throw José out because he won't take off his do-rag. I am so aggravated with this school administration. Everywhere, there are signs posted about not wearing do-rags, no CD players, etc. Why in the world can't Security stop the kids in their tracks and confiscate the contraband? The teachers are forced to be the bad guys and enforce the rules when the guards could bring an immediate halt to the problem.
In the T-L, Lindsey Holden asks me if I still want to teach the same kids next term. She must have overheard my request to Mr. T. when school started. I'm not so sure anymore. I don't know that I can take more freshman antics.

WEDNESDAY, DECEMBER 10

I gave out twenty-five warnings today and yesterday in one class alone. The admonition to us was right on. With the holiday coming up, the kids are wilder than ever.

Intervisitation #2

I intervisit Ms. Dantillo's ninth grade, first semester algebra class during a break. She's a tranquil, confident, and experienced teacher, about fiftyish I would guess. She speaks Tagalog with other teachers in the T-L. That's how I found out the language doesn't rhyme with "tag along." Anyhow, I think she's from the Philippines or thereabouts. She teaches in one of the new small schools embedded within CBHS, Anchor Academy. I have particular interest in seeing her class because I hear so much about how marvelous and all the small school environment is for both the students and teachers. Today, the topic is functions and relations—confusing material for lots of students, even those in the burbs. I'm advised by the math department's mentor, Tami Macumber, not to even try to teach it to my classes since the subject doesn't pop up on Regents exams.

Here are my written comments:

1. Ms. Dantillo did an excellent job of taking attendance and checking homework at same time.
2. Ms. Dantillo was able to maintain a firm but low-key style of maintaining order.
3. Class moved smoothly through the lesson w/o interruptions.

What I didn't say: We're supposed to accomplish the normal attendance and homework in a few minutes. However, I'm having trouble walking and chewing gum at the same time. Just getting the kids into their seats and to quiet down takes awhile before I can take attendance. Also, I'm still torn between having the kids hand in daily homework, an enormous time-consuming task, and checking the work at the kids' seats. If I check the homework *in vitro*, I invariably get drawn into excuses about why it's not done from most of the kids and queries on how to do a problem from the others. By the time I'm finished, the period is half over.

Call it sour grapes, but it seems to me that Ms. Dantillo's class has a fraction of the troublemakers that dwell in mine. But she has a couple of them, and to give her credit she never loses her composure. Always calm. This is the real key. I could use a good dose of "serenity now" as *Seinfeld*'s George Costanza's dad said. Here's an example. A tall, husky boy gets up and starts walking around the room in Ms. Dantillo's class. He looks a little spaced out, and his size means you can't see through him. I know immediately what I'd do. I'd tell the kid to sit his butt down or I'll have it tossed out. Or something to that effect. And worse, I'd be vexed at his show of disrespect in front of the others. What does the masterful Ms. Dantillo do? Absolutely nothing. She ignores him and keeps on teaching. In a bit, he takes a different seat than his first but causes no other disturbance. He repeats this behavior a few minutes later and throughout the period. Never a peep out of Dantillo. Nerves of steel. A few children do fool around, nothing like the bedlam I experience, but still mischief. Ms. D. handles it with aplomb and expediency. One or two kids chitchat throughout the period. Left alone entirely. The class goes on. When we get to the cooperative learning part of the lesson, many kids are engaged in the lesson. Several aren't. Nothing's perfect, but I'm impressed with Ms. Dantillo and hope to imitate her competency. But I'm also convinced that these small schools selected the best children in the pool to pull aboard into this new school initiative.

I throw José out again. Too many times the kids get recycled back into my class by the guards. They don't want to deal with *los problemas* either. Luckily, José goes out and stays out this time. In another class, the kids start mooing. Yes, mooing. They act like cows to get my goat.

In the T-L, one of the teachers tells me he learned to write on the blackboard without looking at it. He kind of writes backhanded.

Writing while keeping your eyes on the students also cuts way down on the paper wad air bombs, he informs me. It has another benefit, he says. "Stops the mooing."

THURSDAY, DECEMBER 11

"No Talking Please

during an exam or I'll take your paper and give you a zero." I lay down the law and stick to it.

Mostly.

Besides trying to maintain control, I'm trying to expose the class to a future life in college—if they get there. None of them has any sense of what a real academic climate is like. Alvin doesn't take my warning seriously and gets bounced out for blabbing. On his way out, he calls me "Mr. Ass." With a name like Klass, I've heard this a zillion times before. When I was ten.

Another kid guffaws. I start to get huffy with him, too, but he wins me over. "I was just laughing, mistah. I had to get it out." He gets off scot-free. I know I should treat all children equally, but I can't argue with the physics of youthful mirth.

FRIDAY, DECEMBER 12

Intervisitation #3

I intervisit Lila Korkna's class for juniors in intermediate algebra.

Lila came to the United States in 1992 from Albania where she majored in economics. At first, she worked as a housekeeper here but for the last six years, she's been teaching. She went to school to get a master's degree and complete her math courses. She was already plenty good at math anyhow. Iron Curtain societies may have stunk, but they drilled their children in mathematics like kids here study NBA scores and the latest Adidas shoes. Back-talking to teachers was an unknown form of suicide there. Their strict discipline doesn't sound so bad to me now, here in the Bronx.

Kind of short and plump, Lila is a pleasure among the math-teaching compatriots, with her good nature and willingness to converse on any subject. And I really love her melodic Albanian accent. The topic: Solving motion problems involving quadratic equations. I'm expecting a mostly well-behaved class since it's a midlevel course. So much for my intuition again. The class starts with sixteen kids but over the course of the period, another five wander in. For all my visits, I sit in the back so as not to interrupt anyone. But more importantly, I hope that the kids will forget I'm there so I can see what really goes on. What goes on in the back of this class?—slackers reading the newspaper. They're sitting right next to me but couldn't care less that I see them goof off. One of them gets caught by Lila and slinks out of the classroom before any disciplinary action can be inflicted. Regardless, many of the kids are engaged.

My written comments include Lila's rejoinder to a boy's putdown of a girl's intelligence—she answered a question incorrectly.

"It's not smart and dumb. It's people who do work and people who do not work," Lila snaps back.

True enough.

The class gets out of hand for a moment. What I don't submit on the intervisitation form is Lila's other, pithier remark

"If you don't want to listen—go. I can teach the class with just one student!"

Now she's talking my lingo! I absolutely buy into that line of reasoning with goldbrickers. I feel that way every class. Another thing impresses me. Lila doesn't sweat the small stuff, like minor talking amongst the kids. I almost always get visibly annoyed to the detriment of the lesson's continuity. I'm also envious of her legible writing on the blackboard. Chalk holder or not, mine's not improved.

Losing It

I've become unhinged. I'm taking the daily struggles way too personally. In my 14th period class, Ronald scrunches up his face in his uniquely devilish manner and starts to horse around. His expression makes me want to scream. I not only want to scream, I do.

"Take that smirk off your face and shut up." I suddenly explode, my face etched with crimson.

I'm not done. I crack in two the pencil in my hand, charge up to him, and fling it down towards the floor. But one half accidentally bounces off his desk, nearly striking him in the face. He's cowed, indeed. So am I. My God. I realize I've gone over the edge. We had just been warned in the faculty meeting that verbal abuse is technically corporal punishment. If that's the case, then I'm guilty and I'm worried. I back off of Ronald for the rest of the class, but don't really need to. The rage in my voice and face did indeed shut him up—for today anyway. I have to get a hold. I vow to never let myself get out of control again.

Written Statement
December 12, 2003
To Security:

My freshman student Alvin Torento has engaged in disturbing his math class for the entire term and has been asked to leave the classroom on several occasions. I have previously spoken to his father about his unsatisfactory behavior. Yesterday, December 11, 2003, he engaged in antics, including talking during an exam, disturbing the papers on my desk, calling me "an ass," and finally leaving the class during the test before I had a chance to call Security. I recommend that disciplinary action be taken by the school concerning Alvin.

Sincerely,
Ric Klass

SATURDAY, DECEMBER 13

My Introduction to Teaching

Today is the birthday of my late father and my older brother, Jim. My sibling first introduced me to a teacher's perspective while I was in college. He had already been uninvited back by one farmtown high school in Ohio. He passed out copies of *The Catcher in the Rye* to his English class students against the direct orders of the principal. It actually was more in-your-face than that. The principal had already confiscated them individually from Jim's kids. During lunch, Jim went into the principal's office, retrieved the alleged pornography, and handed them out again. For rural Ohio, Salinger's book was considered racy in those days. It was goodbye Jimmie-James. My recollection is that this episode made the newspapers around the state. Student censorship and all that stuff.

I think it was my sophomore year in college. I'm on Christmas vacation and visit Jim's high school English class in yet another rural Ohio town. It's the day before their holiday. We enter the first class to students giving Jim a standing ovation—I don't know why. But I am impressed with his popularity. Maybe Jim put them up to it, but I think the applause is for what's in store later in the day. In that class and the succeeding ones, the kids rehearse a skit. They pretend to quietly study and then stand up one-by-one while making a musical farmyard sound. Cuckoo. Cuckoo. The skit ends with them bobbing in a circle and then suddenly plopping down, pretending to study again. A school play, perhaps? At noon, all his kids meet in the lunchroom, scatter around the cafeteria, and start the playlet. Except no one knows about it in administration or the faculty. The skit creates an explosion of laughter and glee from the entire student body. The halls are buzzing. In the afternoon, Jim tells his kids to go outside—explicitly for the purpose of throwing snowballs. Then he swings open the doors of other classrooms and shouts that school is dismissed. Please go outside and play. The entire school empties out in about two minutes. No one is left to hear the stern demand from the principal over the loudspeaker to return to class. Jim was not invited back to teach there either. My own mother used to say to me before I left for school in the morning, "Remember, honey. Don't take any crap from your teachers." For Jim and me, a lack of reverence for school officials is hereditary.

MONDAY, DECEMBER 15

My Crony

My coworkers peg me for something of a wallflower. It's my conservative demeanor and lack of enthusiasm for gossip. They don't know that I was voted class clown in the 8th grade. Nothing's changed. Comedies almost always feature a compatriot alongside the main protagonist. My life's comedy is no different. While I'm naturally reticent to reveal much of my real self in a business setting, I enjoy having a sidekick—an audience to my ranting, raving, and general grumbling. My school buddy is Glenn.

Glenn grew up near Yankee Stadium. "That's why I'm here in the Bronx," he quips. We're teaching mostly the same courses and share copying work assignments, quizzes, and so on. We also trade personal barbs for fun. I make the mistake of poking him too hard.

The point-of-entry push for short mini-lessons and kids-teaching-other-kids-something-they-have-no-clue-about has become a running joke between us.

"Glenn, there was a meeting last night of the Committee On Un-Point-of-Entry Activities. I'm afraid your name was brought up." We're in the T-L alone and Glenn's not really paying attention to my McCarthyism gag but perks up a little when I mention that his name was brought up.

"By who?" he wants to know. My performance must go on.

Me—very straight and serious sounding—"The committee. I tried to protect you, Glenn, but your open hostility towards our point-of-entry mandate hasn't gone unnoticed by the higher ups."

I now have Glenn's full attention. I've got a decent poker face and Glenn's not 100 percent sure if I'm talking about a real event or engaging in my usual T-L burlesque. "I hope I've talked them into giving you another chance. But I don't know for sure." I think I'm unbelievably hilarious—Jay Leno, move over. Glenn starts to become truly agitated until my quivering cheek gives me away.

"You know, Ric, you really are a piece of crap."

I'm aghast that such a tasty joke has gone so flat. He's truly incensed. At what? It's a hah-hah. Now between periods, other teachers start to pile into the room, but Glenn's not done.

"You really are shit, Ric."

I'm stunned and my cheeks turn hot. Our jokes are private—not meant for the entire faculty. Now I'm steamed. I don't go in for public insults, especially crude ones. The others look at each other quizzically. Are Glenn and Ric going to get into a fight? I say nothing and walk out. I resolve to back off on kidding Glenn and maybe break off our friendship. I definitely don't want a repeat of today's embarrassment.

A Perfect Exam

It's really the student's responsibility to take makeup tests, but I press Shaneika to take the test she missed last week.

"Please let me take it here. I don't want to go to another classroom."

"I don't know, Shaneika. I'm handing back the tests now."

"Don't worry. I'll just sit in the corner by myself."

I give my dubious consent as she heads for the corner. I start to hand out the graded tests to the other kids. To help them learn the material, I put correct answers with the full solutions in red ink on their papers when they get questions wrong (which is almost all kids and all of the questions).

While I'm teaching the class, I'm oblivious to Shaneika and her exam. Next thing I know it's the end of the period. As she hands me back the test on her way out, I'm thinking, "One thing's for sure. She'll never get the last question right."

I look at the last question and I almost topple over. She correctly answered the question that no other kid got right. I quickly look at the other answers—they all seem correct, too. Shaneika got the last answer right on the makeup test that no one else got right in all my sections. She copied from a corrected test and filled in my own answers. She cheated right in front of my own eyes! Goddamn it. I'm so pissed off I can't see straight. Now what do I do? I didn't catch her red-handed.

I Don't Care for Him Either

I've discovered in the T-L that teachers try to like their students. Or at least not actively dislike them. Lindsey Holden admits with anguish that she just doesn't like one of hers. She feels bad about it. I know that many of my children, especially the ones that I send to Security, feel I have it in for them. Occasionally, I even tell a class that, uniformly, I like all of them. But what can I do? For the benefit of the kids that want to learn, I can't just allow the class to be disrupted. Conduct yourself like a student and all is forgiven. I mean it, too—even Derek who's sullen, arrogant, and impudent. Because of my own reactionary feelings, I try to go out of my way not to single him out for persecution. However, today I reach the end of my rope.

Written Statement
December 15, 2003

To Security:

My freshman student Derek MacAdams has engaged in disturbing his math class for the entire term and has been asked to leave the classroom on several occasions. I spoke with his mother on December 10, 2003, about his poor attitude. Today, he engaged in antics including talking. When I told him he had to leave the class and called Security, he left the classroom and shoved me out of the way to escape being led to the Deans' office by Security. I recommend that disciplinary action be taken by the school concerning Derek.

Sincerely,
Ric Klass

TUESDAY, DECEMBER 16

Intervisitation #4

OK. I'm just going to say "visit" this time—as in English. I visit Paul Lanier's third semester algebra class for sophomores. He's in his second year of teaching after graduating from Columbia University. He majored in history with a math minor. His goatee with sideburns, long brown hair, and buttons bearing the union slogan "UFT Fair Contract Now" trumpet to us, his putative comrades, the real love in his life— "the revolution." He can keep the buttons—I wish I had his hair.

Once again, I'm impressed with the low-key and self-assured manner that comes from experience. I write down all kinds of complimentary snippets in my written comments. Yet, I also feel a little gratified—maybe I'm not doing such a bad job by comparison. For one thing, it takes Paul sixteen minutes to get started with teaching the class after taking attendance and checking homework. I timed him. Practically none of the kids do the Do-Now; there's background noise of chatter going on while Paul checks the homework; and when he turns his back, kids start pitching wadded-paper baskets into the trashcan from the rear of the room. What can I say? Misery loves company.

Boot Camp

Pre-Bronx, an inspiration trooped through my brain—boot camp. My tutoring experiences and what I had read in the newspaper convinced me that many urban kids weren't prepared for high school. So . . . why not get them ready? I drew up a plan for a twenty-day summer program consisting of a corporate-sponsored light breakfast (McDonald's would be my target), followed up by alternating sessions of math, vocabulary, reading, and social skills. The camp would provide summer jobs for math teachers and bootstrap the kids into being better prepared for what lay ahead in high school. I had high hopes. I would use my B-School skills to land pilot grants and ultimately get the NYC Department of Education to adopt the idea in a big way.

Scholarships for gifted children and magnet schools like the Bronx High School of Science exist now. Also programs to usher a few of the most motivated ones into prep schools (aka "independent schools"). These fixes can't help more than an insignificant percentage of the kids. Boot Camp became my Mercy College term research paper. I turn it in today.

I no sooner hand Harriet my ambitious project than realize by how much my proposal misses the mark. It suddenly occurs to me—the kids won't go to summer school voluntarily. And, if they do attend under duress, they won't pay attention. Unless one has faced their daily wall of resistance, academic proposals like mine are just that—academic. My plan is no different than the cooperative learning presumption—no doubt a Ph.D. doctoral thesis put forward by misguided administrators.

I toss and turn all night about getting bested by Shaneika.

Justice for All

The world is set upon its feet again for me today. I finally get around to grading the papers on the last test. Sure enough, Shaneika not only gets the last answer right on her test—she notches a perfect score—but with one little problem I hadn't noticed earlier. Her 100 percent correct answers are for a different test. She copied off the wrong exam, not knowing I had handed out three test variations.

WEDNESDAY, DECEMBER 17

Puzzles

I can't figure out Mikel Hobart. He arrived late in the term and immediately started making mischief—that is, when he shows up, which isn't often. Yet he strikes me as innately intelligent and capable of doing the work. About two weeks ago he wrote me a note saying I should be firmer with the *other* kids. They're interfering with his ability to concentrate and learn. Fine. I had a short meeting with him after class and told him I'll try harder, and why doesn't he do the same. Then he disappeared. Mikel materializes today and reports he had been suspended. He intervened in a fight to protect a smaller student. I believe him. It hurts to see these children with potential get dragged down by every conceivable misfortune.

I'm forever searching for strategies to deal with these fledglings. When I have the slightest whiff of inspiration, I march into Mr. T.'s office. Usually I make the same comment or a minor variation, "We've got to have smaller classes." He nods in agreement as he continues his oppressive chores managing the math brigade.

Only fifteen kids show up for 12th period and I go to town. The mini-throng goes to the blackboard and loves it. Their busy little hands aren't doing the devil's work and they actually enjoy being engaged for a change. At the end of the period, one girl announces that this was her "favorite class."

Sure enough, in the *NY Times*, I start to read an article about a successful inner-city school. In the first few sentences, it says the school has fifteen kids per class, and I stop. Really, no more need be said.

Sensational headlines make a hullabaloo over dedicated teachers leading their charges through the murk. Right this second, I think a Barnum & Bailey pinhead instructing only fifteen of these little nudniks could get the job done. After all, didn't I this afternoon?

For the Record

I continue to document the daily high jinks. I don't know what good it does, but at least it makes me feel better and that's something:

> Written Statement
> December 17, 2003
>
> To Security:
> My freshman student Jamir Ransom has engaged in disturbing his 14th period math class in room 250 consistently this term and has been asked to leave the classroom on several occasions. Yesterday, December 16, 2003, he engaged in constant talking and horseplay. I tried moving him to different seats in the classroom, to no avail. When I told him he had to leave the class, he cursed and insulted me and turned off the lights on his way out. It was almost completely dark in the room since it was about 5:30 P.M. I have left a message at his home concerning his behavior. I recommend that disciplinary action be taken by the school concerning Jamir.
>
> Sincerely,
> Ric Klass

Written Statement
December 17, 2003

To Security:

My freshman student Charles Walton has engaged in disturbing his 14th period math class in room 250 consistently this term and has been asked to leave the classroom on several occasions. Yesterday, December 16, 2003, he engaged in constant talking and horseplay. I tried moving him to different seats in the classroom, to no avail. At one point, he was jumping on the desks. When I told him he had to leave the class, he cursed and insulted me on his way out. I have left a message at his home concerning his behavior. I recommend that disciplinary action be taken by the school concerning Charles.

Sincerely,
Ric Klass

THURSDAY, DECEMBER 18

Who's on Trial Here?

Mr. T. eavesdropped on some of my students. He says they're "O.D.ing on Mr. Klass," but like the blackboard work.

Okay. Tomorrow is a test day just before Xmas vacation. I will go over the actual test and assign it as homework prep but just not tell my angels that it is in fact *the* test. A little present to Santa Klass' helpers for the holidays.

Angels, indeed. Despite not being religiously observant, I still find myself thinking:

"Maybe I'm the one being tested. Maybe they *are* baby angels put on earth to see if I can stand up to the challenge and help them fly. Maybe their failure will really be mine. What if God is putting me on trial and not them?"

I really think this sometimes. No kidding.

FRIDAY, DECEMBER 19

Going Backwards

I've tried to reach twenty-four homes in the past ten days. Only one of the calls was congratulatory.

Jared Thompson genuinely had been trying to improve. I spoke to his mother ten days ago to tell her just that. She was so thrilled. I also call her today, this time to tell her that Jared has relapsed into doing poorly and misbehaving. One step forward and a jillion steps back. Do I ever feel dispirited. Other teachers warned me not to be too hasty making positive calls. The high recidivism rate makes most kids' progress transitory at best. I can't help myself. I'm anxious to bring some light into my students' lives, so I'm quick on the praise whenever I get a chance.

I get a note from a guidance counselor that Janelle Marquez is upset because Johnny Carton is harassing her with insulting comments. I will fix his wagon.

It's only a few days until Christmas and I find I'm beginning to like more of the students. Even the louts. Maybe it's the season. They are, after all, just big ignorant babies, but babies foremost.

But as I look at their faces now, more joyful than belligerent, I dwell on their life ahead. What is facing most of these children? Sometimes after yelling at them, I've told them that the truth is that I feel more sadness than anger at their behavior. A sobering revelation for them and me. The class always quiets down for the remaining time.

Last Test Before Xmas

Near the end of each test today I try to sell the kids on going to Saturday school and tutoring over the holidays. No interest. It includes breakfast, lunch, and free Metro cards. Still no takers.

"How about you, Aurora? Why don't you go?" I plead.

"I don't know, mistah." My test is spoiling the fun of thinking about vacation, and talk of more work isn't sitting well with her.

At the end of the day, I look over some of the tests. Since I gave them sample questions and answers yesterday, I'm expecting good marks. My stomach sickens. My present for the holidays is that they mostly all failed anyway—even though they had the exact test in hand the day before. Phooey!

SATURDAY, DECEMBER 20

Catching Up on Union Reading

I happen to read minutes of the UFT Action Plan from the December 17th delegates' meeting. I don't know how many of us read these forebodings, but they're scary:

"Resolved, . . .

The United Federation of Teachers will move to close temporarily any school or site where there is a clear and present life-threatening danger to the students and staff until such time as the immediate danger has been alleviated."

I don't know how my other union members feel, but I'm not exactly relieved to read that the NYC public school system even needs this kind of resolution from the UFT.

MONDAY, DECEMBER 22

Fresh Air

To paraphrase G.B. Shaw's witticism about Tallulah Bankhead, a day without CBHS is like a month in the country. I missed my first day of school today. My former business affairs linger on. Nonetheless, going down to Wall Street feels good and even though the chores interfere, it still beats going to CBHS. I left math puzzles for my substitute teacher with the explicit instructions that completed ones would be rewarded with chocolates the next day.

TUESDAY, DECEMBER 23

A Canteen Carnival

I start the day in the cafeteria with an English muffin I brought in to save money. And, anyway, I like the Thomas' brand. The ones they sell here taste like cardboard. I'm normally content here except when my reverie gets interrupted by a particular loudmouth teacher. Sad to say, but he's a regular patron here, too. He's now playing a guitar and singing a not very yuletide version of *I'm Leaving On a Jet Plane*, plus Spanish Christmas songs. For an encore, a jazzy Spanish *Silent Night*. Two female servers join in the caroling by beating on pots and pans with the bent and dented fake silver service. Another scrapes a drum beat on a potato peeler.

The ladies in their white uniforms and netted hair march all round and round through the kitchen and out the other side to the steaming platters of food already prepared for lunch. At first, annoyed at having my trance disturbed, I soon break out of my unseasonable attitude, sit back, and enjoy the spontaneous fiesta.

Later, Brandi, one of my favorite and most upbeat students, gives me a tie. She wants to go to both law school and medical school, but she's failing my class. What can she be thinking? Anyway, I'm touched by her thoughtfulness. Ordinarily, I wouldn't be caught dead wearing this thrift shop reject, but I plan to wear it tomorrow to show my appreciation.

Call to Arms

At lunchtime, I read the UFT house organ, *The CBHS Log*. After a gentle nudge to complete and return union membership cards, it launches into a *"Warning."* I'm informed that "charges of corporal punishment under the Department of Education are on the rise," and it gives advice on how to handle such matters.

Among other notices, the *"Overcrowding"* item lets us know that the UFT decries shoving more small schools inside our already crammed big schools. The cat is already out of the bag. As long as the Bloomberg administration has the reins, like it or not, big schools are on the way out and small schools are in. But the overcrowding won't be alleviated, even when the massive schools like CBHS are dead and just a memory. There will just be the names of more schools on the front door.

Reading on, there's a *"Be Vigilant"* notice, typical of the union approach to school matters. On one hand, there is the legitimate need to inform their constituents about vital issues, but the union accounts seem unduly negative on almost every subject. "Over the counter admissions continue without thought to anything that is logical." I certainly can attest to that. New kids poured into my classes right up until final exams. But then, on the other hand, antagonism takes over with this admonition, "Watch your class size numbers and report any that go over contractual limitations or compliances."

Other similar alarms appear throughout this cheerless epistle, "Be assured that your executive board will remain a staunch sentinel regarding any and all of your personal information." Is Big Brother after me, too?

The messages go on: "On December 10th, arbitration will commence for those denied sabbaticals last spring." I wonder if I can go on sabbatical before working a full year . . .

"We cannot do battle without the bullets you provide." So much for pacifism among the pedagogues.

"In the event that someone from the Office of Special Investigation (O.S.I.) shows up and wants to speak to you, *do not* (the organ's emphasis, not mine) do so without proper union representation and *never* give them any written statement they want you to author." Have I unknowingly entered some secret cabala? I put down the bulletin. The revolution can go on without me for the rest of the day.

I guess that, at heart, I'm not a union guy. The confrontational tone of these messages irritates me. It's true the city's administration doesn't go overboard meeting teachers half-way. However, these notices go over the top.

Noki, my best student, tells me that he's going home to Pakistan and won't be back until after final exams. He asks for math work to do over vacation. Ouch. The only kid who's solid in math in any of my classes has left for the term. I spend the day with my groups, giving them chocolates and puzzles. My other present is no homework over vacation. Not really that generous since most don't do homework anyway.

It's my last class before vacation and already dark out. Even so, I'm not permitted to let the kids leave yet. I see Harley, a Spanish teacher I've gotten friendly with, walk by, carrying a guitar. I wave him in and he sings Christmas songs in Spanish to the kids. They seem mellow as they sing along with him and dance and sway to the hymns. They feel content. As for me, I feel rescued.

School's out. It's moonless outside as I walk slowly to my car in the night's opacity. Suddenly, a young man, dressed in black and looking like a street bum, grabs my arm. Thoughts of "Am I going to get stabbed? Maybe he'll just want money," immediately spring into my mind.

"Hey, mistah. Can you get a cab around here?"

"I don't think many come 'round here," I answer briskly, yanking my arm away and not stopping to look at him. I keep on going. I'm annoyed that he touched me. When I finally reach my car, I think I should be more thankful I wasn't a mugging victim. I should have shown more courtesy to him. It strikes me that Christmas vacation starts now. "God bless us all, every one!" I say out loud, laughing at my own humbug.

WEDNESDAY, DECEMBER 24

First Day of Christmas Vacation

I'm breathless. Intoxicated that I won't have to face *them* again for thirteen days. Yet, filled with trepidation. The two-week vitamin pill dispenser I use also acts as a relentless reminder that *tempus fugit* as it empties. I fear that the aggravation, anger, and sadness that swelled in me over the past three months will surface again with renewed venom.

I could never have predicted this. Me, Ric Klass, filled with worldly knowledge, a fat academic resumé, and tons of bonhomie was sure to set them straight at Central Bronx High School. Yet, here I sit, paralyzed at the thought that my tedium and angst as a babysitter/prison warden and, by-the-way, incidental and ineffectual teacher of mathematics, would fall to me once more before I can blink.

What am I now going to do with the rest of my life? How did I get into this mess?

MONDAY, DECEMBER 29

A Safe Distance

My wife and I go to our friends' house for dinner. I find that people are fascinated about my decision to teach in the Bronx. Sort of the same kind of enthrallment as going to a horror movie, I suppose. Terrifying, but safe. As usual, when I tell about my experiences, they, too, heap praise on my obvious generosity. I say, no, I'm just stupid. They think I'm kidding. I'm not.

Doyle

I'm home from the city where I settled a lawsuit hanging over me for the past three years. I shook hands with my adversary and we're friends again, despite the dispute and my none-too-small cash payment to get him out of my hair so I can go on with my new life—whatever that's going to be. On the way out of my attorney's office, the managing partner asks me how it's going, teaching in the Bronx.

"Challenging," I reply with my standard answer.

"You know, I plan on doing the same thing some day when I retire from law." Right.

Later, Doyle, the young man I tutored some years ago, calls to tell me that he has completed his degree requirements from Fordham University. He is graduating with a high GPA and won a finance student contest competition. He tells me that my believing in him had made all the difference to him during the years. He had gone to night school, raised two children, and become a store manager to earn a living while completing his degree.

I knew he was making progress in school because of occasional calls from Sandy, his former high school guidance counselor. He told her he didn't want to talk to me until he could say he had succeeded in his mission. I wasn't altogether pleased about that. Maybe he thought I'm so rigid, only complete victory could win my adulation. That's not the case at all. Honest to God: Hats off to him for even being in the race at all. He won my respect long ago completing even a year or two of college. In a way, it's a shame that he didn't know that, but maybe not knowing helped him stay in the race until the finish line.

His phone call of happiness crowns the day. I see a glimmer of hope for my kids at CBHS. Maybe I won't quit on them just yet.

WEDNESDAY, DECEMBER 31

Shared Joy

I call Sandy to share our jubilation over Doyle's success. I express my current dilemma in the Bronx. She tells me her school has a new biology program with a maximum of fifteen kids per class, and it's working very well.

But she also says, "I'm frustrated with the kids who failed and won't come to my English class."

Despite a much different environment, Sandy's problems at Mamaroneck High School don't seem very different from mine.

FRIDAY, JANUARY 2

Marking Time

Just three more days of vacation. The thought makes me nervous and I flush red. A *NY Times* front-page headline broadcasts that schools are resisting the Bush law, "No Child Left Behind."

SUNDAY, JANUARY 4

Tomorrow, School Starts Again

I spend a good hour and a half transcribing the classroom attendance for the past three weeks of school into my grade book. What should take ten minutes recording the absences in a "normal" school becomes agonizing labor even with my wife's help.

"Okay. Twelfth period. José B," I call out. "Absent on the first, second, third; late on the fourth, absent on the fifth; late on the ninth and tenth; absent the fourteenth, fifteenth, and sixteenth; late on the seventeenth and eighteenth; absent on the nineteenth," my wife drones on. Her disgust over the pitiful attendance record matches my own. Is it any wonder he's failing? And this is a repeater class!

My fraternity brother, Ken, who I think is something like 564th in the presidential succession line as a result of his high-ranking job at the Justice Department, emailed me today: "So, tell me more about your new career, teaching."

My response: "Challenging, to say the least. Most of the kids will drown with or without my help. Teaching math in the Bronx is akin to giving out multicolor Band-Aids to earthquake survivors."

Note the standard "challenging" adjective. I don't think casual inquiries really justify a more truthful reply of "hair-raising," "frightening," "infuriating," "gloomy," and the like. Do people really want to know how you feel when they ask, "How are you?" I go to sleep depressed. Can I face *them* tomorrow? I consider how I got myself into this mess.

FALL 1992

Doyle

On a sunny September afternoon, a chance meeting with Sandy Weinman, head of special education at Mamaroneck High School, changed two lives. At a local Village Green gathering, we were working the table for the Democrats. She told me that a nice boy she advised had just awakened from a Rip Van Winkle slumber and announced that he wanted to go to college. His parents didn't speak English fluently; they didn't know the education drill and hadn't been able to plead his case. Technically in his junior year, he wasn't doing well in any of his courses. He was enrolled in remedial math and not going anywhere in algebra, a requirement for a New York State Regents diploma. "I'll tutor him," I said. Like that. But first I wanted to interview him.

We met at a diner. I mentally saw myself as a platoon sergeant, Lee Marvin in *The Big Red One*. Or maybe Lou Gossett Jr., kicking Richard Gere's Navy butt in *An Officer and a Gentleman*.

"This is going to be boot camp," I sternly told him.

"Okay."

"Do you know why I'm volunteering?"

"No, sir." An extremely courteous, personable, and handsome boy, I noted.

"For the same reason you'd throw someone a life raft if you saw him drowning." I wanted to be as dramatic as possible. I had a young son and if I was going to devote time to Doyle, he'd better be serious. "You can only go out Friday and Saturday nights. Saturday and Sunday will be for homework," I continued.

"Okay."

"And another thing, the only way you can ever, *ever* repay me is by doing well."

"I understand."

I explained to him that although he didn't know it, he was in a race—for his life, for scholarships, for admittance to the best schools and the best jobs. Most teens don't know this. Advantaged children from the manicured suburbs are born running. They will go to college, get good jobs—have a life worth living. The ghetto kids don't even know there is a race.

I tried hard to shake his resolve, but couldn't. I thought this boy might be worth my efforts. So every Saturday morning for nearly two full years, I picked him up at 7:30 at his home and drove to McDonald's. In time, some of the staff greeted Doyle in Spanish and asked me how he was doing. The amiable cashiers let me have endless coffee and never bothered us. Later on, I even made him quit the football team because I said it might interfere with his studies.

The first order of business was to get Doyle transferred into algebra and out of the remedial math class. A couple of weeks into it, Sandy told me that the algebra teacher thought that Doyle should go back to remedial math. *In loco parentis*, I arranged a meeting with the teacher. Friendly guy except that in front of my protégé, he announced that Doyle just couldn't hack it and would probably fail the upcoming quiz. I was irate that he would blatantly undermine Doyle's confidence—and right in his face. I enlightened him: My young charge would pass his course and wasn't quitting.

For the next several evenings, I tutored Doyle. I'll never forget how overcome with emotion I felt when he got a 100 percent on the quiz. Doyle had done *me* a favor I'll never forget. I decided that some day my final career would be helping great adolescents like Doyle.

On one occasion, I met with the special education committee at his high school and gave them hell. Doyle was just getting shoved out of the system—off the plank. He should have been tutored all along. And what nerve, not encouraging Doyle to study Spanish. I was afraid that his lack of literacy wouldn't let him take advantage of being bilingual. The committee accepted my complaints good-naturedly, although that didn't help the boy much. He had clearly suffered without a parent to take his side with the administration. I wondered how many children endured the same fate. No one to help them through the system, be their ombudsman. Doyle stuck to his regimen with me. About a year and half later, as a result of his Regents' scores in math, Doyle was awarded a scholarship to The State University of New York at Albany. Man, oh man, was I elated!

FALL 2002

Time for a Change

After about ten years, any occupation begins to smell like yesterday's fish to me. I'm getting bored in my investment company in Greenwich. And the clock is ticking. If I'm ever really going to teach high school math in an urban school, I'd better start now or I'll be too old a fogey to do anyone any good. I know how to get things accomplished: Prepare myself, find out the requirements, and complete them.

Abuse and Violence

Part of the rigmarole of getting licensed to teach in New York State includes attending two seminars—one on child abuse and the other on violence prevention. The seminars are conducted at a depressed-looking training facility in a downscale community, at least for affluent Westchester County, home to Hillary and Bill, not to mention really hard-core rich people like Martha Stewart and George Soros, or movie stars Glenn Close and Susan Sarandon. The instructional depot itself seems to me more like a holding tank for deviants than a seminar facility. But like the others, I trudge through the unlocked gates, down the corridor, and into the torture chamber. Cookies and coffee on long tables ease the lobotomy to come.

Anyhow, at least the punishment takes place a convenient twenty-minute drive from home. Why punishment? I figure that since I have a couple of graduate degrees, years of business experience, and college teaching under my belt, the public school system is lucky to get me. The required seminars, tests, and education courses serve as nothing more than harassment, a kind of educational fraternity pledge system where the future teachers are paddled under the ridiculous guise that it's good for their development.

The instructors in both seminars solve the most urgent question facing us: how to prove our attendance in order to receive credit from the New York State certification police. We complete a form to be returned after the session, showing proof positive our warm bodies were there.

The attendees range in age from what looks like college kids—must be graduating education majors—to the almost retired like myself. It's clear that everyone, including the instructors, want to get the obligation over with. The child abuse program emphasizes that in more than

90 percent of the cases, the victim knows the perpetrator. The U.S. statistics in the handouts turn my stomach: 2,000–4,000 children die each year as a result of child abuse, 19,000 cases of abuse and neglect are reported annually, and so on. We're taught how to identify abused children. The instructor makes a point of our legal obligations to report suspected child abuse to our supervisors and perhaps the police, or both. At the seminar's end, I'm not sure which.

I see it as a premonition now: The violence prevention program just might be relevant to my teaching in an urban setting. Again, the handout statistics aren't heartwarming. Every day in America: 17,152 public school students are suspended; 2,556 babies are born into poverty; and 3,356 high school students drop out. From the seminar's point of view, in-school violence includes bullying and abusive language in addition to physical aggression. Overall, the seminars' topics ring gloomy and foreboding. At each seminar's conclusion, the prospective clutch of teachers fly the coop by pushing their way out of the room to freedom and feeding time.

WINTER 2002

The Great Job Hunt

I decide that it's time to start looking for a position. While I'm convinced that I want to work at an urban school where kids really need my help, I know that it pays to check out the marketplace. I begin by contacting prep school placement agencies that I find on the Internet. I'm trying to keep my options open, but my heart isn't in it. I first discover that private schools now call themselves "independent schools." To dodge the elitist connotation of "private," I suppose. OK. A rose by any other name.

After faxing, emailing, and snail mailing my resumé to all the likely suspects, I get two nibbles. Sandy's recommendation, referring to me as a "master teacher"—so much baloney—must have helped capture their attention.

Turns out despite my feelings that yours truly has a surfeit of qualifications, the headhunters and independent schools don't necessarily agree. Here's the skinny: The most important qualification for teaching high school is—what else?—high school teaching experience. They're right. Let's face it. You don't need to be an MIT grad like me to teach algebra. College degrees and academic accomplishments mean almost nothing, especially in the Bronx.

How High?

We all read and hear the constant drumbeat in the press concerning our nation's need for new math teachers, especially in New York City. That demand apparently doesn't seem to deter the New York State Department of Education from making us jump through hoops to get a temporary license. Despite my degrees, the DOE requires I still have to take three tests to qualify. They are the CST, LAST, and AST-W. I still don't know exactly what the letters stand for, but they consist of a math test, a kind of teacher's liberal arts exam, and a writing test, respectively.

I take two of them, the AST-W and CST. I'm told the scores themselves aren't reported to your future schools, just whether you've passed. I know I did okay, and probably much better than that, but I'm feeling indignant that I had to even take them. And they took all day on a Saturday!

Headhunter #1

I meet with Jim and Cornelia Iredell of Independent School Placements at their home on Manhattan's West Side. Charming place. Charming people. But not all that encouraging. I have no high school teaching experience, and private schools want *and can get* the best teachers out there. Why? Because they pay the best? Noooooooo. Because anybody with a brain in his head, which excludes me I suppose, wants to teach smiling and willing students in a cozy, safe setting in a good neighborhood. That's why. Nevertheless, the Iredells will give float to my resumé and see if they can find a fit for me in high school heaven. I don't really want to teach in an independent school anyway, but leave somewhat crestfallen and a little better educated myself.

2003

JANUARY

Mug Shot

I arrive at the NYC DOE Center for Recruitment and Professional Development in what I guess is downtown Brooklyn just as lunchtime hits. Many moons ago I consulted for the Department of Housing and Urban Development in Washington, D.C., so I should know that any time around noon means a lengthy siesta for government workers. Afraid of losing my place in the long line, I don't leave for coffee or a snack. Eventually, I'm fingerprinted and photographed. At least there's no lineup.

Still Hunting . . .

I make a myriad of calls on openings at five different public schools in the Bronx, including one to the Bronx Leadership Academy deep in the heart of the eponymous borough. I may be in great demand in the NYC public school system, but I quickly learn no one is beating down my door to see me or even get my resumé.

Headhunter #2

Today I meet with Tim Hemphill of the Education Resource Group at the Ringha Hotel in Manhattan. Although he's located somewhere in

Pennsylvania, on the phone Tim seems knowledgeable about teacher placement in NYC independent schools. By this time, I'm savvy to use the word "independent" instead of private. When I enter the hotel suite, ERG is in the midst of schmoozing prospective clients (the schools themselves), and interviewing other deadbeats like me looking for a job. Tim says much the same thing as the Iredells. Doesn't hold out much hope but will try.

FEBRUARY

Job Interview #1

Tim comes through with an appointment for me right away. And it's practically walking distance from my house. It's premature, I know, but I start to fantasize about the easy commute. Rich kids are people, too, I try to convince myself. So today I meet at 8:45 A.M. with Lynn Chandler, the headmistress at an all-girls', Catholic-affiliated prep school. Teaching at an all-girls' high school strikes me as a little iffy for a first-time male teacher. I have one sibling—a brother. And although I have my own daughter and a wife of more than twenty years, I still feel I know almost nothing about girls—or women either, for that matter. Well, Ms. Chandler is very professional. She clearly knows her job. The follow-up letter to the headhunter pretty much sums up the meeting:

Tim,

Met today with Lynn and Martha, head of the math dept. I spoke to them separately. Both were very cordial. My guess is that Martha would prefer someone with high school teaching experience and that Linda would prefer someone with experience teaching in an all-girls' school. They both assumed from my background that I have a command of the subject material, but Martha emphasized that knowing and teaching aren't the same thing—quite true, I concurred.

Possibly because of my background in business or my confidence in being able to teach well, Martha expressed concern that perhaps I would not be open to learning their approach towards teaching and working in the math dept. on a team basis. I tried to convey my sincere desire to be open to their techniques and approach. I'm not sure Martha was convinced. I also told Martha I was happy to teach any level mathematics from 9th–12th grades, including AP calculus.

My discussion with Lynn focused on their premise of teaching and working with young women. After a cordial interview, Lynn said that she had more candidates to interview and consider, and would get back to me.

I very much appreciate the interview because it helped me to better understand the concerns and issues of an all-girls' school, and independent schools in general. I'll let you know what they say when they get back to me.

Thanks for the introduction and your efforts,

P.S.

Tim,

One additional comment: Inasmuch as this is a career change for me, Martha wanted to know if I was a serious candidate. On a positive note, I do think she took at face value my response that this fall I will be a high school math teacher.

Ric

What I didn't say to Tim was that I asked Ms. Chandler what I thought was a probing question, "What's the biggest problem a new teacher will face here?"

Without batting an eyelash, she immediately replied, "The parents."

The Rich don't pay big tuition bucks for their progeny to get anything but As and entrance into Ivy colleges. Very logical. As we were talking, I wondered if I really wanted to have to deal with the egos of wealthy moms and dads. Also not in my letter to Tim, Martha asked me what other kind of positions I was pursuing. I told her that if I didn't work there, I would probably teach public school in the Bronx. To wit, "I wouldn't do that if I were you." I ignored her advice, but in retrospect it had much to recommend it.

MARCH

Job Interview #2

I have an appointment to meet with Arianna Dantine, head of the math department at Harden High School in the Bronx. Finally, I get down to the business of employment in an urban school. There's a small fly in the ointment, however. I'm asked on the phone if I would be committed to an entirely student-centered approach to teaching. I hedge my bet by talking around the question. I'll do everything I can to support the department, I reply. And how about cooperative learning? I'm queried. Uh oh. Are we talking about the blind leading the blind here? The Latest Push?

Regardless, I'm determined to resist my instinct: "That's not the way we used to learn." I want to be a good teacher and even have this old dog learn new tricks.

The drive from home to Harden takes nothing flat down Interstate 95 to the northern edge of the Bronx. Identifying exactly which building is the high school and which is Co-Op City is another thing. They look the same—sterile and claustrophobic. Parking's jammed all around but I get lucky when a car pulls out. Endless wandering down wide, littered corridors and up an elevator finds me at the appointed spot. After a brief chat, Ms. Dantine and I quickly get into the cooperative learning thing. I try to disguise my heretical feelings and welcome her offer to show me a math class in session using a student-centered approach. I'm willing to have my mind changed.

Ms. Dantine and I enter, mid-period. The teens are arranged in groups of four. Exactly two out of the thirty children are engaged in any activity remotely connected to the study of mathematics. Most of them are gabbing about their social life or dozing. What amazes me the most, however, is that the kids sitting next to me and the *head of the math department*, don't even try to fake it. The teacher tries to gain control of the classroom at one point, but fails, even after almost shouting over the roar.

Ms. Dantine notices that the scene isn't making a particularly good impression on me. She tugs me into another advanced class where I'm assured the teacher is more experienced. She's right. Some of the kids are paying attention and even taking notes. But hey! Teach is standing at the front of the pack delivering a lecture. And the troop is all seated in rows— not in groups. After Ms. Dantine and I exit, I not so diplomatically point out that we were watching a traditional class. Yes, but that's not usually how she teaches, I am assured. But I don't feel assured. I feel vindicated.

Job Interview #3

Before I even get to my appointment at the Bronx Preparatory School, I'm ready to like it. The day before, I read an advertisement for a high school math teacher at a new charter school in the Bronx and immediately fax my resumé. Just as quickly, Kristin Jordan, the school's director, calls back and arranges today's meeting. The Internet tells me that Ms. Jordan, a young Exeter and Brown grad, has raised millions for her new school. Impressive. We take a walk through the halls and peer into the classes. The kids are dressed in uniforms, and to a child, are paying close attention to the teachers. Between periods, the children, all of color, I think, march in crocodiles to their next class. Wow! Please come back to teach a sample class.

Demo Class #1

A few days later, I'm back for a demo with eighth graders. The tykes are a trifle young for my brand of teaching, but I do manage to get a girl to do a problem on the blackboard who, I'm told later, has never volunteered before. My secret? I whisper in her ear that I'd help her at the board and not-to-worry. The upshot? I'm told: Don't call, we'll call you. They don't. Everyone wants to teach in a school like that, I tell myself.

Certification Evaluation

I'm still a bit confused about the qualifications to become a licensed teacher in New York State and decide to check with the powers that be to make sure I know what's expected. The DOE service line meets my expectations. The numerous messages and numbers I punch up are designed to discourage one from ever making the mistake of calling again. The phone labyrinth has a particularly unhappy surprise ending. After about fifteen minutes of listening to messages, thwacking up various extensions and whatnot, my call terminates with, "We're too busy to answer your call. Call again," or something like that, and hangs up. I'm self-employed and won't get fired for wasting time during business hours, so I don't give up. Miracle of miracles, I finally get through.

The long and the short of it: I need some education courses, the LAST test (already scheduled for May), and I need to meet the foreign language requirement. Foreign language requirement? Although my bachelor's degree didn't require a language for my major in aeronautics and astronautics or my minor in lit., the NY DOE does. Perhaps classical Greek would come in handy teaching math in the Bronx. Or maybe not. At least I don't have to complete that requirement until I get my permanent teaching certificate in a year or two. The irony is that I've been trying to learn Spanish for the last twenty years. My wife and I even took classes at Georgetown on Saturdays for a few semesters. I like languages. Along the way in night schools, I've taken French and German as well. I even tried to teach myself Japanese and Swedish. But, even though I have an interest, I have no ear for languages. This isn't even the worst part. Much later, I discover that I've screwed myself for even asking to be evaluated by the NYS DOE. The college where I'll complete my education courses will automatically request the DOE to certify me. Now I'm flagged as missing the language requirement. It would have been a Monopoly card to PASS GO. But, no. I had to ask.

Live and learn.

APRIL

Job Interviews #4 & #5

I meet with Ken Gaskins, Principal of Bronx Leadership Academy, and am I ever impressed. I'm introduced to some of the other teachers who are as enthusiastic as they are young. One of them, *très* gung-ho, volunteers to give me a guided tour. The kids, quiet and polite, wear uniforms. No metal detector at the school entrance—a matter of pride commented on by Ken and even the amiable guard. Ken and his staff, in just a few years, have created a small public school with an impressive graduation and college acceptance rate. Something around 80 percent. BLA lies nearly adjacent to the Cross Bronx Expressway in a busy, if not a bit seedy, commercial neighborhood. While the parking story isn't great, on balance it looks like a fairly safe place to hang my hat. I'd like to get a position here. I will be teaching a demo class to demonstrate my skills, if any, in the next week or so.

The next week, I head to a meeting at Bronx Leadership Academy II, modeled after BLA. I take in the sights of the decaying neighborhood. There's no doubt that I'm in the heart of the troubled Bronx. BLAII opened last year as one of the new small schools in New York City. It's embedded in the once stately Morris High School, which organizationally is being broken up into smaller high schools. It's my first introduction to this sort of jumbled arrangement and I find it a bit schizophrenic and confusing.

After passing muster by the guards and through the metal detector, I notice some students wear uniforms and some look like rejects from MTV gangsta videos. BLAII is on the second floor. Despite guards on every floor, I wonder whether it's safe to walk up the stairwell.

Here's another thing. On one hand, I want to teach in an urban school. The other hand is telling me to do it where I stand a good chance of not getting pummeled, stabbed, or worse by my students. I had never even been in the Bronx before I made this midlife career change. When I've driven by especially rough-looking areas there on the expressway, I've always hoped that fate wouldn't choose this spot for my car to break down. I want to choose my battleground where the recruits and I both have the best chance of surviving.

Meanwhile, I'm supposed to meet today with Mrs. Franklin, the principal of BLAII. But she's called away on some emergency and instead, I meet with the resident school mentor who I think is a retired principal. I arrange to come back and teach a demo class here, too. With all the commotion going on in the other schools in the building, I couldn't even guess if BLAII would ever catch up with its predecessor.

MAY

Getting an Education

While hunting for a job, I haven't yet decided how I'm going to meet the educational course requirements for a temporary teaching license. I can't teach in any public school this fall without meeting them. I have different directions I can go. Lehman College in the Bronx and one or two others have programs for change-of-career blokes like me. None seem to have any interest in granting me transfer credits for previous courses I took earning two master's degrees. That frosts my butt, too. I mean, really. I have two degrees in engineering and an MBA.

This new career has become hell week with push-ups and jumping jacks. Can't I just show them my fraternity pin? Taking exams, seminars, educational courses, and now scrounging for a job doesn't add up to a tad of the appreciation on anyone's part I thought I might expect.

I call the United Federation of Teachers, which represents NYC public school teachers, for advice on educational requirements. A UFT rep happens to mention that Mercy College has a program especially suited for someone wanting to teach in the Bronx. I've driven by Mercy's beautiful Westchester County campus along the Hudson River. This image seems more to my liking and I immediately make an appointment with the head of the program, Esther Wermuth. The next day, Esther (she asks me to call her that) graciously welcomes me into her office and yes, of course, she can arrange to have some of my graduate credits transferred. This is more like it. I am being treated like an experienced professional and so I fill out the application registry right then and there to enroll in the master's degree internship program. Classes start this summer.

Referrals

Tick tock. The numerous *New York Times* ads tell me school hiring holds full sway for the fall. Alleged demand for NYC math teachers notwithstanding, I'm going to have to hustle to secure an acceptable position. Even with my supposed impressive credentials, I may not be able to be picky. While I think it would be great to teach at BLA, tenured teachers have first dibs on job openings. It seems that the new NYC small school initiative has sparked a kind of gold rush mentality among the seasoned pros. But maybe it's more like rats jumping sinking ships to hop on more seaworthy vessels.

While I'm in her office, Esther kindly puts me in touch with two leads—the principal of Central Bronx High School and the principal of Diana Sands School, a middle school—both in the Bronx.

Demo Class #2

I return to BLA where I'd really like to get an offer. First, I sit in on a freshman algebra class. I'm at the back where one of the lads is obviously having difficulty doing an assigned problem. I work with him. I like helping out the child, and I feel that we have some rapport. This change of career voyage seems a good idea. Teaching in the Bronx will work out fine.

When I meet the instructor for a few minutes before my demo class, she's boiling over in her own dilemma. I eavesdrop as she tells another colleague how she's tried for years to pass the LAST test required for her position but failed to do so. Now she has been told that she either passes or gets booted out of the NYC school system. I'm scheduled to take the exam myself next week. I've seen samples of the LAST test but decide not to tell her how easy I think it is. She might not find that encouraging. Sounds to me like there's going to be one more position in the math department. In any event, we don't have time to chat about my upcoming performance. I'm next on the agenda.

After a brief intro by the regular teacher, I get going with my spiel. I'm a little rusty for the lecture portion. The subject is exponential equations. I've put on a better show in my time. For one thing, teaching bell-to-bell proves far easier to say than do. How much do you try to teach in forty-one minutes? I'm also not sure what I can assume the kids already know. I don't want to be either over or under their heads. I use a borrowed projector for some transparencies I have prepared. But as I present the lesson, I don't feel I'm connecting with the students. I knew the material cold decades ago. But that was *decades* ago. I run out of steam five minutes before the whistle blows and turn the show over to its usual mistress. She asks for and gets polite applause for my appearance. Like I said, I've done better. They'll get back to me.

Job Interview #6

Later in the day, I meet briefly with one of Esther's referrals, the principal of Central Bronx High School. He immediately pawns me off on Mr. T. when we meet for the first time. Despite his innate good breeding, he's running around at full gallop. It's nearly the end of the school year and he's revving up his coterie of instructors for finals and monitoring the required New York State Regents exams. Between taking a breath, he informs me several of his staff are leaving so he's got slots to fill. Because he's so busy, I feel he'd like to get the new hiring over and done with. He says to me, please return in a few days to show him a sample class. For the Bronx, this big school is not half-bad. The neighborhood's a little down at the mouth, but there's housing stock in the neighborhood that shows it once was, and maybe even now is, a decent place to live. I could do much worse.

Demo Class #3

I teach a first-year algebra lesson in Denis Friend's class at CBHS. Denis is young and strikes me as a good guy. Very welcoming. I start right into the session without an intro from him. By this time, I'm getting into the rhythm of a forty-one-minute class. Also, Algebra I is pretty trivial even for a guy like me who hasn't looked at it for some time. Mr. T. sits in on the session at the beginning. I do a lot better job teaching this class. I hope he appreciates the fact that I immediately tell the kids in no uncertain terms to get their behinds in the chairs, take out their pencils, and start taking notes. While in my heart I feel deeply for children, I don't like sass or fooling around on my time. My way or the highway as far as discipline is concerned. On the other hand, maybe he'll think I'm too rigid for this environment. But since Mr. T. has several positions open, I feel I'm likely to be offered a job here.

Demo Class #4

I demo teach freshman algebra at BLAII. But first, I observe the math teacher instructing a previous class. He's from one of the Caribbean islands and I have trouble understanding him. I'm not sure if the kids understand him or not. I guess they're used to his thick accent. The students in BLAII all wear white shirts. The shirts aren't necessarily tucked in and the ties aren't tied in what I'd call a Windsor knot, but it sure beats the sloppy hip-hop attire of the other kids in the building. A boy sitting next to me asks if I'm going to teach in his school. I say maybe.

"I hope so, mistah. We need help here and want to learn," he explains plaintively. I'm touched. I feel that I'm definitely on the right path. Before leaving, I'm told that the new teacher funding isn't definite yet. They'll call me. But they don't.

Enrolling

I've squeezed into the Mercy College teaching internship program at the last moment. I complete the registration at Diana Sands middle school where I'll take classes this summer, instead of the bucolic setting in Westchester. Oh, well. I was kind of looking forward to rejoining academia mixed in with riverside strolls. I make the most of the registration session by conning one of the administrators into letting me take a graduate Education Law course instead of one of the required undergraduate education courses meant for elementary school teachers. But I can't dodge all of the requirements. I'm forced to enroll in "Evaluation and Assessment," "Cultural Perspectives," and "Integrating Technology into the Classroom," or some names like that.

Last LAST

I take the LAST test, the SAT equivalent for teachers. It's a no-brainer but I hope to hell it's the last test I have to take to get a job in this city. Another afternoon wasted.

Paperwork

After multiple calls to BLA without a commitment, I accept an offer from Central Bronx High School. I rationalize the choice as being far from the worst school I could land in. Mr. T. seems gentlemanly, the neighborhood appears to be fairly safe—without the bombed-out look of some Bronx neighborhoods—and the commute is only twenty minutes or so from my house. Not bad at all.

I scurry around to complete the necessary paperwork. Esther lets me barge into her office to obtain a letter from her proving I'm eligible to be hired by the DOE. It says I have the Mercy College imprimatur for sponsorship under their internship program and that I will be taking the required education college courses this summer needed for an internship license to teach in NYC. Then I hand carry the letter to Linda Fuego, Assistant Principal of Organization at CBHS. I'm going to get to know her better. She forks over her own letter and I'm off to the DOE. After cooling my heels there for the better part of an hour, I'm told that Esther's letter notwithstanding, I haven't yet met the requirements for a license. Come back when I've taken the necessary courses. How would I be treated if there weren't a demand for math teachers?

Police Record

I return to Brooklyn. The professional inker, who placed each of my digits on the fingerprint cards, smeared my prints. I bring my receipt from the last visit so I won't have to pay the $80 fee again. I also fill out OSPRA 104. This form authorizes NYC to check out any criminal history with the

FBI and the DCJS. I don't know what DCJS stands for, but I hope they think I'm an all right sort. Once upon a time, I had a job-related top-secret clearance from the FBI, so I'm not too concerned.

My only run-in with the police occurred more than twenty years ago, a few weeks before my wedding. I was driving five mph over the speed limit in Washington, D.C.'s Rock Creek Park. After hearing my excuse that I was a little dazed due to my upcoming nuptials, Officer Goldberg said, "All the more reason for you to keep your wits about you," and slapped a ticket on me. So much for my life of crime.

Join the Club

It's never too soon to earn brownie points with a future supervisor. I volunteer to help Mr. Tqiqi's staff grade the New York State Regents Math A exam. Not such an easy test, it seems to me.[2] The CBHS kids do terribly.

It's a beautiful day today. I join the math department at their annual end-of-year lunch. It's held at a seafood restaurant on City Island. I squeeze in at one of the long tables next to Rob Simmons, Victor Gallo, and Joel Farmer. The last two are long-time CBHS war-horses—Victor has been there since 1986. Rob has worked there for a couple of years. It's at this lunch where my real knowledge about teaching in the Bronx begins.

I can't disguise my enthusiasm. I sound like a hopeless romantic, waxing on about how I'll help those needy kids. Meanwhile, I'm thinking the school year is over. These poor guys probably want to talk baseball or something—anything but shoptalk. I don't care. I'm ready to spew my ignorance about the entire spectrum of problems teaching urban children. The three of them indulge and educate me, too. Joel and Victor are cynical about teaching. For them, life at CBHS revolves around getting past the mindless bureaucracy; the overcrowded conditions; saving, at most, a few kids a year; and completing their tour of

---

[2] The New York State Board of Regents later voided the test. Practically the whole state failed or did miserably.

duty before retiring from the education rat race. Rob, a tall, thin, and contemplative sort, takes a low-key "I do whatever I can do" point of view. Maybe it's because he hasn't taught for as long. All three are mildly amused at, but not actually dismissive of, my ambition to raise most—not some—of my students to a much higher level. We have a heated discussion on the topic for a good two hours.

Victor does give me one piece of advice I take to heart. I shouldn't wait to grab a locker for myself when school starts. The teachers snarf up the free ones in an instant. Come to school prepared with my own locks and secure my bunker. I resolve to do just that.

JULY

McSchool

I decide to enroll in the night classes at the Mercy College's Bronx annex: two courses in the first half of the summer and two ending mid-August. I figure I'll do the homework in my backyard during the day and soak up some sun at the same time. That way I won't be miffed about wasting my summer taking Mickey Mouse education courses. Luckily, Mr. Rodent only shows up for the "Cultural Perspectives" course taught by a new teacher who has just arrived from the Dominican Republic. She's clueless about how to teach the course and wastes our time complaining about not getting her paycheck. When asked why Puerto Rico has such a high birthrate, her answer is that the inhabitants are "just happy people." So help me.

To my surprise, I find myself enjoying the education law and technology courses. Every profession has its own lingo, and the education racket is no exception. In "Assessment and Evaluation," I learn about Bloom's Taxonomy, multiple intelligences, rubrics, and HOTS (higher order thinking skills). Stuff like that. I also appreciate that in these condensed summer courses, the instructors don't force us to spend a lot of dough on textbooks that we'll never have the time to read or digest. They copy handouts for us instead.

The most memorable session occurs when the law course lets out a little late. I make a practice of parking at the McDonald's across the street. One night after class, I find my car surrounded by yellow tape. Minutes earlier, a bandit robbed the Golden Arches, followed by a shootout near my car. The unlucky slob never had a chance. A stakeout by the thief would have exposed a police station the size of a suburban mall right around the corner. After parking my rear for an hour waiting for the photographer to show up, the reigning detective takes pity on me. I drive off without police pics of my auto.

AUGUST

The Paper Chase

I wait in line for hours at the main Bronx branch of the DOE to fill out the official eight-page job application for CBHS. There are tons of applicants here. After several hours in line, it's too late to be evaluated. Come back tomorrow.

I'm back today. It's just as well because I was missing some of the required forms yesterday. Before arriving, I had to have a notary affirm that I owe no child support. I also bring additional forms to be checked off by an evaluator:

1. My CST, AST-W, and LAST scores.
2. Proof of fingerprinting.
3. Yet another letter from Mercy College attesting to the fact I have now completed the required courses.
4. OSPRA 104. My take on this unintelligible form? I am giving the U.S. consent to spy on me.
5. Still another nominating letter to teach at CBHS from Linda Fuego.

6. My authorization to allow NYC to do a credit report on me.
7. Certificates of completion for the child abuse and violence prevention seminars. I knew to hang on to these.
8. My various college transcripts from eons ago.
9. The notarized form affirming I don't owe child support.

As long as I'm here, I try to up my salary by filling in a "Salary Differential" application showing prior applicable professional work. I'm sure everyone I worked with on the moon shot when I was right out of college has gone on to other lives—if they're living at all—so I submit a copy of my Apollo Achievement Award. This merit certificate has a value of zip to the NYC DOE. Everyone in the Bronx must have one.

Locks—Any Bagels?

Next week I launch my new career at CBHS. On the school premises, I'll also be taking tutorial classes with an assigned Mercy mentor at CBHS. I need to stay in the internship program to keep my license. Taking Vince's advice, I buy four identical combination locks to stake out my locker sectors. I'm psyched to teach. I also wonder if there's a decent deli in the neighborhood.

Hola

I think I already have a clue about my future at CBHS. Just for practice, I teach the last forty-five minutes of a summer math class. Mostly kids who have previously failed take the course. Many doze or barely keep their heads up. Juanquier Entero, their teacher, works primarily with the Spanish-speaking kids who apparently speak no English. I really envy Juanquier's bilingual abilities. In a way, I'm glad I have a language requirement. I'd like to be able to speak the ancestral tongue of the 40 percent or so Hispanic children at this school.

Before presenting my lesson, I help some of the other kids who complain to me privately that the Hispanic kids get all the attention. I take the podium and draw an example on the board of a rocket ship coming back from the moon. I tell the kids that if they get the wrong answer they've killed the astronauts. Forever drifting dead in outer space because they ran out of fuel using the wrong data. Catches the attention of a few of them. A little drama never hurts. At the end of the period the kids take off, except for one smiling black boy who comes up to me and says he really likes my teaching. Very nice of him. And Juanquier compliments me, too. I'm feeling good.

And that's how I arrived at CBHS. Full of hope and other misconceptions. Christmas vacation is over and tomorrow starts the battle anew.

MONDAY, JANUARY 5, 2004

The Impact of Being Earnest

Our Lady of the Apocalypse sends out a letter today to "The Students and Parents of CBHS." She lets fly with, "Welcome Back to School! I hope you had a fun and relaxing break." I think, "What a warm and chatty way to talk to our constituents." It goes on to say that Mayor Bloomberg and School Chancellor Joel Klein " . . . have agreed to provide our school with additional help to improve discipline and safety . . . This attention is a positive development for our school." And so on. Well, well, well. So our principal apparently twisted the mayor's arm and got him to agree to designate CBHS as one of the twelve most dangerous schools in New York City, or at least that's the way the news media reported it. We're on the "impact list" for schools with high crime, absenteeism, and suspension rates and it's a *good* thing, according to Ms. Fuego. I look out the window in search of pigs with wings.

Up to the Challenge

This week, I'm determined to take no nonsense. I have only ten days to review for final exams that cover the whole semester's work. Kids who won't keep quiet and behave will have to go. I'm feeling upbeat. I had a good night's rest, unlike most of this entire school term. My attitude is a new one.

But the break has been salutary for the kids, too. They're energized as well and in the mood to be up to no good. Nevertheless, I find that Antwan and Natalie turn around in their behavior and seem pretty humane today. Glenn's return hasn't been good: "Some little bastard has stolen my Delaney cards."

Good Advice

In Mr. T.'s office, I meet Akmed Soo. A black, late fifties, deeply baritoned Regional Instruction Specialist. I'm sure this title disguises his real job, administrative spy. Nevertheless, he seems like an OK guy so I take this opportunity to pitch a bitch about my students.

Akmed tells me not to complain. "If kids behaved, you wouldn't have a job. Everyone would want well-behaved children. We have so much vacation time. Just maintain your cool and then the kids are powerless," he advises.

He's obviously heard complaints before and he's not done with me. "Don't give handouts because they won't take notes. Use the overhead projector at all times so you can face them and keep your back to the wall. Keep them copying and busy." Despite his title as some functionary, Akmed seems to know what he's talking about.

TUESDAY, JANUARY 6

The Great Robbery

Ronald, a rat-faced daily irritant in the 14th period, is hell bent for leather as darkness wears on. His eyes seem to glow sulfur yellow and his little sharp teeth both exaggerate his smallish frame, making him seem to be a real-live evil gnome—and that's exactly what he is—I swear to God. He smiles grotesquely—at what, I don't know. It's 5:00, pitch black outside, and the mob is restless. Forty-five minutes to go before the mutual hazing the students and I give each other ends. This is my birthday present, I guess.

I know what—time for peppermints! I stash them on the seat of my chair, safely removed from most of the kids, and go to help the students individually. I return to fetch candy for some half-hearted progress on the part of a few of them—but the treats have disappeared! Only a few lemon drops in my pocket remain. I try to keep a straight face but the kids, waaaaay ahead of me, already know what's up. What's happened? Who's guilty? My other habitual nemesis, Alvin, sitting close to my desk, seems a prime suspect. The forced, empty look on his face, obviously trying to stifle laughter, betrays his knowledge of, if not complicity in, the heist.

In the meantime, Ronald floors me by volunteering to answer a question on the board. I meet his half-assed attempt to do something correct for a change by offering him a lemon drop.

"No, I want a peppermint," he says, gritting his teeth in his own peculiar way that for some reason drives me nutso.

I've been robbed of the peppermints so I offer the lemon ones again. Composing myself despite my general aversion to this nudnik, "These are good lemon drops." I try to sell him.

"No, I want a peppermint."

Yours truly just doesn't get it. Ronald knows damn well I don't have any peppermints. He's merely hamming it up for the benefit of the class by demanding it. That isn't all. Now how does Ronald know it was the peppermints that were stolen and not some other goodie? *Because he was the one who stole them!* That's how. How do I know all this? Because there's no honor among thieves nor among the juvenile imps in the Bronx, either. After class, Alvin and several others rat on Ronald. Ronald threw the cargo out the window when I happened to turn in his direction earlier. Sure enough, I look out the window and see the red-and-white-striped evidence strewn about—a gift to the rodents below from one above.

Alvin squeals because he knows I would suspect him. He wants to earn his demerits from me legitimately, I suppose. The others are correctly afraid that I'd turn off the candy spigot. Thereafter, Ronald knows I know. Although I never say a word about the hijacking, on several occasions the little liar swears his innocence, thereby confirming his guilt.

WEDNESDAY, JANUARY 7

Copious Copying

The three copiers in the T-L get beaten into a pulp on a daily basis. It's no surprise these workhorses are out of order today. For the umpteenth time, I see the Canon repairman. I'm astounded at what he tells me. In the past two years, the copy machine he's now working on has printed three million copies. I ask him to repeat the number. Wow! To save money, the school system buys these heavy, four-semester text-books for the math department that almost none of the kids will tote around. So the teachers hand out copies of daily assignments instead, as textbook surrogates. How much moolah can the taxpayers be saving?

Allen, a teacher I know who's also going to Mercy College for his master's degree, tells me he has forty-four kids in his physics class. I guess I shouldn't complain about my class size. Janet, one of the social studies teachers, tells me that our common student, Khalid, has just been suspended. A biology teacher listening in says, "You have Khalid? What an idiot!"

THURSDAY, JANUARY 8
Learning New Tricks

If nothing else, teaching at CBHS has taught me some humility. Experience really counts in reaching kids. Sitting down with Will Gerard in the T-L, I tell him that my kids just can't get the knack of solving even simple equations. Will has taught high school mathematics for seven years. Before that he worked at an AT&T lab in operations research. His group there was getting moved around so he took a parachute. He suffers from a colon polyp and diverticulitis. At a graying sixty-two, he looks older. Will certainly knows some math and takes pride in his excellence at teaching.

Do I know the SAMD method? No. "S" stands for subtract, "A" for add, "M" for multiply, and "D" for divide. He goes on to show me an excellent visual method for helping kids learn to solve simple problems. I wish I had known this earlier in the term. Is it too late in the semester to introduce this method? Will says try it. I leave the T-L wondering to what degree my lack of expertise contributes to my problems. Could Will take my classes without a hassle?

Here Come the Mounties

I send more lamentations to Security. I wonder if anyone even reads them at this point. Maybe I should entomb my sad missives in jars and float them out to sea like Kevin Costner did in *Message in a Bottle*.

> Written Statement
> January 8, 2004
> To Security:
>
> My freshman student, Angeline Cortes, has engaged in disturbing her 10th period math class in room 313 consistently this term and has been asked to leave the

classroom on several occasions. Today, January 8, 2004, she engaged in constant talking and horseplay. I recommend that disciplinary action be taken by the school concerning Angeline.

Sincerely,
Ric Klass

Written Statement
Jan, 8, 2004
To Security:

My freshman student, Kelsie Pines, has engaged in disturbing her 10th period math class in room 313 consistently this term and has been asked to leave the classroom on several occasions. Today, January 8, 2004, she engaged in constant talking and horseplay. Previously, I have tried to reach her home but could not get an answer. I recommend that disciplinary action be taken by the school concerning Kelsie.

Sincerely,
Ric Klass

I have to call Security to jettison Dexter. Our resident precinct dispatches four constables. What the fudge! I'm either left hanging to dry or saved by the Royal Canadian Mounted Police. My students think I am *some* kind of asshole.

Time's running out. I'm looking for as many to pass the final exams as possible. I also decide to use a ploy of Rob Simmons'. Convince them not to quit. Let them know that if they can learn enough to pass next semester's course, the principal can reverse their grade for this term and they'll pass for the year.

FRIDAY, JANUARY 9

Life is Fair—Here

A teacher in the T-L tells me that when kids say they're not being treated fairly, he retorts, "This is the one place that is normal. You do fair work and you get a fair reward. Do well and you will excel. Guaranteed. Nothing else in your life is like that." This theme strikes home for me. I determine to use it. Then a Dean comes in the room: "Administrative higher-ups are in the building. One girl wouldn't leave the visitors alone, so we cuffed her after she hit a policeman."

Again with the RCMP

The day didn't have to end this way. I ask Jamir three times to put away the CD player. He looks defiantly at me and refuses. Goddamn it! I get mad so easily. I could have just moved on with the lesson, but now I'm looking for blood. I stick my head out the door and call for a Dean.

My friend Dean Candie comes in and demands the CD player from Jamir after I point him out. Immediately—it looks like Jamir sneaks the digital annoyance to his buddy Charles sitting next to him at the back of the room. Charles moves several seats away to try to avoid the impending disaster and now transports the forbidden electronics to Deanna, another math victim. Deanna beams with delight—she's part of the fun. After repeated denials from Jamir that he has the device, Candie calls for reinforcements and now three policemen position themselves at the doorway.

It's Friday, bitter cold outside, and the big hand on the clock is now headed north for 6:00. The absolute dark of the night vacuums all the life out of the classroom. The raid's show of force shocks the kids. They glare at me. Now *I'm* the enemy. This really stinks. I'm knocking myself out protecting the ones who want to pass from the mindless, loud-mouth orcs and guess who is public enemy #1?

Candie and the police nearly have to drag Jamir out. They seize Charles as well. I try to protest to Candie that I'm not sure Charles is involved in this particular debacle, but Candie will have none of it. He also saw Jamir hand the CD player to Charles.

Charles has been an immutable problem for the entire term—a determined truant and a persistent buffoon. Yet, despite his rare appearances in this particular conclave, he strikes me as intelligent, completes some homework, and tells me he's trying to reform. I started this week looking for survivors. I was hoping that Charles would be one of them.

After hauling them away, Candie comes back. "Write up something for me on them. Are they failing? Include that, too. We're going to suspend them."

I try meekly again for Charles. "Well, Dean Candie, thanks so much for your help." I never neglect to butter up Security. If they decided not to come to my aid when called for, then what? "Do we need to include Charles? He didn't really start this."

Candie looks at me quizzically. "I saw the same thing you did. Jamir slipped the CD to Charles. They're both failing, aren't they? What's their attendance like?"

"Both pretty spotty," I admit dejectedly. Now I've lost a potential contender. The kids look at me like they would lynch me if they could.

Time is up. Almost no review for the final has taken place. Instead, we all witnessed a police raid. The kids run out the door, except Celia, one of the more or less better students. She takes her time and files out last.

"Have a nice weekend," I call out hopefully, but Celia frowns, snubs me, and keeps on walking. For crying out loud! Why can't they just come in, sit down, take notes, and shut up? Pay a little attention to what's going on! What is so blessed hard about that? That's the easy part. Failing is what's hard. I keep saying these things to myself. What I should have said to them. But I *have* said these things to them. They won't listen.

I nearly sprint to my car parked a long way off. It's Friday and I didn't find a place at my usual "secret" spot. I'm frozen by the time I get in. "Thank God It's Friday" doesn't begin to express my relief at surviving until the weekend.

MONDAY, JANUARY 12

"No More Freshmen

for me," Mandi Dantillo happily peeps in the T-L. I couldn't agree more with the sentiment but I keep my own counsel on the subject. I'm not a certified teacher and still work on an intern's license. But I swear to myself that I'll return to industry or sweep streets before I face these freshmen agitators again.

I run into Dean Candie at the faculty meeting where I convince him not to suspend Charles. "He's trying," I tell him.

I've been mulling over the fact that Kobe is transferring to one of the new small schools upstairs next term. Having a couple of passing students has made the term at least barely tolerable for me. And I really miss Noki. I could always count on him to understand the lessons and help the others. It hits me that the better students are headed out of CBHS. The better ones here are not Bronx High School of Science quality but at least they can eke out a B or C. What will be left when even *they* go? The teachers will have classrooms where not one student understands what's going on. Having even just a few cognoscenti provides an anchor for some measure of civilization. When no students understand what's happening, I know the *Götterdämmerung* will materialize. CBHS will essentially be a special education facility without the special resources and small classes. Teachers will flee like mad. I'm already about to jump ship anyway, but what about the long-term teachers who built a career here? I want to find out if the administration realizes the devastation that's being put in motion.

Written Statement
January 12, 2004
To Security:

My freshman student, Johnny Carton, has engaged in disturbing his 10th period math class in room 313 consistently this term and has been asked to leave the classroom on several occasions. Today, January 12, 2004, he engaged in constant talking and horseplay. He is flunking this course but refuses nevertheless to take notes or hand in homework. Previously, I have tried to reach his home but could not get an answer. I recommend that disciplinary action be taken by the school concerning Johnny.

Sincerely,
Ric Klass

Not all letters flying around this school are negative. Lindsey Holden shows me this letter from one of her students:

Ms. Holden   1-12-04

I am sorry for the way I acted today. I promise not to act this way again. I know you was very upset today but I hope you can forgive me. I will sit down and do my work without talking from now on. I wrote this letter to show you that I do have respect for you not only as a teacher but as a person as well.

There are nice kids here.

TUESDAY, JANUARY 13

Our Filthy Microwave

Mainly college-educated professionals populate the T-L. They have, I suppose, at least average intelligence. This fact must account for the quarter-inch-deep layer of food debris and stains in the microwave oven. I'm frankly shocked that someone—anyone—can't take just a few moments to clean it. I don't have the time either, it seems, and so carefully place my half-empty cup of cold Dunkin' Donuts vanilla-flavored coffee in a relatively scum-free landing pad for thirty seconds. The smells of spilled pasta, yesterday's fish, and what sickeningly reeks of a Spam-and-mayo combo overpower the dark bean aroma I crave. Not-to-worry. The foreign pungency doesn't seep into my precious liquid. The D-D caffeine rescues me again. I'm braced for my next class.

Before I exit, I hear that last Saturday 10,000 people, including 2,000 kids, showed up at CBHS for a Bronx high school fair. The kids were trying to gain entry into the small school academies. These experimental conservatories of education subtly eliminate the misbehaving children through discouragement. For example, they tell the kids that they will have to take four years of math.

I'm very depressed. Charles, the intelligent boy whom I rescued from Dean Candie and targeted for a turnaround, goes out of control again. "Just sit down and be quiet," I beg, to no avail. I'm preparing my classes for finals. Coddling them is more like it. I don't have time to put up with nonsense. Finally, Charles gets up and starts to do gymnastics in front of the class. Now I have to call in Dean Candie again. He recruits a second Dean to assist in hauling Charles out. He won't dodge getting suspended this time, which means that he won't participate in the review classes and will go belly up. It doesn't have to be this way.

After class, I leave despondently. Dean Candie is standing there. I tell him that I gave Charles several chances to quiet down but he wouldn't do it. Candie's sympathetic with my disappointment but not surprised at the conclusion. The ups and downs with Charles have driven me wild. I can't justify my foolish decision to teach here.

When I get home, I read in the *NY Times* that three charter schools in NYC are in trouble; one of them is recommended to be closed.

WEDNESDAY, JANUARY 14

No Copying, Please

In the T-L, I make multiple versions of the final exams. I don't want cheating. I've discovered it a few times and it infuriates me. Afterwards, I stop in to say hello to Lucy, the payroll master. Lately, I've gotten into the habit of mumbling to myself, "Maybe I'm the wrong guy for this job." I must have said this near Lucy because she comments that she knows I'm going to find a way to leave CBHS.

A fistfight between Orane and Ricardo breaks out before class even starts. Ricardo gets a bloody nose. I don't see who starts the fight. Despite my loud calls in the hall for help, no police show up. I march into Mr. T.'s office to complain. I'm still upset, go next door to the T-L, tell Glenn what happened, and compose a written statement. Suddenly I realize I've forgotten to go to my next class. I rush upstairs, not at all ready to go on.

THURSDAY, JANUARY 15

They Won't Be Helped

at least not my Albanian duo, Korem and Gujix, fooling around in my repeater section.

Me, exasperated, "I'm trying to help you pass!" I shout at them, to their amusement.

This is not what I expected at the beginning of the term. These two boys are smart. At the end of the day, I expected them to shape up. I was dead wrong. But not even my calls home to their parents have made any difference. I keep forgetting that this is why they're here in a class for torpedoed kids in the first place. But they're not alone. Most of the kids in all my classes refuse to be helped for finals.

FRIDAY, JANUARY 16

Looking Out

The week ends on a high note. I'm harassing Mr. T. in his third floor office for the 182nd time. I drone on about my difficulties when I notice I'm standing about three feet from a gigantic hawk preening itself. It's just outside the window on a branch and paying us no notice. I'm close enough to sense its focus and solitary strength. I'm uplifted for the coming holiday.

Big Weekend

with my wife in NYC. We celebrate our anniversary on the three-day Martin Luther King Jr. holiday by booking a room in a nifty hotel in the theatre district. For dinner, we're sitting comfortably in a banquette at the swank Café Bouloud with a view of the candlelit room, its gorgeous flowers, and beautiful people. I find myself thinking about my students. What a different world this is from theirs. Can I light a path for even some of them?

SATURDAY, JANUARY 17

A Busman's Holiday

Still on our mini-vacation, we visit the "Children at Risk: Protecting New York City's Youths 1653–2003" exhibit at the New York Historical Society. The Protestant and Quaker fervor in 1805 led to a Free School Society for NYC's deprived children with the motto, "Let every child at every moment have something to do and a motive for doing it." The organization evolved into NYC public education in 1853. The positive intentions of the group included housing for children in order to insulate them from outside influences. No good deed goes unpunished and theirs was greeted with mixed emotions of suspicion, anger, and relief. The underprivileged, with some justification, felt their children were being stolen from them.

A poster at the show highlights a disturbing statistic: In 2003, there were 1.6 million children of all ages living below the poverty line in the U.S. Enough to rank as the fifth largest city in the country.

This evening we take in a Broadway play, "Wonderful Town." Senator Edward Kennedy sits a few rows behind us. Later at dinner, we see actor Matthew Broderick at a nearby table. My enjoyment takes a holiday for a moment. I'm thinking that I don't see any blacks or Latinos at the theatre. Will my children ever attend plays?

SUNDAY, JANUARY 18

The Holiday Ends as It Started

with a hawk. This one swoops down in front of my house, chasing a squirrel and nearly slamming into a guest who has stopped by.

MONDAY, JANUARY 19

Back to the Grindstone

The kids return to a week of final exams. I start high in spirits, but as the day wears on I'm getting nervous. I know so many kids are going to fail. The exam equations didn't print out of the computer correctly. I make the changes by hand on all of them. Almost all of the math department calculators are stolen so I have none to hand out to the kids. The experienced teachers know to hang on to scarce resources and husband the few that are left. I'm even out of pencils. I bum some from other staff. I've already handed out hundreds.

TUESDAY, JANUARY 20

Test Review

My exams last for one period. In my double period classes, I use the first to review. Even so, the kids won't let me help: they talk, fool around, refuse to take notes, pass letters—*et cetera, et cetera*. I could scream. I want them to at least pass. All they would have to do is just sit still, watch, and listen. I'm spoon-feeding them the exam. Even with a history of defeat, any dodo could see the benefit of paying attention when the teacher is going over the test. But they don't.

I bump into one of my students in the hall who was a no-show for the exam. Even though he missed it, Gavin tells me he wants to take the final. He has no chance of passing but I'm touched that he finally wants to try. Next period, Christian imitates me by banging on the table. The truth of his parody makes me laugh, too. It's probably the closest we've been the whole term to understanding each other.

Mr. T. advises me to let kids have more time on the exam if they need it, even though the official schedule says otherwise. Whatever is best for them. He knows the priorities and cuts through the bull.

In the following class, Derek saunters in late. He's not through high-fiving buddies when he asks me a question about a problem already solved on the blackboard. I tell Derek that if he passes next term he will retroactively pass this term, so he should keep trying.

I ask myself again—are these kids hellions or furious angels?

WEDNESDAY, JANUARY 21

Mistah

The kids at CBHS don't call the men "Mr. this or that." The male teachers are "mistah." No last name. No letter R at the end. I don't know what they call the women. I know it seems trivial, but this, along with their chronic flow of solecisms and vulgarities, drive me over the edge.

Rob Simmons says he was insulted at first because students called him "mistah" and not his name. This guy's affronted . . . and from a hard-scrabble childhood.

Two White Flags

wave in my repeater class. Gujix and Korem have unofficially quit trying—so they tell me. What a pity. All they had to do was show up and keep their traps shut. This really smells.

And the bathrooms stink today, too.

THURSDAY, JANUARY 22

More Exams

Victor tells his kids not to forget to change feet to inches on the test problems. On one exam, the students simply made twelve feet equal to twelve inches. As Victor tugs on his beard, he muses, "It's a shame we don't have more vocational training for these kids. At least they could earn a living when they get out of here." He often acts the cynic, but he's concerned about his students.

During the last exam, I watch Johnny Carton carve soap and take his ballpoint pen apart. But he doesn't turn in his test. Korem doesn't do his, either. Instead, he distracts the other kids. I kick him out.

FRIDAY, JANUARY 23

When the Battle's Lost and Won

My students continue to have tests in their other courses, but the agony of math exams is over for the semester. I try to make peace with them by bestowing candy and puzzles. Aurora comes up to my desk and tries to kiss me! I politely ward her off. That's all I need, a sexual harassment case against me. Nonetheless, maybe the children don't dislike me as much as I think.

The regular classes end today, but next week the math department has to proctor the New York State Regents Exams. I first need to examine all my students' tests and hand in their final grades for the term early next week. I grade Tiqnaz's and at least one of my worries is over. She's been struggling the entire term with her math. Her English wasn't strong at the beginning of school, but it's improved significantly since then. Her hopes of going to medical school will be crushed if she succumbs in mathematics. I've continued tutoring her at lunchtime and after school in the library. She's trying so hard. I'm thrilled she did well enough on the final so I can pass her for the term.

Jamir, a tall, sturdy lad, has been an ongoing problem for me. I've booted him out numerous times. I even got him suspended once. Towering over me, he puts his arms around my shoulders and gives me a big bear hug. "You're still my nigger," he says affectionately. I feel bad that I've helped him so little. I should have found a path to give him a boost instead of the boot.

Lights Out

The last class of the semester is over. It's Friday. Everyone has run out of the room. Except Alvin, who's hanging around for some reason. Despite the fact we've been at each other's throats all semester, I like him and I think the feeling is mutual. He helps me erase the blackboard.

When I get to the door, a request, "Alvin, would you be so kind as to turn off the lights?"

"With pleasure, *Mister Klass*." Lights out.

End of the first term.

MONDAY, JANUARY 26

To Pass or Not to Pass

them. That is the question. In my spare time, I'm grading tests and doling out grades. My conclusion? I toe the line on the point system. Below 65 fails. I try to assuage my guilt by bestowing a Certificate of Merit to one student who clears only an "85"—not the "90" gold standard.

Exactly seven kids pass the final exams—12 percent of all the students that took it. Nearly half of my class register didn't even bother showing up. Rotten defined. And I know I must acknowledge my part in the kids' shellacking. I ask around, wanting to know how the other teachers with freshmen faired. They didn't do much better, if at all. Kreshak had 8 percent of his kids pass; Casey, my Irish colleague, about 18 percent; Lankin, 22 percent; and Amigas, 15 percent.

I hope for a better schedule and better results next term. If I'm assigned freshmen again next semester, I'll quit and go back to investment banking—run a lemonade stand. Anything but.

Whan-key-a

Why does the staff call Juanquier "Whan-key-a," as though his name is French? He's Latino. The "r" is pronounced. Juanquier Entero never stops smiling. I ask him why everyone says his name wrong. He doesn't know. He doesn't care. It's no wonder he's liked by all who know him. He doesn't come by academia naturally. He was still living with his parents when he got married and worked for ten years in various jobs, including UPS, the airport, IBM, and check cashing. Later, he needed more *dólares* and segued to teaching. He's worked here for six years while attending Lehman College at night. Juanquier lives in the Bronx and says he loves it here at CBHS. When he is not correcting homework or grading tests, he's cleaning the tables, fixing the copiers, or trying to repair the PC bugs or the HP printer.

Regents

Colleges, and maybe even workplaces, won't really consider a kid a *bona fide* high school grad without a Regents diploma. Anyway, the math department is now in the throes of proctoring and grading the exams.

I'm given one piece of advice about monitoring the Regents: "Tell the kids to answer the questions."

Sounds obvious, but it isn't. Very often, a student will set off through the maze of a problem, only to answer with the results of an interim step. For example, the sum of Ann's age and Juan's is twenty-five. How old is Juan? A kid will find Ann's age first. Say it's twelve. And then he/she will write twelve when the correct answer is thirteen. Happens all the time.

After conducting the tests, we start grading. We're going to spend the rest of the week on the exams. You have to be a handwriting expert for the job. I helped Mr. T. grade Regents last summer, so I know the drill. All of us grading the tests scrounge for points to award the kids. A point or two can mean a Regents diploma. Or not. There's an official rubric for scoring. "Rubric" is teacher talk for the grading guide. We stretch the rubric just a little. A kid writes down an equation? Give the little squirt a point! Draws a diagram? Another point. Even so, most don't make the cut and fail the test.

One boy's answer on the test became the high point of the day for all of us. A diagram illustrates two different paths for a car to drive. The exam supplies data on mileage and velocity.

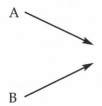

Which is faster? The boy chose A, the top path, because the car would have to drive uphill for choice B. Yuk, yuk. As a group, we talk about giving points to the kid for making us laugh.

But we don't.

TUESDAY, JANUARY 27

Sweeping the Place Clean

I get this note from our chief of Security:

> Memorandum from Freddy Girano, A.P. Security:
>
> As you know, Central Bronx High School has been designated an "Impact" school. As a result, we are gong to intensify our sweep efforts. However, hall sweeps can only begin when most of the students are in class. **Please stand at your door at the late bell and usher your students into the classroom.** This small, but very important, action could significantly improve the climate of our school building.
>
> Thank you.

I can see the administration headline coming now: "Security at CBHS would've been just great if only the teachers had stood at their doors as requested."

I also get my last term's grade report back from the main office. Twenty-eight out of eighty-four kids passed the first term in my classes. Just 33 percent. And I was going to lift 80 percent of my students to Level 3 or 4. I feel deeply the malfeasance was mine and not my students'. But they didn't help much, either.

I should feel somewhat uplifted by the few successes. Kenya's determination to do well propelled him to a 70, when in the beginning of the term I was certain he'd stumble. Good for him. Sweet Tiqnaz, who aspires to be a doctor someday, can keep her candle lit by at least passing. Intense Joselyn managed a 75, impressive for her. Demarco badly tripped in the final and, alas, failed the semester as well. I'm not proud to say it, but it served him right. On the other hand, Alvin and Khalid didn't make it either, and for that I'm sorry. Kobe notched an 85 and Noki a 92—not good enough for their innate talent.

FRIDAY, JANUARY 30

A New Leaf

isn't my favorite movie, although I did like the performances. In the denouement, Walter Matthau converts from a life of hedonism to a career in teaching. Right at this moment, that choice seems like a mistake to me. Anyhow, the title fits the day. I finally get my course schedule for next term. I'm basically getting screwed. I had worked the late session with twenty-seven classes per week last term. We're supposed to teach only twenty-five. No problem, Mr. T. told me; I would get the morning session with twenty-three classes for the spring. Union rules, you know.

Well, I get the morning session all right, but I'm scheduled for the standard twenty-five classes. What happened to the twenty-three classes I was promised? Mr. T. lamely apologizes but when push comes to shove, it's tough tushy for me. At least I have no freshmen. Only sophomores and upperclassmen. Hurrah!

SUNDAY, FEBRUARY 1

Gettin' Ready 'Cause Here I Come

I prepare for classes on Monday by buying a box of 100 clear plastic transparencies for the overhead projector. The low salary makes me feel unusually stingy. I keep the receipt in a special folder to turn in at year's end as a credit against the $200 given to me for expenses.

I decide to get off to a good start for the new classes by designing a weekly form for each class with the names of each student in alphabetical order. To save time while in class, I set up an elaborate letter system for the types of bad behavior I anticipate:

T = talking, H = horseplay, A = absent , a boxed date = asked to leave class,

T = tardy (oops, I use T for two different infractions!), U = unprepared,

N = not taking notes, L = late

I realize that I should lob in a few positive abbreviations just in case the occasion arises—a rarity that might coincide with a meteor flying in the window:

V = volunteered, B = worked on blackboard, W = worked w/other students

I'm one of twenty-two Americans who doesn't religiously watch the Super Bowl. But my son shows some interest and we sit and watch a pretty exciting first half, including a Janet Jackson exposé of sorts. At halftime, I notice it's almost 9:00 P.M. Can't be knocked out tomorrow.

SEMESTER TWO

MONDAY, FEBRUARY 2

Starting Over

First day of the new term. My schedule is 7:50 A.M. to 1:11 P.M. I rise at 5:00 A.M. I must have coffee before school and even more importantly, I must get to school by 6:15 A.M. or I'll never find a parking space. If I'm early, I can park right in front of the entrance and make a fast getaway at the end of classes. Arriving late and not finding a spot is out of the question.

Before leaving, I need to fax something to my attorney. A lingering virus I can't get rid of in my computer makes it slow but still useable. It freezes and I've got to fool with it and reboot. My former life still haunts me. I can't seem to escape to my new life, if I can call it that. Minutes are ticking away. I'm perplexed that I got up early to get coffee and now I might have to do without Dunkin' Donuts vanilla—cream only and no sugar. Mission finally accomplished, I run downstairs to make two no-fat cheese sandwiches with low-fat Pringles on the side. I never even used to eat lunch, but for some reason I get starved at school. Maybe because it's real work.

I want to buy the coffee first and enjoy a more-or-less leisurely drive sipping the caffeine, but the D-D nearest me is in the wrong direction. If I go that way, I might miss a parking spot. Instead, I disconsolately head right for school and go to the D-D a few blocks away from CBHS. Now I'll have to balance the briefcase, fairly huge lunch bag, and medium-sized cup all the way to school. The empty halls greet me with dismal silence.

For this term, I'm assigned five second-year algebra classes, two of them for repeaters. I start out the day with a wise guy sitting in the front row, Ahmed Mattingly. I'm instantly reminded we're in the Bronx.

"Say, were you born with that name?" Yes, indeed, here and now begins the initial onslaught of the term with this comedian.

I give a remarkably low-key, flat-toned response, "Yes, I was."

Then, "And what does E equals M C squared mean?"

"Well, the question is more appropriate for physics rather than a math class, but it means that if one multiplies a mass by the velocity of light squared, you get its energy equivalent. Would you like me to review Lorentz transformations for you now?"

"No, thanks." Children are always so amazed when an adult knows something that they just learned five minutes ago.

After they endure the agonizing ritual of completing Delaney cards, I stun the kids by daring to assign homework, give handouts, and even teach for a few moments.

TUESDAY, FEBRUARY 3

Rise and Shine

Today I get up five minutes earlier—4:55 A.M. I'm taking no chances that I won't make it to Dunkin' Donuts before my scramble to school down Rte. 95. After putting my lunch in a brown bag, and restocking my soda can cooler holder with diet drinks, I carefully note the time— 5:41 A.M. I want to calculate the exact latest time I can get up.

WEDNESDAY, FEBRUARY 4

Do They Have Tails?

I get a nasty surprise today. In my mailbox, I find that one of my classes is changed from a second-year algebra class to a special ed class. What??? I plead my case to Mr. T.

"I don't have any training in special education."

"No problem."

"What do I teach them?"

"Whatever seems appropriate for the children. They don't come under my purview. Talk to the SPED department head about it."

I feel greatly relieved. Not!

Will they be the unfortunates in wheelchairs I see on the elevator? Mentally challenged, they call it now. I start to perspire. I'm not proud of it, but I'm squeamish around the disabled. Especially children, may God beatify their nurses and caretakers. Somehow I've jumped from the frying pan into the fire.

In the T-L, I tell my plight to anyone who will listen. Nobody's interested. As I cast about looking for sympathy, the phone rings. No one answers. Victor warns me to stay put. It might be the main office looking for coverage, someone to replace a missing or sick teacher. I'm always learning new tricks here in the T-L.

THURSDAY, FEBRUARY 5

Fear of SPED

I wake up anxious. I'm afraid of the special education class I'll face today.

I'm determined to have a better relationship with my students this term. I open with an ersatz Borscht Belt warm-up gag. I tell them I'm 135 years old, but people tell me I don't look a day over 130. In every class, I repeat the joke to no laughs whatsoever. Maybe I *am* going on 135. I also emphasize that I'm here to serve them, even though I'm but an impoverished schoolteacher. Ahmed, who's no dummy even though he's already a bother, practically calls me a liar by pointing out my designer eyeglass frames and BMW keys.

I cover three sections of the same subject this morning. I feel like the star of *Groundhog Day*, repeating the same stuff over and over again.

The real surprise of the day is the SPED class. I arrive just on time at the appointed classroom. It's locked. But, of course, I don't have the key, so I hustle down the stairs to the main office. Key in hand, when I return the door's already been opened. I'm out of breath and find six perfectly normal-looking kids fooling around. I am sooooo relieved. No two-headed monsters. Only run-of-the-mill ones. Maybe better. Cory, Jerry, and Elton seem civil—alert even. Cory is downright friendly and his outgoing and chatty demeanor makes me wonder why he's here. Dalia strikes me as intelligent but combative. And what a mouth on her! Possibly reincarnated from an Irish longshoreman maybe. I suddenly note we're in a tiny room. The kids can't sit more than ten feet from me. I do notice they have a hard time getting focused, despite my prodding. Not typical when there are so few of them. Maybe this is why they're in this class. I really don't have a good idea about it at all.

Meanwhile, I'm not sure what I'm supposed to be teaching these kids. The letter designation of the class indicates second term, sophomore math, but from today's session I doubt that these kids are that far along. So I take a trip to the special education department to see Harold King, the assistant principal who runs the shop.

King keeps me cooling my heels for about ten minutes. When he invites me in, "It's Harry," he says. Fine, Harry. Harry strikes me as tolerable, but he, too, has no clue as to what I should be teaching the kids. It's his department, I say to myself. What the hell does he mean he doesn't know what I should be teaching?

"Whatever you think," he offers. This is just great. These sad sack kids don't have enough problems—no, a totally untrained SPED teacher walks in to ruin their lives some more.

So I say to Harry, "How about a course in third-semester math? They probably can use the review, even if some are further along. This way, they'll be prepared to take the Regents next year."

Sounds good to Harry. I get the sinking feeling that my students in the SPED class accidentally fell into some kind of educational *Twilight Zone*. Although I have no training in SPED, I do know from my summer courses that each one of them has an IEP, an Individualized Education Plan, that lays out their problems and needs. I could check up on their backgrounds to see why they're in the program at all. But I don't. I decide to treat them as perfectly normal kids in every way until proven otherwise. I have no idea whether or not I'm doing the right thing.

FRIDAY, FEBRUARY 6

Plough Ahead

The math department gets a round of applause from Santino. "Good job teaching," a pat on the back and all that rubbish. Nobody buys it except for two women—both of them new and young. I want to start using the overhead projector this term but the elevator isn't running again.

Ms. Abrahamson has been tinkering with my classrooms every day so far this term. Today, I get two changes.

MONDAY, FEBRUARY 9

Only Bad Answers

I'm in the second week of the new term, but my roster of students keeps changing. During one class, Dexter Shunt, an obese and genuinely mischievous kid from last term, dashes in and stands at the door, pretending to be lost and retarded. Before he completes his noxious performance, he recognizes me and scampers out.

I try to encourage children to ask questions. I want them to be fearless about what they don't know. To be inquisitive. "There are no bad questions," I tell them. "Only bad answers." I antagonized some of my own teachers in high school by my endless questioning. I always managed to find an exception to the rule, whether in English grammar or in math. I resented their irritation and I'm not about to repeat their behavior. Not on that account anyway.

TUESDAY, FEBRUARY 10

Making a Getaway

I arrive early and trod the mostly deserted halls towards the administration office. First, I check to see if my punch card is turned to the "IN" position. It's been moved again to another part of the pigeonholes.

I'm IN already today, according to the card. But sometimes it's turned to OUT. I'm not sure what will happen if it's left in the OUT position. I slide over to my mailbox. A form in Times Roman font size 5 (no magnifying glass is attached thereto) informs me that my SPED group has been assigned to yet another classroom. The scheduling is supposed to permit teachers with three classes in a row to remain in the same classroom. It doesn't work out that way for any teacher I've spoken to. Most are running like I am from floor to floor, one class after another, every class in a different room.

Just as I'm walking into my first class, a student excitedly reports that a teacher was shot late yesterday behind the school. I'm depressed. Man, I've got to walk away from here before I get carried out. I find out later that the rumor is false, but for some reason I'm not relieved.

I arrive at the new SPED classroom. Good news—it's the same cozy quarters where Ms. Grainger teaches her students. This agreeable surprise gets balanced by waiting fifteen minutes for the door to be opened. No key came with the new room assignment. My students straggle to the locked door every few minutes. Although they were supposed to be notified of the new classroom (I don't know how), just to be sure, I put a sign on the old door telling them where to go. Frankly, I'm surprised that any of them show up at all. In the meantime, my kids start to wander off through the halls. I'm not sure why the kids are in SPED. So I worry, without any valid reason really, whether it's safe for them out meandering around like this. I lamely try to start the class right there in the hall: "OK, kids. We were talking about adding polynomials at the end of the session yesterday . . . " One of the girls gapes at me as if I were ET. I stop in mid-sentence.

Between classes, I'm finally relaxing when Kenya pounds on the T-L's door. He begs for an endorsement from me to gain admittance into a Virginia private school. I spend about half of my break filling in part of the academy's application form. I'm pleased to be an accomplice in Kenya's jailbreak. Kenya also takes the opportunity to boast about winning a school poetry contest. He flashes a $25 book certificate. I'm immensely proud of him.

When free myself, I stroll by one of my students, talking seriously to two teachers. She looks like she's about to cry. I wonder if it has anything to do with the black eye she's sporting.

I run into my last class a little late and put the kids to work. I'm feeling good. Just forty-five minutes until the end of the day. A little prep for tomorrow and I'm off for home to read the newspaper and relax.

"Norton, please erase the blackboards. Sean, hand out the homework lesson for tomorrow. Please start on the Do-Now now. Do problems one through six on page 189 of the handout," I rat-a-tat commands. It's good to be king. These are older students in this class and it shows. Very little outward hostility, if that. Some are seniors and mostly concerned about getting out of CBHS and their life ahead.

I peer down the sixty-foot, double-bowling-lane-sized art room now being used for my M$40 (fourth semester) math class.

"Lunna, I see you hiding in the back again. You know I like to pick on the kids who try to escape there," I tease.

She squirms a little. Lunna's quiet and genial. But her dull, stringy hair; weight problem; and pockmarked face probably don't contribute to her popularity. She's no doubt hiding from her fellow classmates and not me in the back of the room. I don't know if she's bright, or for that matter, if any of the kids are since I haven't tested them yet.

At the bell, Norton hands in homework not due until tomorrow. I'm not sure why he's even in a repeater class. He gets all the questions. Norton tells me he's joining the Merchant Marines or some service like that. I like him. And Sean, too. He reminds me of a young Sidney Poitier. They're both laid-back seniors. It's more like teaching an adult class. In fact, I've warmed up to most of the kids in this section. One boy says math is his favorite subject. Fishing for compliments? I ask why he likes it. "Because it's so easy!" Not a bad answer. It's what I'm trying to drill into the kids' heads about twenty times a day.

WEDNESDAY, FEBRUARY 11

Greeting the Day

Amber Firenzi joins me early each morning in the T-L. She drops her share of blue talk, too. I think it's cute on a young Smithie. Together, we watch the rising sun filter through the dirty windows of the lounge.

"I'm glad you're here to share the morning, Ric."

Not a bad start to the day.

I find a note from a SPED student's mother in my mailbox asking that at the end of each period, I sign a daily notice signifying her son's presence, homework, participation, etc. It occurs to me this is a well-written note. She didn't come to parents' night, but I respect her concern. The do-gooder side of my brain heartily approves of this parent's interest in her child. On the other hand, I muse that it's a good thing not every parent wants me to complete a daily checklist. I would never reach my next class in time—scheduled by Ms. Abrahamson on some distant universe.

THURSDAY, FEBRUARY 12

In the Groove

I'm getting into the rhythm of my new schedule. The manager of the Dunkin' Donuts where I now go to get my coffee at 5:41 A.M. greets me warmly, immediately puts on a pot of vanilla and in a minute or two, pours out a cup before the whole batch is ready.

It's a little after 6:00 A.M. and I find a spot on the still vacant street right across from the entrance to the school. I couldn't print out my test last night. I'm praying I left the CD in the T-L. I open the CD-ROM slot of the PC. I'm almost certain it's there since no one except me even uses the CD-ROM on this computer. It comes out empty. I'm bonkers with agitation.

"Where in hell is that CD-ROM?!!!" I know some envious math teacher has stolen it, but I put up a sign anyway: "Has anyone seen my red New

York Math A CD-ROM? - Ric Klass" in the hopes that my note will browbeat the thief into returning the loot. A little paranoid, I wonder if putting my name on the sign will convince the rotten bastard to keep it. Now what? I can't print the test for tomorrow without it. I'm fit to be tied.

Later, I hit the UFT lounge without any hope at all to see if I left it in the MAC. I tried to use that machine yesterday, without luck. I just don't want to learn to use one more electronic gadget. I'm mildly upset that Apple is even alive. Doesn't Steve Jobs know that MACs have been dead for two decades? After plunking an alien key on the incomprehensible keyboard, the CD-ROM drawer opens up and out pops my red New York Math A/B disc. Life is good—for the moment. Still not forgiving the MAC, I mentally allow that Jobs does deserve some credit for IPOD and Pixar's success.

I hustle back to the T-L and take down the plea for the return of my precious software before it draws any attention. Here, I'm double-teamed by Don Lankin and Morton. Lankin is sick and wants everyone to know it. Feverish, headaches and yet, still with the lame jokes. Morton sits down quietly next to me—for a moment. And then his jabbering starts in, too.

In the 6th period, I announce a quiz for tomorrow and hand out review problems. The students who usually talk their heads off now scream for me to go over the test. Not what I had in mind for this session, but I comply.

FRIDAY, FEBRUARY 13

Shedding Fear of SPED

Not so bad for Friday the 13th. Several students do well on my quiz today. A couple of 80s, a 97, and Shaylee racks up a 100 percent.

Most amazing is that the SPED section ranks as my best overall class! Several kids on the roster never show up, but four of the seven or eight regulars are smart. Jerry is a machine. If I were to ask him to solve 500 problems right now, he'd get right to work and steamroll over them. He's pretty taciturn, though. If he says five words in a session, it's a lot. From appearances, he looks like an idiot savant I saw once. I think on *60 Minutes*. Dalia likes to fool around, but she's also extremely bright. She does best when she thinks the other two good students are getting ahead of her. Amiable Cory has more than a little math talent. Elton is the biggest goof-off, but a nice boy and also very able. He likes to put his arms around me and tell me what pals we are. These kids like me. And I like them back. They love it when I tell them they're my best class. What are they doing in SPED? It can't be intellectual inabilities. Maybe they're socially maladjusted or something. But there aren't any Prince Charmings in my other classes, either. I still don't want to see their official records. I think I'm doing OK without them. One thing I do notice is their aversion to being seen by their peers in the SPED classroom.

A sign on a can in the T-L asks for donations: "Sign a petition in solidarity with the workers at the Oyster Bar." OK. Maybe I'm a snob or something, but what do bartenders and waiters at a restaurant at Grand Central Station have to do with my job teaching in the Bronx? I'm not anti-union. God knows how unfairly teachers would be treated without one, but this kind of union activity is nothing more than a big turn-off for me. My guess is that Paul Lanier, our self-styled Marxist, has a hand in this. Maybe I should lend him Solzhenitsyn's *The Gulag Archipelago* or *Cancer Ward* so he can find out what communism is really all about.

SATURDAY, FEBRUARY 14

First Day of Winter Vacation

I'm determined to grade the test papers early so I can enjoy my vacation. Amber declines to give tests before the holiday. She didn't want to work on her time off. Maybe she has the right idea.

MONDAY, FEBRUARY 16

Glad to Make Mistakes

Lucky me. I learned one of my life's most valuable lessons just out of undergraduate school. I hated to be wrong or even admit I was ignorant of something. My college was loaded with kids like me. Anyway, here I was, a lifetime ago, right out of college, working on the Apollo project at McDonnell Douglas Astronautics in Huntington Beach, California. My unit covered the electronics for the third-stage firing rocket. My supervisor's boss surprised me with a question. I now have no idea what, but I didn't have a clue to the answer. I tried to talk around the question—fake it.

"Listen, Ric, all I want to know is if you know the answer to my question or not?"

I stalled for a few seconds. "No," I finally mumbled.

"That's all right, I'll find out from someone else." He smiled and walked away.

I had an epiphany then. It's okay not to know! Many years later, I had a partner in a real estate company in Washington, D.C., who was a sweet guy except—he could never, and I mean never, admit he was wrong or didn't know a fact about anything and everything! We all know these people. I used to be one of them. These days, I like to think I've gone the other direction. Now I don't claim to know anything. And every day I know even less because I've forgotten what I might have known the day before. It's far less stressful. I pity the dismal guys on the dark side.

At CBHS when I'm solving a problem on the blackboard, I don't mind a bit when I make a mistake. I welcome the opportunity and sometimes even create one. I make a big deal pointing out my boo-boos to the kids.

"See, even the math teacher gets it wrong," I announce happily. "It's OK to be wrong." If I'm lucky, some of the kids laugh and make fun of me. I just smile. I need to remember to smile more.

To a stranger, many of these kids seem tough and mean. I'm convinced that even the worst of them is just scared. Constant disappointment has made them timid. They won't answer questions, do homework, or study because their defense against more of the same drubbing is, "I just won't try." I want them to try, take a chance. If they must, then be wrong. If they keep trying, soon they'll get it right. I encourage them to take a shot at answering questions in class, "Do the homework, even if you make errors. It's really OK." Sadly, not many take me up on it. I'm too late.

TUESDAY, FEBRUARY 17

Not So Good

I wake up aggravated. I feel that I was partly to blame for the low test marks on transformations—maybe more than partly. These kids are in a Regents prep program and everyone in the school administration takes Mathematics M$40 courses seriously. Good scores will pull the school out of the fire and the inverse is also true—bad scores will keep us in the frying pan. To make matters worse, I awake realizing an easy way to demonstrate the material.

The subject was rotating, moving, and transforming objects on a coordinate plane. My mini-lesson on the subject was too abstract. All I had to do was draw a triangle and turn it around to show how the axes changed. Simple. I want to go in on Monday and show them, but I'm a little afraid they'll want to murder me. "Oh, NOW you tell us. We want to take the test all over again," they'll scream. I just spent three mornings of my vacation grading the tests. Should I do it all over? The info was on the handouts I spent hours copying and collating.

"Let them eat cake," I grumble to myself as I munch my morning rye toast. "And anyhow, they'll get another crack at it on the midterms. Maybe I just won't count the test too much." The rationalizations pour out all day—the stopper in my brain's been yanked out. By bedtime, I'm akin to 10,000 economists stretched out end-to-end—I still haven't reached a conclusion.

Later, I meet my brother at the Metropolitan Museum. At lunchtime in the cafeteria, Jim overhears a child asking her mother, "Is this a four-star restaurant?" Jim thinks it's cute. I'm thinking that it's a good bet most of my high schoolers have never set foot in this temple of art so close to their homes. And never will.

WEDNESDAY, FEBRUARY 18

No Escape

I actually try to take a real day off by taking my daughter to the American Museum of Natural History. It's a good opportunity to forget about CBHS. I'm not bothered by the fifteen-minute wait to the museum parking garage, nor am I shocked at the same extortionist rate charged by other lots in the city. I won't get away for less than fifty to sixty bucks if we spend a few hours here. Just relax, I say to myself; at least it's not teaching.

Upon entering, I'm immediately struck by the throngs of crying, squirming, and hyperactive children of all ages. Any rational person would expect to see all these moppets, but somehow I'm unprepared for it and not a little exasperated.

The first item on the agenda is twenty-four bucks worth of tickets to the Exploratorium Exhibit—theoretically an educational haven where children can learn to love science by hands-on experimentation. In fact, it's total chaos. The peewees push and shove the experiments in every way except as intended. Most are toddlers incapable of sharing with their peers or taking the time to read the explanations of gravity, air and water currents, centripetal force, etc. Instead, the munchkins careen helter-skelter around the large room, mostly shoving the displays to see if they'll topple. I can't seem to escape good intentions for children gone awry.

We're hungry after this jaunt to the limits of knowledge and after several directional errors, find our way to the cafeteria in the bottom pit of the museum. It's feeding time for the varmints and the cafeteria is packed with strollers, slobbering infants, and their older unwashed and ill-mannered siblings. I have a hard time stifling my revulsion. It's clear to me while wolfing down my $.50/oz. salad plate that my experience at CBHS has made me negatively hypersensitive to kids of all ages. And maybe even made me a bit of a misanthrope for good measure. Yesterday at the Met, my brother smiled good-naturedly at the comparatively few tots we encountered. I wrote this off to his being single and without his own children—a status enabling even the cold-hearted some amusement at seeing the young alive in the wild and not on a sitcom.

When we finally make our escape from the museum, I vow to come back only during nighttime hours when the density of rug-rats is likely to be minimal.

SATURDAY, FEBRUARY 21

More Paperwork

I spent the last weekend grading papers, and now I have to record homework. I'm ambivalent about the fact that there's relatively little to grade and record considering that I teach five classes. I really should have pounds more from my 134 students on record. On a percentage basis, I have just as much turned in from the SPED kids as from the other classes. If they can somehow avoid negative assumptions arising from being SPEDs, they might end up with the upper hand by having small classes. I really don't know if a taint will follow them through the educational system or not.

MONDAY, FEBRUARY 23

So Ye Be Not Judged

On the way to work, a radio station announces an "adopt a school" program. Who are they kidding? I wonder.

I share my 8th period classroom with Ms. Tottle, a thin, short, and graying art teacher who has class just before me. She often stays in the room to clean up the crayons, paints, and other paraphernalia of her subject. Ms. Tottle started teaching at CBHS in '63, leaving to raise her children, and then returned in '86. "By then, this school was already a disaster," she tells me.

She compliments me about my teaching, but adds, "Kid are animals. They don't know anything."

Earlier in the year, her negative comments about our students offended me. No more. I see her students engrossed in drawing, creating. I know she tries to expose her kids to aesthetic expression. I have too many of my own downbeat, unspoken thoughts about the students to judge her.

The office transfers out four of my students in this class but they want to stay with me. How bad can I be?

TUESDAY, FEBRUARY 24

Hackneyed Jokes and Other Minor Irritations

The T-L seems a microcosm of the world at large. Take Don, for example. Good intentions, amiable, but a persistent and consistent punner whose lame jokes stretch back to early television—Milton Berle stuff or worse. And he doesn't ever stop talking. But he's not alone. Morton's blabbermouthing never quits, either. Now these are intelligent and educated men who annoy the hell out of me. Guys like this reside at every watercooler in corporate America, I suppose.

I'm just not used to it. My years of working mostly alone in my office have come back to haunt me. I can't focus, read, write, or keyboard with people running off at the mouth incessantly. Is it me? Maybe my haughty attitude creates non-existent problems. Maybe I think I'm too good for this place—above it all. Just a lofty spirit that's descended from on high to instruct elflings, teachers, and administrators alike. Yeah, that's it.

And no toner again in the copiers.

While two of my classes seem on an even keel, my 6th period section has become this term's nemesis for me. It's a fourth semester algebra class and intended to serve as the preparation for the Regents exam in June. An important milestone for the students. This period is also my largest section and 30+ kids regularly show up. In several specific instances, I'm sorry they do. Two kids I ask to pipe down just up and leave. One of them slams the door behind him. I chase him a little way down the hall and shout, "Was it something I said?"

Back in the T-L, Morton starts his non-stop commentary again.

WEDNESDAY, FEBRUARY 25

A Danger to Society

As if things aren't bad enough, last night I find out I might be next on the list of the Axis of Evil. The *NY Times* reports that none other than Education Secretary Rod Paige likens the National Education Association to a "terrorist organization." The UFT may not be far behind. Will I be forced to identify other teachers? Name names?

Holly Golightly

said of one of her frequent visitors, "I speak Yiddish better than he speaks English." She could also have been talking about the students at

CBHS. It's no wonder that Johnny can't read—he can't talk, either. The kids' conversation is barely intelligible outside their ghetto niche, although I know that TV has expanded their jargon to the outside world. That would be fine if they could also speak SEU, Standard English Usage.

The word "ask" serves as the school's shibboleth. The kids, and many of the staff, I might say, evidently can't say it properly. I resist my impulse to jab a mispronouncing student with, "You're not going to *ax* me in the head, are you?" How are these kids ever going to fit into the world at large, land a good job, advance their dreams? Their argot automatically casts them down.

Every so often I make it a point in my classes to say something like, "Math is important, but even though I'm a math teacher, reading is the most important thing you can do to advance your education." I don't fool myself into thinking my exhortations amount to much, but at least they hear the message from me and not just their English teacher. When I corner one of my students in private, I always ask them about their reading habits. Do you read? What do you read? Read comic books if you must, but read every day.

In my troublesome 6th period class, Shana, the ringleader of the Philistines, shouts out, "Why don't you teach?" and walks out. This after coming in late, kibitzing with friends, and then reading the newspaper after I halt her yakking.

THURSDAY, FEBRUARY 26

Begging for Calcs

My conversion to calculators for kids is complete. The tactile, visual, and psychological influence of having a calc in hand makes an impact on some of them. But that's only when I can cadge a few from the math department. I'll take any edge I can get. But there aren't enough to go around in the math department. I pitch Mr. T.: Can the math department buy more to hand out? Not enough money in the budget. I hear some teachers hoard them for their own classes.

The little electronic toys are only a few bucks so I'll exhort the kids to buy them. If they can wear designer jeans and the most expensive basketball shoes, they can spring for these. Except, they won't. I remind, beg, and threaten. Still they won't get them. I even make a point of writing down their names on a phony list to be used to penalize them on the final grade for not bringing them to class. No luck. I explain that I will intentionally have problems on tests that can only be solved by calculators. I am wasting my breath. I feel so stymied. They won't lift a finger to help themselves.

In the hall, I bump into Noki from last term. We're glad to see each other. He decided not to transfer to one of the new schools. I'm afraid he's gotten comfortable being at the top of a very small heap. I also run into some of my other kids from the fall semester. They hug me. Two of them had been openly antagonistic. I begin to realize that my role here is more a parent or social worker than a teacher. "Do I want to be a social worker?" I ask myself. This is what my job at CBHS has turned into.

FRIDAY, FEBRUARY 27

You've Got to Accentuate the Positive

I pick up my outreach log and decide to make someone feel good today. So I call Roxanne's mom. Roxanne is one of our rare demanding types who insists on getting an education. She wants her questions answered and on the double. Sometimes it's a distraction from the rhythm of my instruction, but good for her! She and CJ are almost my only hopes for success in 6th period out of thirty-plus kids. I congratulate the mom on her daughter's good behavior and progress.

They don't say TGIF for nothing. Evidently, my kids say it first thing in the morning.

And don't show up.

One of the administrative spies shows up for my 8th period class and demands to know: Where are all the kids? With a straight face, I tell him that one is in jail, another is a prostitute doing tricks at this very moment, another moved to Puerto Rico, and yet another came down with sickle cell anemia. He turns around and walks out, evidently satisfied with knowing the facts of the situation. Who knows? Maybe I guessed right.

In the T-L, Rob Simmons tells me that when one of his kids stomped out, he locked the boy out. Now this kid wants back in—he forgot his book bag with God-knows-what inside it. A co-conspirator lets this buddy back in the rear door. Meanwhile, Rob hurls the book bag out in the hall. While the bag gets the heave-ho, the co-conspirators steal Rob's attendance sheets. The fun never stops at CBHS.

I'm feeling in the Friday groove myself today. Finally, I have all the keys to my classrooms.

MONDAY, MARCH I

Euphoria Slips Away

from me. Kids are late to class and when they do come, they schmooze with each other like there's no tomorrow. Absenteeism soars. Vidal, one of my favorite students, takes a hike when I ask him to stop playing around. Nobody hands in homework. Hats and do-rags abound.

It's not just me. In the T-L, Janet says her kids stopped coming to class. The ones that do show up are inattentive. Her theory: Once the nice weather arrives, school is over as far as our boys and girls are concerned.

TUESDAY, MARCH 2

Hats Off

Some kids thrive on their disobedience. In the 6th period, Adam Rivena refuses to take off his baseball cap. Every single day. I've approached to him after and before class and tried to reason with him. "Well, Adam, you know I've got to enforce the rules. I'm a teacher here. How about our not getting into the hat thing anymore?" No way. He must spite me. It's in his contract with Lucifer.

Ari is another one. Always late to class. "The bus doesn't get here in time."

"How about catching an earlier bus?" I query. He nods his head that maybe that's not such a bad idea. But he never does it. Comes in late every day.

Kris is yet another character in this Damon Runyon comedy called CBHS. I blame my pal Glenn for this headache. She was in his section. When she wrote a letter to Mr. T. complaining about him, Glenn immediately had her exported out of his class into mine.

The following is Kris' letter to Mr. T., now making me the target of her disaffection:

> From: Kris Powers
> To: Mr. Tqiqi
>
> Right, now I am in Mr. Klass [sic] math class and he teaches worst [sic] than Mr. Martin, because he gives us homework on what he doesn't teach us and then he stops during lessons and tells us stupid stories that we don't need to hear, and right now I am not understanding anything that he is teaching me.

She knows the system. She also knows the best defense is a good offense. I give her credit for the period after "Mr" and a spirited attack against me. Back in the T-L, Glenn gloats over the fact that he made his problem mine. I write my counterattack:

Written Statement
March 2, 2004
To: Mr. Tqiqi

My 2nd period M$40 student Kris Powers came to talk to me today after class and said she was not learning the subject. I suggested she come see me the 9th period for tutoring. Her response was that she does competitive dance and cannot attend. I then suggested she attend Saturday classes and her response was the same—she cannot attend. I then was in the process of asking her what her suggestion might be when she abruptly turned around, left the classroom, and evidently promptly went to your office to write a complaint.

Today when doing group work in class, she made no attempt to ask for help, even when I went around the room asking students if they needed assistance.

Part of her written complaint was that I tell too many stories. My story today was an explanation that when solving the problem of the day concerning triangles, a student should write down all the facts about triangles they know, such as the sum of the angles adds up to 180°, before giving up on solving the problem.

Her first day in my class was February 25th when she arrived late. She was also late the following two days on the 26th and 27th.

Sincerely,
Ric Klass

WEDNESDAY, MARCH 3

Gospel of Math

I can't help myself. I preach to these kids. In my heart, I'm an evangelical in the original sense. The word from the Greek means "bringing good news." And that's what I want to do. Tell them the good news that they can have a life worth living. For my sermon on the mount today, I draw on none other than Bernie Cornfeld. He preached regularly to his dominion and asked his financial disciples, "Do you sincerely want to be rich?" I leave out the fact that he spent eleven months in a Swiss slammer.

Everyone except maybe Mother Teresa, priests, and teachers want to be rich. So what did Cornfeld mean when he said "sincerely"?

A couple of kids in each class take a stab at it.

No matter what they say, I say, "That's right. If you're sincere, you do what it takes to reach your goal. All of you have told me you want to be doctors, lawyers, engineers, or have some other successful career." I omit references to the kids who want to be drug dealers. "But to reach your goal, you must take notes, pay attention, and do your homework. That's what it means to *sincerely* want to be somebody."

I don't know if what I'm saying falls on deaf ears or not. There's no visible response. Career teachers tell me the kids are listening, even if they don't show it. I hope so. Shana Cantrow gives me one distinct response in my 6th period class.

"Why do you keep wasting our time? Teach! All you ever do is tell your stupid stories."

This from a girl who either reads magazines in my class or engages in unrelenting yapping with Stan Gabriel—when she's here, that is, which isn't often. And she hasn't passed a single quiz or handed in a stitch of homework.

"What's it to *her*, anyway," I think. Still, something tells me Shana is smart and could do well if she wanted to. She dresses like a hippie.

Definitely not stylish in the CBHS sense. She seems a loner, despite her conversations with Stan. I wish I could preach my gospel privately to her but she won't talk to me after class. It makes me sad that I can't reach a potential convert.

In the T-L, there's talk of gang wars among the students in the small schools here. On a positive note, it seems to me that I'm seeing fewer baggy pants. Are styles changing? I hope so. Maybe I'm just becoming visually immune to them.

THURSDAY, MARCH 4

The Aroma

infuses every cranny of the T-L, and it's not pleasant. Between periods, teachers pile in. Everyone stares at each other with an "it's not me" look. Now all point their noses in the direction of the culprit. A stink of one or more days' heavy perspiration emanates from the pores underneath the unwashed shirt of one Victor Gallo as he obliviously pours over the *New York Post*. We nod to each other knowingly but no one says anything. We move to the far corners of the room. In one of them, Don whispers to himself like a drunk with the DTs. Community life in the T-L definitely has its downside. Victor imparts some advice: "Tell your students who won't study, 'This is what you're going to have to learn next year when you repeat this course.'"

Join the World

I'm making progress with the SPED kids. Even a couple of the truants start to show up more or less regularly, but they're so far behind I can't see them passing the course.

At one point, Elton asks me, "Can I be mainstreamed?" The others perk up at the question. It's an exciting moment. They all want to make a break for freedom. I don't know the answer, the administrative requirements of how he got in, or how he'll get out of SPED.

"Why are you here?" I ask the entire class. No response.

FRIDAY, MARCH 5

Teaching to the Test

I plead guilty to teaching to the exam tomorrow. I don't just go over the topics, I give the kids a sample test that has exactly the same questions in the same order. Only the numbers are changed a bit. An automatic guarantee for high scores? Most of the kids don't look at the handouts or at my solutions written on the blackboard. The other freshmen and sophomores' math teachers follow the same practice with the same result.

Mr. T. observes my 2nd period class. I assign the kids to groups with specific problems to put on transparencies for the overhead projector. They like writing with colored markers on the plastic sheets. The groups stay on task and do the work along with some kibitzing. They present their solutions but no one takes notes on other groups' answers. In our post-observation conference, Mr. T. doesn't have that many comments. I've done worse. I'm still not following the point-of-entry model because I stand up and teach too much. He corrects my habit of asking for questions at the end of class. Most of our kids don't like to admit they don't know something or are just too shy to ask. He suggests that, instead, I pose questions for the students to answer. Right on.

Wayne, a non-special education boy, transfers into my SPED class. He's a senior who hopes to graduate, and this class fits his schedule. He needs the math credit to graduate but doesn't show any particular inclination to do the work. One thing he is inclined to do is make sure his friends don't spot him in a SPED class. He tries to tape paper over the window, but I put a stop to it. After my experiences last term, I want to make sure guards can at least see my bloody corpus so they can call an ambulance. So Wayne hides from the door. He's not alone in not wanting to keep his SPED class secret. It's definitely uncool to be here, and I'm told it subjects the kids to ridicule by their peers. When I relate this to Mr. T., he says to let them know they're lucky to have small classes.

A rash of heart attacks among the students' parents breaks out. I find out that Shana's dad is seriously ill and has been for some time. Maybe that's why she's so difficult in class. I'm sorry for her. I'll try to be more understanding. In the T-L, I hear of other students' parents with the same malady.

Tonight I meet Doyle at a diner. He tells me he's graduating this summer. I'm gratified to share in his triumph.

SUNDAY, MARCH 7

Ups and Downs

A few kids improve. Arjun scores an 84 percent on the last test and Jocelyn a 94 percent. Ketchum Saunders writes on his quiz today:

" 'I'm going to try to pass, now.' (his quotation marks)
Help me!"

What a jolt! He looks half asleep most of the time. It chokes me up to see that, deep inside, these children want to succeed but don't know how to go about it. I'll try to help the boy.

My rule of thumb coming to CBHS was that 80 percent of the kids could achieve and graduate. I stick by this percentage, despite my difficulties reaching them. I get this love letter from Jackson Sabot in my SPED class. He's part of the other 20 percent. My sense is that he fell behind in his education so long ago that it would take intensive individualized help for him to progress. If he were willing. But he's not. The note's unsigned, but I know who it is by the handwriting and substance. He's angry with me for interrupting his reverie.

To: klass
Fucking
dork
I was Fucking
Thinking
To my
Fuckin selve
u stupid Asshole

The note is heartfelt, if nothing else. Sort of poetic, too—the way he arranged his thoughts on the page.

MONDAY, MARCH 8

How Can I Help?

After the period is over, I go up to Ketchum who wrote the plea for succor yesterday.

Can he come for tutoring during any of my free periods? No.

Can he come see me after school? No, he works.

OK. Can he go to Saturday classes for free tutoring? No, he works then, too.

What the hell can I do for this kid? He says he wants help but won't/can't put any time into it. He looked sleepy today, too, despite his cry for help. It occurs to me now that his job probably drains all his energy. Ketchum is not alone in this dilemma. Many of the kids work because they must assist their families or in order to dress well—an extremely important element in their lives.

It's been a typical day: Ahmed asleep in class, Ari twenty-five minutes late. Twenty-nine kids show up for 6th period—way too many with so many of them disruptive. And then there's Blaze. Judging from her clothes, jewelry, and décolletage, she considers herself something of a fashion plate. Today she's busy with her makeup. After completing her toilette, she complains about my inadequate teaching. Pity. She drew the short end of the straw picking me. I skipped the education course on "Math and Lipstick Applications."

In my SPED class, Cory Gardenia gets a 94 percent and Dalia Armiger gets a 92 percent. In the 8th period, Reynaldo Santiago gets an 82 percent. But I'm concerned about the coming nice weather. Another thought pops out. If I stay at CBHS, my lack of seniority will probably stick me with freshmen again.

I start my search for a new position tonight by applying for jobs I saw in the Sunday *NY Times*.

TUESDAY, MARCH 9

Light!

It's light out when I pull out of the driveway this morning. That means summer's coming and so is my own deliverance.

What Really Matters

I confiscate this letter today passed between two girls. It speaks of their main concerns:

(*n.b.*: written without periods or capitalization of new sentences)

G1: what happen?

(my translation of this question is: "What is it that you'd like to know?")

G2: just out of curiosity how is the relationship w/ that kid is it serious or puppy love?

G1: serious/puppy love

serious ➔ when we are alone

puppy love ➜ when alone or around his family

G2: oh! I know so ya are still on kissing and lovey/dovey but when you are alone its intimate that's great cause soon he will be serious when hes wit his friends then that means hes falling in love then ya will have 1 break up its painful then ya will get back together and then ya will be in loves it great then painful at the same time but the pain won't hurt.

I wish I had made this up.

WEDNESDAY, MARCH 10

A Pointed Question

When it comes right down to it, whether or not my students technically have passed freshman algebra, most don't know any math. Not the basic multiplication tables, not solving even the simplest algebra problem. But I am starting to make some headway using the SAMD technique Will Gerard showed me. So I think maybe I should hand out compasses to the kids to use in geometry. It's another visual aid and it's a manipulative. A "manipulative" is our jargon for a hands-on tool. Luckily, I'm getting a master's degree in education or I wouldn't know the arcana of my new profession. Anyway, I bring up my bright idea in the T-L.

"What? Are you crazy?" Victor asks me. "They'll take those pointy compasses and kill each other and then finish you off for good measure." I consider his diagnosis and go to Mr. T. for a second opinion. He's not so keen on the idea, either. It so happens Bill Kojac, our most experienced math teacher, is standing by. I can get compasses with soft points at the supply counter in the kiddie cafeteria. Supply counter? I didn't know we had one. I have assiduously avoided the cafeteria as one would avoid a booby-trapped snake pit. OK, so I hike down to the basement to the supply counter. The guy running the shop tells me there are only fourteen left, not the thirty I ask for. And they're fifty cents apiece. But what the hay, it's almost the end of the year. Go ahead and take them all for free. Nice man, but I guess it beats having to keep track of them as inventory.

I bring my plunder back to the T-L. The gab of the day centers on the advisability of jumping ship to a new school. There's no union at the small schools, one teacher says. Another points out many principals are a pain in the butt. In a school as large as CBHS, the principal doesn't have time to be on your neck. We don't discuss what kind of pain in the rear we have here.

THURSDAY, MARCH 11

Spring in the Air

In the T-L, I hear truancy is way up. Rod Bonano tells us he caught kids making out in his classroom. Rod sees me making three versions of my tests to prevent cheating. We get into a discussion of the merits of multiple tests. Rod doesn't bother. "Who are they going to cheat off of?" he asks. Good question.

FRIDAY, MARCH 12

Comes a RIF

The talk of the day has the new teachers in a panic. CBHS is shrinking to allow for the growth of the small schools sharing the building. Layoffs are coming but no one knows how big. First to go will be the new untenured staff. People like me. Basically, I'm indifferent to the news. While I have sophomores this term, I'm still the new boy on the block and will be assigned freshmen next year. This fact leads me to an inevitable conclusion. It leads me out of here. My applications for a new teaching job already float on the Internet.

A giant fat guy joins us today in the T-L for the first time. He's lugging around a massive cart—really a mobile office. He's moved the tables so it can fit into this small room. I'm annoyed that I can't sit in my usual spot. Along with his instructional materials, his wagon's chock-a-block with liter bottles of lemonade and giant bags of mixed nuts. While stuffing his face, he interjects comments into the various conversations going on.

I have other matters on my mind, anyway: I'm more concerned with my difficulty teaching loci, points that satisfy an equation. I have an ongoing hurdle. It all seems so easy to me that I frequently move too quickly from one topic to the next. Even so, I'm just barely staying even with the mandated daily schedule for the term. I can't get ahold of the overhead projector today. Someone else snatched it before me. I uproot Elton from my SPED class for fooling around today. The guards recycle him back, lickety-split. Instead of being angry with me—which would be my reaction—Elton hugs me and says he's sorry. Nice boy.

When I stroll into my last class of the day, I find Ms. Tottle in a dither. Some kid threw one of her valuable art books out the window. Was it one of mine? I swear fealty that none of my darlings would do it. Anyway, I'm always first in the room and nobody sits near the window. I pray I'm right. I like this group and wouldn't want to see any of them charged with theft.

MONDAY, MARCH 15

Arrogant Me

I get a call in the T-L to come see Harry, the SPED head. When I show up, he's not in. I'm asked to go downstairs and speak with the SPED scheduling madam instead. I introduce myself. What's up? I inquire. This convivial woman doesn't know me and clearly is having some difficulty coming to the point. By this time at CBHS, I've come to realize that friendships can smooth the way. But we're not friends. The point: They want me to pass the SPED kids in my class. I'm ashamed to say I get huffy with her. I let her know that my students will either pass the tests or fail. I strut out like a stuffed shirt. But before I get back to the T-L, I confess to myself what a putz I am. These nice people work like dogs to help kids with troubles, and I act like a jerk. Am I some self-styled Ayn Rand fountainhead? I could've at least been civil. This job's turning me into a gargoyle.

More aggravation. My fourth semester kids can't even solve $2x+3 = 4x$ and the Regents exams are coming soon. That's not all. This entire year, the administration has required teachers to enforce a no hats or do-rags policy. But today is: Hats Day! All the little ones can wear anything they like on their noggins. What b.s. this is. And what kind of lesson is it? Our principal has a screw loose . . . I suppose tomorrow will be Snub-Nosed Revolver or Swiss Army Knife Day. I am going insane.

I get another call. The SPED guidance counselor asks for a written update:

> Written Statement
> March 15, 2004
> To: Mr. Tiranio:
>
> Following up on our conversation today, the following students that you counsel have not appeared in my 5th period YM$4 (special ed) class or only rarely so:
>
> Jaylon Parrias
>
> Josue Torento

In addition, Dalia Armiger and Alissa Recuse have been excessively absent. I believe it is because they were suspended.

Cordially,

Mr. Klass, Math Dept.

TUESDAY, MARCH 16

More Tsouris

What my students don't know fills every book ever written. Especially their textbooks. Kris doesn't know how many inches there are in a foot. Others don't know how to calculate the area of a rectangle. Third grade stuff.

And the microwave is disgustingly vile.

Enemy at the Gate

I'm sick and tired of students wandering late into my class. Some even drag themselves in only moments before the bell. But I had pretty much solved the tardiness. Until today. Starting a couple of weeks ago, I've made latecomers get a pass from Security to enter my class. My rooms are in the back of the building on the upper floors so that it's a good ten-minute trek back and forth. Most of the chronic laggards now arrive on time. Too much trouble to get the pass. But today Shana, Abel, and Adam, three of my big-time agitators, arrive late at the same time. And they scream bloody murder when I won't allow them in without the visa. They march right to the assistant principal's office to post charges against me. Mr. Santino does the right thing. Or so he thinks. And gives me hell indirectly through Mr. T. for barring entry to these upright citizens. Make sure Klass doesn't do it again. Mr. T. won't intervene on my behalf. He's a great guy but his political instincts keep him out of the fray. Mine keep me in it. For a shot at some administrative support, I make a beeline to Mr. Girano, the security pasha. We haven't exactly hit it off this year but he's sympathetic to my tardiness solution. Notwithstanding, he lets me know NYC regulations forbid preventing students from entering their school unless suspended. By extension, that applies to the classroom, too. He knows the regs, all right. Darn.

Nothing comes easy here. The simplest act becomes an effort. That's why the experienced teachers coast on a minimum-energy platform. Always low-key, they let the crashing surf roll over them. For sure, they live longer that way—except the ones teaching freshmen that can't stomach their kids.

WEDNESDAY, MARCH 17

Nut House Day

Wayne, the senior who transferred into my SPED class for a certain passing grade, gets the message. He either works or I'll sack him. He transfers out. Meanwhile, some of these students are doing well, others can't begin to hack third semester algebra. They're at a fourth- or fifth-grade level. If I were more experienced, maybe I could teach what's called in the education racket, "differentiated instruction." In English, it means teaching more than one subject in the classroom. Frankly, I'm not up to it. Besides, I've got several fairly talented kids making real progress. Teaching each kid something different will mean the good students will learn less. So I approach Harry for help. I want a paraprofessional to help me with the slower children. I get this bright idea from Katherine, the leader of my weekly UFT professional development group. My sessions there have turned into therapy.

I make my pitch. I need an aide so that I can help both the better students and the slower ones, otherwise both groups will suffer. Well, Harry nods his head knowingly and says, "You don't understand kids, Ric. These students are used to not learning. Don't sweat it." Oh. Please forgive my ignorance. The SPED children have been stepped on for so long they don't even know they're not getting a good education. I'm mad as a hornet. I go to Mr. T. and make my case. Can he get me some help in my classroom? He says he'll take it up with Linda, the principal. I don't have high hopes about getting her assistance.

Ahmed, the sarcastic David Letterman of my sections, walks out of my class today. I decide to call his parents for a little home support. Neither his Delaney card nor my class registration lists his telephone number. I'll try a new tactic another day.

Keep Your Eyes Wide Open

The UFT meetings provide a welcome relief, although they take from my free time. Jean, a funny, divorced science teacher in a new school upstairs, joins me in this weekly gabfest. The feelings of anger and frustration we share help to make me feel I'm not a freak. Jean used to teach at a preppy Catholic girls' school. I find it incredible that she would leave to teach here. On the other hand, maybe an ex-investment banker is the wrong guy to point a finger.

Today's theme turns on "with-it-ness." An attribute I'm definitely without. With-it-ness is the ability to always sense what's going on all around the classroom. A teacher's sixth sense, as it were. Personally, I'm more akin to without-it-ness. While I'm engaged in a task, I'm so focused a bomb could go off without my knowing it. When I read a book, my wife has to take hold of my arm to grab my attention. Just repeating my name makes me feel as though someone has been pounding on my brain. Anyway, I learn with-it-ness is key to maintaining good discipline in a classroom. Otherwise, bedlam can break loose. Unpleasant situations can be avoided. Man, do I ever need to avoid "situations." The good news is that I can practice improving this trait. I resolve to do just that.

THURSDAY, MARCH 18

Unobserved

Mr. T. conducts another class observation today. Once again, Linda is a no-show. Kind of a shame. The session goes well and even the kids say they like the class.

FRIDAY, MARCH 19

Hoping and Hopping

A stoned kid threatens Glenn in his class today. Glenn stands in front of the boy and casts down the gauntlet. "Walk around me," Glenn challenges. Glenn was hoping the kid would throw a punch so that he could return the favor legally. Eventually, the police charge in and yank the inebriate out of the classroom.

"That didn't sound like such a good idea," the voice of reason, me, tells Glenn. "What if he were armed? What if you hurt him? We're not insured if we instigate a fight." What I don't say: He doesn't look like a contender, in my opinion. But you never know. My what-ifs leave him unmoved and unrepentant. He's still plenty mad, even though the episode happened hours ago.

I must be dozing. As I'm solving an equation on the board, Kris, who openly can't stand the sight of me, informs me more than a bit cattily, "We did that problem yesterday in class." I'm shocked that she was paying attention.

Tqiqi can't help me with the SPED class. "I did what I could, but Linda can't help. No money in the budget. I don't know what to say." Surprised I'm not.

Tonight I go upstairs to bed feeling anxious. A devout man would pray for an aide in the SPED class. Minister David Niven in *The Bishop's Wife* comes to mind. The pastor wanted heaven to give him a new church. His angel, Cary Grant, only gave him unwanted guidance. On this consideration, I turn around and head to the kitchen for a cheese sandwich. Angst makes me famished and at least I'll find what I'm searching for.

SUNDAY, MARCH 21

Mr. T. calls me at 6:00 P.M. He's observing me tomorrow during the 6th period. Linda will be there. I tell him what I've said all year. "I don't care if Mayor Bloomberg and the President of the United States sit in. I'll do my best." And I mean it (although I'm not all that keen on seeing Bush—not a big fan). If I'm doing a ghastly job, go ahead and fire me. Take me out of my misery.

MONDAY, MARCH 22

Electrocardiogram Normal

By now I would be shocked if Linda showed her face for my observation today. Her Majesty has other duties in her kingdom. It's just as well. At least for Mr. T.'s sake, if not mine. The 6th period is my worst section and the kids raise Cain.

The Dirty Little Secret

in education, kept quiet by teachers, concerns truancy. We're thrilled when kids who don't want to be in school just don't show up. The classes are smaller. The vanishing warlocks are somebody else's problem. Life is good then. We can teach. Only the young, inexperienced, or compulsively idealistic teachers have their heart in chasing down the truants and compelling them to attend. Administrators have an

entirely different view. Per capita attendance per day usually
drives funding for schools. No kids. No money.

Today, I'm cursed in my SPED class. I need to post an SRO sign. Kids I've never seen before show up. Despite the small room, the class quickly gets out of control with the newbies doing their best to make sure none of the others learn anything, either. I know these truant SPEDs have a host of their own difficulties, but regardless, I wish they were out of here so I could continue making progress with the survivors.

All the copiers and printers are down in the T-L. I don't care. I'm here at sunrise and stay late. I'm not going to work at home, too, or I'll dislike this change of career so much I'll call it a day—for good.

TUESDAY, MARCH 23

My SPED class has come to a grinding halt. The new arrivals jamming every nook and cranny toss paper wads, goof off, and stroll around. Anything to keep the focus off math.

Mr. T. tells me I performed so defectively during his observation, he won't even write it up. I feel rotten. I respect his opinion, and I do want to be a better teacher.

WEDNESDAY, MARCH 24

A Rare Admission

"The daily math schedule moves too fast for the kids," I complain to Mr. T.

"We can't do what's sensible. We don't have flexibility," he dejectedly replies. Although not in a Pollyanna way, he's usually upbeat and supportive of the administration. His atypical candor catches me off-guard. If he's turning sour, then this school is in deep doo-doo.

It's a test day. Lately, a girl I don't know from another class has been sitting in on my 5th period section. I haven't challenged or questioned her presence. If she wants to learn, may heaven protect her. Besides, I'm a little flattered that at least some child thinks my instruction is worth something. Today, she wants to take my test and get tutoring, too. Can I say no?

I pick today as a good time to repeat the fairness speech. "Math is as fair as life gets. School is the fairest time in your life and math is the fairest school subject. Get the answers right and you get an A. Get 85 percent right, it's a B and so on. In your entire life, you will never be treated more fairly than by me, right here." I don't get a verbal response but their alert silence tells me they heard me. At CBHS, I can't ask for more.

Disaster strikes. During the 6th period exam, I'm so mixed up I hand out the wrong test. I don't discover my mistake until ten minutes into the period. Moans and cries abound when I collect the wrong ones and replace them with the correct tests. For a change, the kids are justified with their complaints. "Too bad. Life is hard," I think. But then, work-men pound on the door. They need to replace a window. Now my little chickadees squawk their heads off. A cacophony of verbal abuse fills the air. Abel declares, "This is scandalous!" A witty, literate remark goes a long way with me. I'm so amused that maybe I'll pass him this term. On second thought, maybe not. I don't tell them, but I decide not to count this exam.

My professional development group lets its hair down at our session today. We unload our gripes. We all agree that Katherine, our group leader, has become our shrink.

THURSDAY, MARCH 25

Who's He?

Last night and today, CBHS conducts Parents' Day. A total of fifteen family members show up, representing only twelve students for all my sections. Pathetic. Most of the other teachers report spotty parental attendance, too. In some cases, the older brother or sister comes instead of a parent. My guess is that they probably take the role of parent for the student. One mom shows up with her son. Who is this kid? I wonder. I look at the class register. He's on it but has never attended. Not once. I tell her this and also say I really can't comment on him. He's a stranger to me. I discuss the low turnout with Joel Farmer. He tells me that he attended Grandparents' Night at his granddaughter's school, half of which is Hispanic. He says not one Hispanic grandparent showed up for the 100 Latino kids. I have no idea if his experience is typical or not, but I take his word on the math.

In my 4th period class, I sack Travis, one of my most promising potential survivors, along with Ahmed. One bad apple makes the others turn sour, proves too true here.

FRIDAY, MARCH 26

Liar's Poker

I catch several kids trying to copy answers during exams today. It makes me laugh, how innocent they act. "I was just seeing how he was doing the problem," Elton in my SPED class tells me. As if cheating had become officially sanctioned. I stifle my laughing by pretending to cough. I don't penalize him, but I warn him not to try it again. He does anyway, but he's so obvious about it I'm entertained and not annoyed. As Rod Bonano said, who's there to cheat off of?

Good news: The tests have driven away most of the troublemakers in my SPED section. But I still need help with the slower students. I have one last idea to get some assistance. I call Harry.

"Listen, I'm sorry you're not able to help me out with a paraprofessional. I understand. Unfortunately, it's going to mean all the students failing this term." Silence on the other end. CBHS's parody of organization has arranged it so that Mr. T., my supervisor, couldn't care less about my SPED class. It's Harry's bailiwick. On the other hand, I don't report to Harry. He has no authority over me, whatsoever. Now it's a game of cat and mouse.

MONDAY, MARCH 29

Harry Blinks

and this morning I gladly welcome Lana, my new assistant. I feel like gloating to Mr. T. about my organizational gamesmanship, but demur. A new duck can't afford too many enemies. Harry might be carrying a shotgun at the next blind.

Travis asks me for a recommendation to enter a special science program. More good news. Travis seems serous about his education. I'm also happy he's not carrying a grudge about my handing him his pink slip the other day.

TUESDAY, MARCH 30

Eye of the Hurricane

Today, we begin four days of midterms. Although I need to spend considerable time in preparation, the classes themselves seem oddly tranquil, as if before a storm.

WEDNESDAY, MARCH 31

Exam Anxieties

Victor tells me his kids don't know how many weeks or days there are in a year. Somehow, I'm not shocked. As for me, I'm concerned because I neglected to give the exact same review questions as appear on the tests. Even when I telegraph the problems, they still don't get them right.

Security rushes in like a DEA swat team and yanks Roxanne, one of my few star students, out of her midterm exam because she's wearing a headscarf. They saw it when they peeked in the window. What nonsense when all the kids wear hats. It's the administration that's out of control.

Denis Friend updates me on his progress teaching math in one of the new schools. Fifty out of 100 of his students sank the first term. They won't do their homework. Doesn't sound all that different from old-fashioned CBHS.

THURSDAY, APRIL 1

Sacre Bleu

Josue makes a rare guest appearance in my SPED class and starts in with foolishness. But when he sees the others are working, he wants to join in. When the conditions are right and the classes are small, miracles can happen.

FRIDAY, APRIL 2

Not a Miser

Tests are over and spring vacation starts tomorrow. I decide to let the kids coast and not assign homework. They won't do it anyhow and this way I don't play Scrooge. Cory, Jerry, Elton, and Dalia ask again about their chances at flying the coop from their SPED classification.

SUNDAY, APRIL 4

SPED Up

I get grading papers over with. My SPEDs do the best of all my sections.

TUESDAY, APRIL 13

Mars Observed

After vacation, Mr. T. notifies me that another observation is planned. On one hand, I find it a nuisance, but Mr. T. always has good suggestions. I'm taking the day off tomorrow to conclude old business. I think it's the last hurrah for my prior life. I take care to prepare detailed lesson plans for the substitute teacher.

WEDNESDAY, APRIL 14

My Lesson Plans

are entirely ignored by the substitute teacher. Mr. T. makes a big deal about having them prepared for when we're absent. A complete waste of time.

THURSDAY, APRIL 15

Quiero Hablar Español

As if I didn't have enough to contend with, I'm also studying for the CLEP Spanish test, an alternative to taking the language in a college for credit. This should wrap up all my requirements for a teaching certificate from New York State. My preparation has the benefit of allowing me to speak pigeon Spanish to occasional victims. I continue to call homes on a regular basis and keep a log to hand in to the assistant principal—part of the bureaucratic record keeping. No wonder storage companies make such a fortune. Eternally profiting from the unending human desire to preserve records of information never looked at in the first place.

Anyhooo, as a part of the edu-telemarketing mandate, I reach a Spanish-speaking mom on the phone. She seems pleased to converse about her daughter in her native language, despite my gringo garbling. Better yet, the conversation is conducted in full view and earshot of my compatriots in the T-L. They're impressed that I can say more than *buenos días* and even carry on, albeit limply, in something other than math-ese.

In the midst of my efforts, I happen to reach the student and not the parent. Shaylee is one of the few students I have earmarked for survival. I indicated by a solitary checkmark on her report card that I wanted her to go to Saturday classes to ensure high grades for the term. Her parents, inadvertently, interpreted that well-meant advice as an indication of academic trouble. Consequently, she's in Dutch with her folks and begs me to call them to straighten out the story. She knows she is a favorite of mine and has no problem pleading her case. I accede immediately.

I'm calling her home with two purposes, therefore: (a) with the express purpose to tell her parents/legal guardians that she is, in fact, a good student, and; (b) Shaylee should get the hell out of CBHS and apply to one of the small schools or somewhere where she won't be dragged down by her classmates. Since Shaylee picks up and her parents aren't home, I tell her exactly that—(a) and (b). I don't think (b) ever happened. But at least she knows I care about her well-being.

Rumor has it that a security guard at CBHS was arrested for the rape of a sixteen-year-old.

FRIDAY, APRIL 16

A Poison Pen Note

from the principal leaches out of my in mailbox today concerning my absence from school the day after a holiday. The truth was that I didn't know the correct vacation dates and before vacation was over, I even showed up a day early. I had already notified the Administrative Assistant Principal considerably in advance, provided lesson plans for the days absent, and checked again with the secretary to verify everything was kosher. The secretary should've called for an explanation— but an in-writing berating accusing me of inexcusable behavior infuriates me.

"Linda, that incompetent witch, should have remained a high-priced secretary." Forthwith, I dash off my own thinly-polite and not-too-thinly-disguised defiant response. This whole teaching gig has boomeranged into a never-ending series of mishaps, miscalculations, and administratively-mismanaged boondoggles. I'm beside myself with anger. Which I really don't need.

Contrapuntally, a welcome surprise awaits in my SPED class. Dalia, that cursing-a-yellow-streak marine sergeant who looks surprisingly like an attractive, well-dressed teenager, confides that she wants to catch up with the others. Like several of my students, she clearly has brains but no discipline. She has graced our class with attendance only fitfully since the start of the term. The excuses range from illness to suspension from school. A letter two weeks ago from Security, requesting I send them her homework, at least confirms the latest pretext. But here is an actual plea to do better.

In part, her ego is at stake. Lana, the paraprofessional, was helping her and, in general, the slower kids in the class. I was instructing the higher end and Dalia is indignant that she's not in the in-group. I give her credit for never ceding math superiority to any of the other students. Fine by me—if it's ego that it takes to get some motivation, so be it. Besides, she's one of the few kids in any of my classes to turn in homework, even if only occasionally. I give her prior assignments and homework she missed. But, to tell the truth, I'm past getting too excited. My enthusiasm has given way to the reality that even when kids express the desire to do better, it rarely manifests itself into action.

Getting an Upper Hand

Nothing's working with Ahmed, so I try a little psychological warfare when I catch sight of him in the hallway. "I'm sad you're not doing well," I say offhandedly. "I had thought you could do better." Occasionally, playing the devil's advocate works with these kids.

It's taken me almost all year, but I feel on the whole that I've gained control of my own emotions. Only rarely now do I lose my temper. I'm calm and give an eight-weeks-to-go speech to all my classes. Rob Simmons told me his past success had a lot to do with always making the kids think they can catch up. Never let them lose the faith. In his opinion, and I've come to agree, it's never wrong to encourage the children to learn. Even if it's a little misleading. And even if they don't pass your course, their studying now will help them later.

So this is my spiel: "If you do well for the rest of the term, even if you're failing now, and get a gentleperson's score on the final, not a just-passing 65, I'll pass you for the term." Many of my students seem intrigued by my proposal. After loafing all term, they can still catch up. I wait to see the results of my bribe. I can't help myself. I still have hope.

Despite the possible turnaround for Dalia, I still go home carping about the poison pen letter from that inept harpy at the top. To make matters worse, I complain to myself about my own reaction. I should be above caring about it. Oh, no matter. It's the weekend.

MONDAY, APRIL 19

A Call for Calcs

For the umpteenth time, I beg the kids to get scientific calculators. "They're as little as nine bucks," I plead.

Ari begs off with a loud announcement for my benefit and the rest of the class: "I just don't have the money." Although I know he's working the house, I'm always cautious on this point. I know it's the truth for some kids, but not others. I don't dare come off as the rich, unfeeling white teacher out of his element. Although almost without exception the students dress as if about to make a guest appearance on the E Channel, the common pedagogical perception supposes that some families starve to let their kids dress nicely; and as for some of the other kids, they just plain steal their clothes. Ari—a big, bearded, and manly-looking guy—and I like each other. He grins at me as though he had just declared "check" to a chess crony. A few awkward beats on my part, but Ari's lack of preparedness saves the moment for me and permits me my next move.

Before he can stop me, I grab a prized possession lying on top of his book bag and hold it in the air. "Surely the monthly cost of this camera cell phone far exceeds the pittance for a scientific calculator," I suavely rejoin. Laughter from around the room makes Ari smile even more broadly—now enjoying losing the match and allowing me to savor my tiny checkmate. Today, I walk out the door with the trophy. Tomorrow will be a different story for sure.

CBHS's inclusion on the NYC watch list has made the administration more uptight than ever. Our fair-haired principal walks the halls like a sullen specter—surely her new job as principal is on the line. It seems our school had been cited by the muckamucks for every infraction except counterfeiting. Regional DOE watchdogs, spies really, monitor to see if we're toeing the party line on the administrative mantra: point-of-entry model instruction (no teaching, please), emphasis on cooperative learning (blind leading the blind), keep the halls clear (don't let the inmates wander outside their cells), and bell-to-bell classes (keep the little whelps busy or suffer the consequences). Of these four catechisms, the last proves to be a must and one I wholly endorse. The first time I heard this admonition, I thought it served to keep a whip on the faculty—sort of, "Don't let these overpaid boobs slack off during class time," or "Make sure the taxpayers get their money's worth," and all that business. In point of fact, safe and secure classroom management dictates never letting the little fiends under our tender care take a breath. "Idle fingers make the devil's work" couldn't be truer in the ivy-less academic walls of the Bronx.

Rob slouches into the T-L pretty upset—but not for himself. In the last three minutes of his class today, who walks in but a regional investigator catching Rob coming up for air. Rob is one teacher who I know works his ass off trying to do a good job.

"I feel bad for Tqiqi, Ric. He's under a lot of pressure from the office, and you know how carefully the math classes are watched. I knew I should have kept going but I ran out of steam, and the kids had had enough, too." Now this retired financial whiz is worried about what our principal will think. My conservative guesstimate is that he gives up $5,000 a day (yes, a day) to work for our dyed-blonde leader whose previous job skills lead with filling out attendance forms for the prior principal. Rob comes from a financially modest military family in Colorado. Adhering to the rules (mostly) and backing the commanding officer comes naturally to him.

TUESDAY, APRIL 20

Another Rumor

travels through the school. The kids from Columbine High School are visiting here on the fifth anniversary of their fame.

I have a pre-observation review with Mr. T. For sure Linda will be there tomorrow.

WEDNESDAY, APRIL 21

Does She Exist?

Our beloved top banana again doesn't show up for my observation. I give it the old college try in every class, but I admit to myself that I also try a little harder in preparation to make sure Mr. T. looks good. I actually do a decent job this time. I even have volunteers go to the board! Once in awhile, they act like mensches when visitors are in the room. I make an instructional boo-boo in calling a negative number a "minus" something. One term refers to an operation and the other to the signage of a number. No big deal. The mistake I made wouldn't make any difference in the real world, even to engineers.

Another problem of mine: When I ask kids to describe how they derived their answers, I often jump in to finish the explanation. A basic teaching error. But time is short and I'm impatient to get through the material. There's so much to cover and so little time. Once again, Linda thanks me in writing with Mr. T. She enjoyed the classroom visit she didn't attend.

THURSDAY, APRIL 22

Is He Moe?

Ms. Tottle tells me that Mr. Santino, the principal's chief stooge, insulted her in front of her students. She hadn't noticed (or maybe didn't care) that one of her students was listening to a CD. He peeks in the window, barges in, and dresses her down for it so that the class could take it all in. How do these people get appointed as administrators? I wonder.

FRIDAY, APRIL 23

Red Letter Day

I'm greeted by red chalk graffiti on the walls and tables in my 2nd period class. In the 4th period, the security guard in the hall refuses my request to stop Ahmed after he strolls out of class. I hand carry a Deans' Referral Form to the Security office, despite my unwelcome status there.

> Ahmed in my 4th period class refused to put away other materials, sit where asked, etc. I asked a security guard to help me today to take him to the Deans' office, but he ran out of the room. This is an ongoing problem.

MONDAY, APRIL 26

Never Volunteer

Again I open my big mouth. "Do I have an assignment for the Regents tests?" I volunteer, barging into the inner sanctum of the Math AP's office. Mr. T., without looking up and not paying attention, at first says no. Realizing my gaffe, I about-face and hurry out the door, but Mr. T. nabs me.

"Wait up. The answer is yes. Go to room 151 for an assignment," he calls to me before I can make my escape.

Cursing my stupidity, I trudge down to where proctor assignments are handed out. The students signed up for the exam consist of a conglomeration of 10th to 12th graders. Some are sophomores taking the test for the first time, ranging up to seniors who must pass it this third or fourth attempt or not graduate. The originally assigned room for my test has been changed. In concert with the overall disorganization of CBHS, that fact had also pretty much been kept a secret from the kids taking the exam. Many wandered in long after the test should have begun. In anticipation of that, I keep everyone waiting for as long as possible for any stragglers.

I feel like I have the hang of proctoring now. With more authority in my voice than the situation calls for, I demand absolute silence. I'm the venerable old Harvard law professor, John Houseman in *The Paper Chase*, terrifying my charges. The kids display their photo IDs, signify their presence on a seating chart with an initial, and receive graphing calculators if they so desire. I congratulate myself on accomplishing this so professionally. In particular, I won't stand for having any of the calculators stolen, which I make certain by making all such recipients fork over their IDs in barter.

The test is in two parts with a break for lunch. Most of the lab rats dutifully trade their IDs in return for calculators. At the halfway point, I safely stash each ID in alphabetical order in the calculator case before the kids leave the exam room. One of the guinea pigs, who at first resisted giving me his ID but eventually relented, stays in the room to eat his brown-bagged lunch. Now I note with terror that although his calculator is still on his desk, no more IDs are left. (Expletive deleted) me! What the deuce am I going to tell this kid? I was sooooooo careful. Every ID in exchange for a calculator and one-by-one, Goddamn it. No hurrying me until I'm ready for the swap. I break into a sweat. Security has clamped down. Now students need IDs to get into the building and even into the lunchroom. This boy will be infuriated when I don't give his back. I decide to take the high road. I go up to his desk and cunningly ask him for his ID. "Maybe he didn't give me one in the first place," I hope.

"Hey, I gave it to you already, mistah," he responds with no little annoyance.

"I don't think so, my boy," I reply in a staccato, pseudo-British accent. "I carefully arranged them all in order and none are left, so that means you didn't give me one," I reason calmly.

"Bull. What am I supposed to do now without an ID? They're impossible to replace. Man, I won't even get into school." He correctly mirrors my own thoughts on the subject, including the "Bull." My condolences notwithstanding, I glide back to the desk at the head of the classroom with his glare blazing hot on my back.

After an interminable forty-five-minute break, the little scholars pile back into the room and, if so desiring, get calculators again by remitting their IDs anew. "By any chance, did anyone get two IDs?" I call out hopefully. Of course, no affirmative reply. The test resumes and as the experiment in futility drags on, I'm determined to get to the bottom of this mystery. I examine the IDs again in alphabetical order. No such luck.

Well, I reason to myself in my best Sherlock Holmes manner, if the boy had given me his ID it would be just under the girl's ID alphabetically before his. But her ID isn't there, either. She hasn't yet asked for another calculator. I ask for the miss' ID and as I clutch her chewing-gum-covered credential, another ID pops out from underneath the sticky underbody, revealing the missing booty. Mystery solved.

TUESDAY, APRIL 27

Jumping Ship

Finally. I get my name in klieg lights. Layoffs are coming and in the math department HQ, the principal has posted the seniority list starting with the most senior at the top. My name shines brightly in last place. I'm greeted with chuckles by Victor and the other old war horses in the T-L. Despite the no-show of sympathy from my peers, I'm unperturbed. I've got a dozen resumés floating out there already. This term's been no picnic, but it's still paradise compared to last semester. I won't teach freshmen again. Lindsey Holden's name hangs next to mine as the penultimate on the executioner's list. The young neophyte at this sweat-shop takes it badly. Crying, she runs up and hugs me. She wants us to share our shame and misfortune. The soap opera continues as I try to console her. It takes a Herculean effort on my part not to laugh.

But I'm far from alone in my thoughts of making a getaway. The talk is rife with others seeking their own escape. CBHS is being downsized. The process is likely to continue over several years until the school is completely disbanded. Get out while the getting's good gains the consensus. There's more. While cleaning up another dozen new icons on the computer, up pops Paul Lanier's letter applying to another school.

WEDNESDAY, APRIL 28

He's Taking It Well

it seems to me. Failing, that is. In 6th period, Stan Gabriel's comment, "Good job," passes for his standard joke anytime I make an error on the blackboard. I hand back his test marked "F" and repeat his witticism. Not so funny this time.

Don't Be Fooled

People often mistake ignorance for stupidity. It's not nearly the same thing. We're all ignorant about something. Ignorance can be overcome by learning. Stupidity is forever. Ignorance abounds here in the Bronx with the children. Stupid they're not.

Blaze steals her Delaney card when my back is turned. I know she's the culprit. Yesterday, she telegraphed the theft when she asked me how anyone could prove her frequent class absences. Stupid I am.

THURSDAY, APRIL 29

More Psychological Warfare

To Ahmed: "You want to fail? Fail! Maybe I was all wrong about you. You don't have what it takes to be an A student." This is not an off-the-cuff remark of mine, but planned with some trepidation. After throwing a pencil at Ronald last semester and learning verbal abuse can be regarded as corporal punishment, I have some reservations about this kind of barrage. But I've run out of ammo. This is a bright boy who should not flunk and I can't seem to get through to him, even in heart-to-heart talks. He keeps agreeing to come around but doesn't.

I have to eject some unfortunate teacher who was about to conduct a sample Regents exam in my classroom. Abrahamson, the malevolent scheduling troll, strikes again.

FRIDAY, APRIL 30

Outreach Revisited

I'm taking a different tack this semester on home calls. The complaints change the students' behavior for maybe a day or two, and then the kids resume their negative habits. My new mission: persuade my kids to come here for free Saturday tutoring classes. If they won't do homework, maybe at least they'll get some extra help. In the past week, I've reached fourteen homes to press the parents to encourage their child's weekend attendance. I also make daily broadcasts in class that I'll give points on their grade for each time they go. I point out that I'm carefully watching the attendance there. To follow up on that claim, I've been harassing Mrs. Rueno, who runs the Saturday program, for copies of the attendance. A few of the kids begin attending.

Victor tells me that although he makes his required calls, he fakes the outreach log he hands in. Doesn't like to be told to do anything. Form over substance reigns once more.

Today, the DOE surprises the math department with an unwelcome new monthly standardized exam for our students. Forget the fact that final exams are around the corner and maybe we have our own schedules for instruction. The Board of Education has gone hog wild over testing. Now, I'm not one of those anti-test vigilantes. Testing has its place and taxpayers have a right to know if their little sweeties are learning anything besides crude jokes, sports scores, and who's putting out. But enough already.

A Crying Shame

I thought I had a long shot at a new survivor in my SPED class. Jaylon, a mature-looking black boy, started paying attention a few weeks ago. Hard-core truancy has been his long-term undoing. He has a strong natural intelligence about him. And I give him moral support and pep talks up the ying yang. He was responding well. But recidivism has him by the throat. With deep regret, I have to boot him out today for incorrigible behavior. He admits he's changed his mind about passing. I'll wait until I'm alone later tonight to digest my grief.

SUNDAY, MAY 2

Thus Spake The Honcho

Whoopee! I meet the UFT's evil Darth Vader face-to-face: none other than Mayor Michael Bloomberg's School Chancellor appointee, bigwig Joel Klein. He's also the former legal beagle at the U.S. Department of Justice who took on the Microsoft goliath before his current anointment.

It's a sunny, balmy day for a local community college fund-raising salon in a mansion backyard of one of its charitable benefactors. Before Klein's short but punchy speech, I briefly talk to him. Unfortunately, I'm fingered by one of the patrons as a change-of-career math teacher in the Bronx. Too bad. I had wanted to ask him questions that wouldn't be answered too cagily. Klein wastes no time proclaiming, loudly enough for the entire gathering to hear, that I'm another likely casualty of the UFT's interference with his and Mayor Bloomberg's vision for the NYC school system. I hoped to do a little undercover work and all I get is a canned speech. Anyhow, I get to see and hear in person the supposed UFT nemesis.

Here's his pitch to the well-heeled crowd:

1. We are failing one-half of the kids in NYC.
2. Three out of ten receive local diplomas. (He doesn't elaborate, but that means that those 30 percent don't get a sheepskin worth having.)
3. Only one out of ten gets a Regents diploma.
4. NYC has 1,000 schools.
5. Our school system is broken and it's been that way for decades.
6. PONS—plain old neighborhood schools—just don't cut the mustard anymore.
7. Take heart. Under his administration, whole schools are being turned around.
8. Now comes the pitch for the support of the assembled guests. "Do we have the will?" (That is to say, the resolve to fight the unions.)
9. He goes on to castigate what he calls the three pillars of the union: tenure, lock-step pay, and seniority.

I'm shocked to hear such a sophisticated man describe the problems of educating our children in such simplistic terms. His theory hangs on the issue of supply and demand. And of labor versus management. Basically, he sees the whole dilemma as being caused by the teachers and the union. This is screwy.

Only people who believe what they read in the newspaper would buy this line of reasoning. But that's exactly what this affluent group consists of! Come to think of it, if I weren't teaching in the Bronx, I'd buy it, too. One point I do agree with: New teachers get dumped into tough schools without sufficient administrative support. Hear, hear!

One patrician-looking man asks why black kids can't be taught "it isn't white to be good in school"? Like any experienced politician, Klein deftly deflects the loaded question.

After the talk, the president of the community college sponsoring this soirée privately describes a bad omen. Behavior problems have now migrated from the high schools to the community colleges. He had an unprecedented fifty-eight discipline problems last year, including a chair being thrown in a classroom. Mostly pupils from the Bronx.

Later, I converse with another attendee, a member of the New York State Board of Regents. I take this opportunity to complain about the excessive testing required to obtain a Regents diploma. His answer: The Board's overriding theme for urban children is escaping "the tyranny of under-expectations." If children are not expected to do well, they won't. OK. I can buy that, to some extent. But how about the "tyranny of college educated administrators"? Rules insisting graduates cram down useless information. Worse, these courses take the place of teaching practical skills needed by these youngsters to be useful members of society. We agree to disagree.

MONDAY, MAY 3

Is it White to Learn?

One of the rumors among whites that I can't personally confirm is that black kids equate academic achievement with acting white. I have never heard nor seen evidence of this in my classroom. Because I again heard this urban fable at the Joel Klein fête, I decide to ask for anecdotal evidence from other teachers. They share my experience. The 20 percent of my students who are doing well in my classes are mostly children of color. None of them think they were acting white, as far as I can tell. In fact, I post all good exam papers on the wall. Because I'm sensitive to the possibility of peer pressure, I first always ask a student's permission. I haven't had any students, be they black, white, yellow, or magenta who weren't proud to be recognized on the wall. All this, as I said, is anecdotal, but I think worth mentioning.

Here's the real scoop: When kids don't succeed—any excuse will do. All kids want to do well, but absent that, a heaping helping of sour grapes works wonders. Maybe some failing kids do say, "It's white to be good in school." When one considers the lifetime of academic setbacks and disappointment a great many of them have experienced, it's no wonder that "The Legend of Only Whites Want an Education" raises its ugly head.

On the other hand, I would be surprised to find any white teacher in an inner-city school who doesn't find students who think they are discriminated against. "'Cause I'm black" should be put to music because it's a popular tune from all the inattentive, unfocused, and lazy kids. I know the multitude of problems leading children to behave badly, but there it is. We teachers never hear that song from the 20 percent or so making the grade. Only individualized instruction will help us overcome the fundamental problems of the non-achievers' home environment—or we'll never solve the academic fallout for the majority.

In the T-L, Janet Mentari and I discuss racial discrimination as an excuse from our students. Across from us, Ekoe, an experienced, ebony-skinned math teacher from Nigeria, listens in.

"They even say "cause I'm black' to me," she volunteers. "I tell them, 'Who do you think I am, Snow White?'"

In a department meeting, Mr. T. openly announces, "The mice are jumping ship." Teachers have notified him they're leaving for other schools. He might even have to hire more staff as a result. He's back-sliding a bit on an earlier warning to us to protect our own careers. Maybe he doesn't need to get rid of me.

TUESDAY, MAY 4

Much Ado About Nothing

Last week in my UFT psychotherapy session, I sought a little sympathy. I cried over the twenty-seven classes per week I worked last semester, but didn't get compensated with fewer classes this term. Katherine, a union firebrand, became incensed. As a school UFT representative, she's going to lodge a complaint on my behalf. I hadn't really given it much thought. Until today. For the first time this year, Mr. T. is pointedly upset with me. The grievance worked its way through the bureaucracy and landed on his desk. An accusation of an unfair assignment points directly at him. He's the last person in the school I want to offend and he's quietly smoldering. For this levelheaded man, it amounts to a volcanic explosion.

"I just happened to mention it in a professional development meeting when we were all talking about our difficult year," doesn't seem to lower the pressure level. "Please accept my apologies," and "I'll be glad to drop any claims," also doesn't mollify him. It's too late. The eggs are broken. He insists I move forward with the dispute. This is just great. I depart telling him that I will emphasize, of course, what a fine manager I think he is.

I obey Mr. T.'s directions and huddle with Daniel Marsh, the head UFT representative at CBHS. The upshot is that the two of us will meet directly with Linda to discuss the grievance. At this point, since there's no turning back, I'm amused at the prospect of seeing how she will squirm out of doing the right thing. I have complete confidence that no benefit will accrue to me, but I want to witness in person the manner in which I'll get screwed. I am impressed that the union is taking up the fight on my behalf.

I kick out Blaze, our resident clotheshorse, for sleeping in class. Nonetheless, she claims she desperately wants to pass. If talk weren't cheap my kids would be millionaires.

WEDNESDAY, MAY 5

Say Please

I'm still working on my anger management. Instead of "Stop talking or get out," I've learned to say, "Please, stop talking." Now, when I find myself repeating the umpteenth request for quiet, I intentionally say menacingly, with gritted teeth, "I'm asking nicely." The kids laugh at this little performance. I've confessed I'm having trouble dealing with their skulduggery. I'm trying to be more civil to them. Can they do the same? Occasionally, they even volunteer with a smile, "Don't forget to say 'Please,' mistah."

It's a test day. Kamron lumbers in late. He's been late or absent all semester. Another crying shame. He has talent but no discipline whatsoever. Whenever Kamron sporadically appears, he listens to my mini-lesson for a few minutes and then answers all the problems. He is one of the few at CBHS that has talent with a capital T. When I've discussed him with his mother, she's naturally upset that her smart son is letting himself down so badly. Today, he gets a zero on the quiz. In private, many times he swore to me he'd do the homework, come to class, take the tests. Of all the issues, problems, and anxieties I've had here at

CBHS, nothing bothers me more than when a clearly intelligent child stumbles and falls. Tears come to my eyes at the thought of it. Kamron never came through on my watch. I failed in my attempt to break him loose from his self-imposed chains.

THURSDAY, MAY 6

How Would She Know?

Shana loudly announces once more, "This is boring. You can't teach." I know I could do a better job making math more interesting. I certainly have lots to learn. But maybe she should stop reading magazines and pay attention. Just possibly, as bad a teacher as she thinks I am, she'd learn something anyhow.

I flag a hall monitor to bounce out Cory. He's my top student in the SPED class. College material. Good natured, too, but a jester. But, I've had enough of his shenanigans for the nonce. I can't let favorites interrupt the others. Girano, the Security whip, barges in looking for blood. Wants me to write Cory up. Gee, Officer Krupke, I'm just not going to. I'm determined that Cory will survive. He's only had a bad day.

FRIDAY, MAY 7

A Day of Relaxation

awaits me. All my sections have tests today. I just sit back and watch them slog away at it. It's good for them. And for me. I joke in the T-L that I wish every day could be a test day.

Evidently, in anticipation of my desire to join this once honorable profession, New York State significantly increased its requirements to gain a permanent license. Today, I found out I may be grandfathered under the old rules since I entered Mercy College's internship program last June. Under the new rules, I have to teach more years before I can be permanently licensed. I call the state and the union information offices to get the lowdown, but nobody knows for sure. The regs are too new.

MONDAY, MAY 10

Anonymous Letter

to Mr. Lankin, the exasperating vaudeville comic in the T-L :

> May 10, 2004
> Dear Mr. Lankin:
>
> I'm writing this letter to show my appreciation of well you thought [sic] Mathematics. You show me that working to my very potential is everything. Although I've failed you're [sic] class one time before & show me the light that I was the one not doing my work. Now having your class again show that you're a very cool teacher. I've learn more work with in a week than a marking period with some other math teachers I've had before. Before I never listen to any teacher when they are teaching but when you teach you give me a reason to learn. And not to give up you tell me math is not that hard is you make it look hard but it's not.

I spot Austin Looty in the hall. A pleasant, but dull boy I haven't seen in some time in class. "Give up on me?" I ask in a friendly manner. Austin, sweating profusely, looks dreadful. He's obviously disconcerted and confused.

"I've given up on everything," he responds breathlessly.

Austin knows he has ADD but he has no medical coverage. Neither his family nor the school has helped him find any treatment.

"I can't focus on anything, not even my video."

I remember how pitifully he cried when visiting me with his mom on parents' night. He's a sweet kid, really. I'm forbidden to get actively involved in seeking medical treatment for a student. I advise him to go immediately to his counselor for help.

I feel sick to my stomach. "You must have help, Austin. Go with your mom to the school and insist that your counselor assist in getting whatever you need."

After talking with Austin, I'm late for my next class, but not as late as seven stragglers after me.

Another boy writes "Help me" on his makeup test. When we confer, I get the same response as before. He can't come to me for tutoring before or after school. Can't go to Saturday classes, either.

I give my "don't quit" speech in all my classes. If they do moderately well on the rest of the quizzes and on the final exam, I'll pass them.

My resumés cast out into cyberspace land a prospective fish. I have an interview in the late afternoon at an all-girls' parochial school in Manhattan. The clean, sweet-smelling halls and tranquil atmosphere overcome me. This gentility stands in stark contrast to the turmoil I just left in the Bronx. Larry, the avuncular math department head here, conducts the meeting. Larry was also late to the teaching game and now he's retiring—can't take the commute over the George Washington Bridge anymore. In his prior incarnation, he was a successful accountant. We speak the same lingo and the interview goes well, in my opinion. Most of the girls come from low-income families, so teaching here would be a dream come true—help needy kids in a decent work environment. And I would have my very own classroom! No more nomadic traipsing.

TUESDAY, MAY 11

Still No Help

for Looty. We bump into each other again in the hall. He says thanks for the advice, but he hasn't seen a counselor yet.

Jocelyn Cortero, who's been coming to me at lunch for tutoring, gets an "A" on her test. Huzzah!

What's more, the SPEDs bring calculators to class! Even the slow learners. In the Bronx vernacular, "Now thass what I'm talkin' 'bout."

Overall, it's been one of those rare decent days. The evil eye will punish me for today's good fortune.

WEDNESDAY, MAY 12

A Tidal Wave of Feelings

All the blackboard erasers have gone AWOL in my classes. Where could they have gone? Maybe they're in the legendary elephant graveyard along with all the pencils I've given out. In case of emergency, I usually carry my own but I lost it yesterday. Nuts. I pilfer paper towels from the men's room as substitutes.

Mr. T. prepared Regents exam guides for the 4th-semester students, but he's run out. I raise my voice to him in protest and immediately feel repentant. My own gentlemanliness and savoir-faire have sadly gone AWOL, too, this year.

In the UFT professional development mental health session, Jean promises to introduce me to her new school supervisor, the School of Visual Arts principal upstairs, for a possible math position next fall.

Kamron and Ahmed walk out after I chastise them for fooling around. But by now, I'm not upset. My mission is clear—I'm focused on the frontrunners. Those who insist on giving up will just have to grow up before moving forward with their education—or possibly face a most difficult adult life. I've changed more than the kids. I will save the children who can be rescued and resign myself that some will drown in their own past, present, and future. This realization sears my head and heart.

Kris tells me she went to West Point on a school-sponsored cruise, despite her fear of drowning. Her dread gives rise to my own dark vision. I'm partly afraid of negative consequences, but decide to tell my class just how I see them.

"Imagine that you're standing on top of a tall hill next to the ocean. Down below you see little children playing in the sand on the shore. Suddenly, you see a giant wave coming at them. They're in great danger and it's too late for you to climb down the cliff to save them. Instead, you scream at them, 'Run. Run for your lives.' But they just laugh at you and keep playing, no matter what you shout. You watch them all drown and you sob. Sick to your stomach. That's exactly how I feel teaching here at CBHS. I mean it."

My reflections blow my students over. This time, they've all heard me loud and clear. I strike a nerve, but I have no real hope that any change will come from it.

THURSDAY, MAY 13

Hot Daze

The spring weather wreaks havoc for every teacher's classes. The warm, sunny rooms make the kids sleepy. Not much gets done.

FRIDAY, MAY 14

What the Dickens

Not to put too fine a point upon it, but I'm living my own version of *Bleak House*. The case of Klass versus CBHS winds through the procedural *mishigas.* Now Mr. T. tells me he's been insulted directly by Katherine for neglecting in my case to observe the rules concerning extra teaching hours. I profusely apologize without mollifying him much.

MONDAY, MAY 17

Hi, Nigger

a student in the crowded auditorium calls out to me. I'm instantly angry until I realize it's one of my favorites from last term beaming at me. I smile back and give him a what's-for-me rare high five. We're all here because Regent exams are using the regular classrooms. I try to conduct class anyway.

In the rows of seats, I hand out expensive graphing calculators for the students to use during this period. I'm suffering from the delusion that I can teach in this noisy amphitheater. I ask Blaze if I gave her one. "You bet your sweet ass," she replies. I still don't appreciate these youngsters addressing me this way. I try to kick her out with no success. The security monitors in the now overflowing hall are too busy with more severe crises. My pledge to live a long and healthy life free of anger regardless of the infantile ogres in this school goes down the drain once more.

Now I'm bursting-veins-in-the-forehead outraged that someone stole one of the calculators. And after I spent five minutes writing down the names of all recipients. How in blazes did I let that happen? I think I know who took it, but I can't prove it. I mutter to myself for the rest of the day about it.

Katherine tells me I'll receive days, not dollars, as compensation for my work overage. Maybe some time off at the end of the term after finals. Sounds good to me, but I doubt it'll ever happen.

TUESDAY, MAY 18

While It's Hot

Some more kids start to tune in. Down deep somewhere they want to succeed. Can they keep the faith? Last term I would've said yes. This term I've migrated to Missouri. Show me.

I call Ken Gaskins, the principal of the public school I interviewed at last summer where the kids wear uniforms. He might have a job opening for the fall. Meanwhile, Mr. T. asks me if it's OK to give my name to a principal of one of the new schools looking to fill a math slot. Very decent of him to be on the lookout for me.

In the T-L, I'm copying and copying until I'm bleary-eyed.

WEDNESDAY, MAY 19

"I Know How You Feel"

I comfort my compatriot, Darwin. As bad as I think I've had it, if Darwin's telling the truth, he's had it up to his ears. He's bitter about his tour of duty this year. He couldn't face freshmen again next year if he didn't already have them again this term.[3] I don't reveal I have no freshmen now. No point in rubbing it in. I also don't say that I will quit teaching rather than face high school novitiates again.

Daniel Marsh tells me he's arranged an appointment for us to meet with Linda on May 28th. Security conducts another cattle roundup of kids in the hallways.

Late this afternoon, I meet again with Doyle at a diner. He wants to be an entrepreneur after graduating Fordham this summer. He already has a dandy little car parts business operating on the net. He knows my career had been running my own companies, but I'm reluctant to recommend this life for him. I hope I haven't been a bad influence on him. I

---

[3] In fact, Darwin shows up the next school year the first day and resigns on the spot to Mr. T.

point out it's risky and not for everyone. He has babies now. But who am I to say he can't make it?

THURSDAY, MAY 20

More Violence

Glenn informs me that one of his students was shot several times in the leg outside of school.

Lost in Space

I find it hard to describe the helplessness I feel. For some of these kids, no matter what they do from this point on, it's going to be a rough ride. But doable, perhaps. For others, hopelessly behind starting from infancy, they will almost certainly never catch up with mainstream society. Both probable conclusions go down as very bitter pills for me, Mr. Do-Gooder. But my real nightmares come from the kids who could make the grade if they tried even a little. Don't even do the homework or take notes—just come to class and pay attention while you're here! Goddamit, you Kamrons, why must you insist on failure? The whole world is rooting for you. Don't you know that?

I sometimes wonder about the wisdom of my colleagues. Lila has the floor in the T-L where we're all in the mood for comical anecdotes. She told her students that she was the cheating champ in her communist-run high school; so don't try it on her. She had notes on her arms and under her skirt. An amusing story, but she raised the bar for cheating—just the kind of challenge our tots are looking for.

Lila's got comedic momentum, "So this student of mine wakes up. 'Is there a chance I can pass?' he drowsily inquires.

'Continue sleeping,'" she quips to him.

I'm also on a roll today—with the SPEDs, on this singular occasion. They're lining up, wanting to go to the blackboard to do problems. Even

Tristan smiles! I have never seen him smile. Ordinarily silent and non-committal, although not necessarily sullen, he steadfastly refuses to participate with the others. I'm no big fan of cooperative learning, but a little camaraderie wouldn't hurt this kid, I figure. Secretly thrilled at the sight of his grin, I decide to take advantage and whisper in his ear to go to the blackboard, too. "I'll help you. You don't have to be afraid of being embarrassed. We'll do it together."

His sunbeam disappears, "I have emotional problems."

"The only way to fight a problem is to face it. Let me know when you're ready." I surprise myself giving such solid advice so effortlessly. I wonder if I truly believe what I'm saying or am I just full of it?

I give a test to the other classes at the beginning of the period. The kids cry foul after the test. They all know they failed. "It's your fault. You're a bad teacher. You're not teaching us," they loudly protest in a kind of multiracial Greek chorus. A "hang the teacher" mood floats ominously in the air.

For a moment, I feel cornered and almost cave in with some apologetic excuse, but I think better of it and wait for the cacophony to die down before launching my own counterattack. A temporary silence cues me for my soliloquy: "So it's my fault, is it?" Charles Laughton in *Mutiny on the Bounty* comes to mind as inspiration. I will not abide a coup d'état, and I wax louder, "Not teaching, eh? Who in this class is taking notes?" I demand. I look directly in their eyes as I stride around the desks to the back of the room. "Who is going to Saturday classes?" I trumpet as they guiltily shrink back in their seats. Having gained the upper hand, I now lower my voice in a hurt theatric appeal. "And who is asking for my help after school?" firmly shoving the blame onto their immature shoulders. The rebellion has been crushed—for now.

When I describe my recital in the T-L, the veteran teachers cluck their tongues in disapproval. Through inexperience, I foolishly gave the test at the beginning of the period instead of at the end, giving them time to conspire for their treachery during class. Teach then test, not test then teach. Too soon old, too late smart—I won't repeat this nearly fatal mistake.

Elton cheats three times on a quiz. Detecting cheaters isn't all that difficult. When they copy from another exam, they copy everything, including stray marks and exact placement on the answer sheets. Cute.

FRIDAY, MAY 21

Enough Already

This time, I'm going to find Ahmed's home phone number. I treasure my limited free time between classes but I must conclude the chapter on this imp. I try the latest student roster without much hope. It's a non-working number. I try information please and get nowhere. Unfazed, I now speed to two different guidance counselors' offices on different floors. "All Guidance Counselors out until 1:00 P.M." is posted on both.

"I'm sure he's been in trouble with the law," I muse and trot over to Security on the first floor. I'm hopeful. "Say what you like, these security guys are tough and won't take a phony number from Ahmed," I try to convince myself. I'm greeted with a friendly hello from a gal there whom I guess I haven't niggled enough to have her ignore me yet.

"Oh, yes. We certainly know Ahmed quite well here," she merrily chirps.

Raising my hopes, she divulges three different contact numbers for Ahmed. Leaving her office, I land solidly back on earth when she remarks, "And by the way. Let me know if any of them actually work."

They don't. I figure my last bet may be my best and canter to room 101. Even wise guy students dodging telephone calls get sick and the nurses invariably call home. Their weak math haunts them again. They don't put two and two together to calculate that they've left spoor behind them. An open secret among teachers: As a last resort, hunt for phone numbers at the nurse's office. She keeps her own file for our kennel. The nurse is surprised to find that her telephone records are blank in Ahmed's file. At this point, I'm not particularly amazed. When it comes to leaving no trail, he's a pro. Ahmed's outfoxed me. Time's up—I lost the scent. Got to canter to my next class.

Score: Ahmed (3)—Mr. Klass (0).

Business as Usual

One student doesn't know the word "horizontal." Several arrive ultra late to class. One of the SPEDs sleeps and another doesn't know what "one-half" means.

SATURDAY, MAY 22

I grade tests all day. I'm depressed. All failed. My two-dollar-against-your-one bet is that other teachers share my dejection today, too.

MONDAY, MAY 24

Oblomov

Glory be! Blaze wakes up and works up a storm in class! Josue wakes up, too. "This is easy," he says. They're like *Oblomov*, it seems.

"Who wrote *Oblomov*, anyway?" I strain to remember the author, without success.

My trance is broken when Glenn reminds me, as he usually does, that we have a faculty meeting led by Linda and Girano.

Mostly, I'm more interested in finding out who wrote that Russian novel. I ask the English teachers as they file in. I'm sure the elegant Princeton grad, formerly a Wall Street prodigy herself, would know. With some mortification, she admits she's never heard of *Oblomov*. She concentrated on English lit. So much for Princeton, I sniff. Marisa floats in. Our in-the-flesh Ruskie will save me from going batty over this, but I've caught her off-guard. She obviously knows the book, but the author escapes her. "Is it Goncharov?" I offer timidly, not wanting to expose my ignorance to a real former Soviet citizen.

"That's it," she cries excitedly in her dulcet Moscow accent. She's delighted to chat about something interesting and dear to her Russian sensibilities for a change. Now we talk about the novel. She imparts "Oblomovshina" is a Russian expression for their society's inability to wake up to reality. This malady describes our kids as well—asleep for their whole life. Marisa must feel at home at CBHS.

I'm thrilled. This conversation is the first real fun I've had at school all year. Marisa has now warmed to the subject of her native tongue and informs me that Shakespeare is really better in her native tongue than in English.

"How could that be, when English has the largest vocabulary of the languages in the world?" I protest.

"Oh, no," she corrects me, "Russian does." And with that, she recites by heart several passages of Shakespeare's sonnets in English and then compares them with the Russian. She swells with pleasure explaining how euphonious they sound and feel in her native tongue. "Shakespeare's much better in Russian," she offers. I'm knocked out by her literary prowess. I'm too embarrassed to gush how impressed I am with her scholarly excellence in both languages.

The Sweeps

Now in full fettle, the faculty meeting rudely interrupts, forcing us to divert attention to our own Commissar and her unfettered Doberman pinscher. Linda and Girano defend "sweeps"—snaring the students in a sudden school-wide police net.

After the Politburo rests its case, Lila and I deliberate the sweeps issue in the T-L. She hands me, apropos, a memorandum dated today from none other than our high priestess, Linda, and her consort, Assistant Principal of Administration Feori Santino:

> To: Korkna (*N.B.* Is it that I am so old fashioned that I think a memo to a female teacher ought to be addressed to *Ms.* or *Mrs.* Korkna?)
>
> Re: Situations during sweeps
>
> (A pre-printed list of *teacher* infractions!!! follows until it decamps on dear Ms. Korkna's crime.)
>
> **#4. X You did not follow the odd/even rule. Bathrooms: Odd day, open odd periods. Even day, open even periods. Periods 3 and 10 are always closed.**
>
> cc: Mr. Tqiqi

Odd/even bathroom schedule rule? My ass! This memo is the kind of apcray that feeds UFT unrest. Nobody should stop a kid that's "got to go" from a trip to the bathroom. I've threatened to stop kids wandering in and out but when they start to wiggle nervously or stand on one foot, they leave the classroom with a *vale*. Lila tells me the student was "swept," despite Lila's written pass.

Eight other crimes and misdemeanors are listed, but not checked, on the potpourri form, including: letting kids wear headgear, not teaching bell-to-bell, giving out more than one pass at a time . . . and so on. What b.s.! Every day these kids swagger into school through metal detectors and past the guards wearing anything at all and carrying enough electronic gadgetry to shame Circuit City. They strut their stuff in the halls past the police and Deans, and we—the teachers—are supposed to be the enforcers!

The memo concludes: "If you have any questions, or concerns, or if you think that an error occurred, please see me in room 137 or call me at extension 1312." My own letter of complaint to Linda about the fist-fight in my room practically got me hung by the neck until dead.

While I didn't have to explain failing every warm-blooded creature in sight last semester, I'm given a form to explain why I *did* pass some of the kids. Kafka's *The Castle* has nothing on the phantasmagoric land-scape right here in NYC's most delirious impact school. My disruption to the great educational celestial plan occurred by permitting a few lucky ne'er-do-wells a 65 score despite excessive absences. Call me pisher, but they passed my tests.

Forgive Me, Oh Divine Beings Who Levitate This Palace In Eternal Rapture.

TUESDAY, MAY 25

A Veteran of Domestic Wars

fits Ms. Tottle. I dismissed her as a relic when I first met her in the T-L last fall. Evidently, she had lost the faith and needed to move on, I thought. Her complaints somehow seem more justified to me now. All along the hallway hang maybe two dozen examples of her students' work. Some of it impressive. Her daughter, an editor for a women's fashion maga-zine, recently organized a style show for the CBHS students, including boys, interested in design. Ms. Tottle claims she's only here for the money. I don't believe it for a second.

WEDNESDAY, MAY 26

Down but Not Out

I've been angry and depressed over the malaise I face every day. I'm barking at the young pups again. With spring's arrival, I've regressed along with them. I decide that two days of calculator fun and a morato-rium on "talk and chalk" should cheer them up. I give them a chance to learn more about using the T-83 graphing calculators. Even Jaylon perks up and seems to enjoy playing with the electronic toy. I like to fool with it, too. I tell the classes I worked inside the NASA mockup of the command module for the lunar landing. The onboard computer didn't have one-tenth the muscle of a $9 calculator, let alone the $100 unit they're using now. For a change, my war stories don't seem to bore them. Knowing that they hold computing power that can land a man on the moon seems pretty cool.

THURSDAY, MAY 27

A Celebration

I can't get my copying done. All engines are down.

Tonight, Sandy and I take Doyle and his wife out to dinner to celebrate Doyle's graduation. I'm stunned to learn that Doyle's father refused to come to his graduation. Doyle was the first person in his family to go to college. His father thought that Doyle shouldn't get so uppity and that he should be a laborer like him. Doyle made it clear that Sandy and my involvement helped him change his life. Gratifying to hear, but am I sufficiently reenergized to help my kids?

FRIDAY, MAY 28

SPED Powwow

I find a written proclamation in my mailbox. By law, Sabrina, one of the slower children in my SPED class, is entitled to an annual departmental conference to review her progress. It's to take place today in the SPED office during my usual SPED session. The notice also tells me a substitute teacher will be supplied for me. Okey dokey. This might be interesting. On the way to the meeting, I see Sabrina in the hall on the way to my class. She hasn't heard a word about this summit conference. I give her a calculator to practice with for an upcoming test and tell her I'll see her later. I continue on my way to the SPED office, thinking that it's strange she doesn't know about the conference. When I arrive, the office is deserted. After a few minutes, a secretary materializes. I tell her why I'm there and finally, in more than just a bit, one of the SPED caseworkers serendipitously blows in. She then hunts for the assigned caseworker. The correct caseworker now shows her face and I think we're finally getting somewhere.

Is that meeting today? I'm asked. I show her the form. Oh! all right. Let's go find Sabrina, says she.

She's with the substitute teacher in my class now, says me.

Good thing you arranged for one, says she.

Didn't *you* do that? says me.

It's clear to me now that I'm trapped in a sitcom. Without ads, the Nielsen ratings will come in pretty low. But something else occurs to me. My SPED kids, alone in that room, have probably set the school on fire. We hurry up the stairs to my classroom. It's empty. Where are they? We ask around and find out they're probably in the auditorium. I'm not amused. These are my favorite kids and they're being treated like nothing. We track them down in the auditorium where they're sitting happily together shooting the bull. They're enjoying themselves, unaware they've been "dissed" by the school. In my opinion, disaster has been just nearly avoided. I'm not sure of the outcome if they had been left by themselves in the classroom for an extended time. They're not alone in the hall. Regents exams have again taken over many rooms and other classes fill a good third of the auditorium. The caseworker and Sabrina complete the conference right then and there. My presence apparently isn't all that necessary. Both the caseworker and Sabrina dismiss my suggestion that perhaps we might sit where Sabrina will have some privacy. It's not a problem. Now I get it. I'm Jack Nicholson in *One Flew Over the Cuckoo's Nest*. Just one of the patients in this nuthouse.

After the period's over, I drop in the T-L to muse over the human comedy I just witnessed. Yikes! I've forgotten my appointment with the principal and the UFT rep. I plunge down the stairs to find the principal on her way out. Daniel Marsh, who was to be in on the meeting with me, has already left. Princess Linda laughs in my face when I say that it's fine by me to take days off instead of cash compensation for my work overage last term. She's not giving in to anything. At the outset of this accidental farce, I didn't care about the outcome. Now I feel insulted by this porky, incompetent bureaucrat.

In the late afternoon, I drive to my second interview at the parochial school. I meet with the headmistress, or whatever they call her. She's a nun and impresses me immediately as a dedicated educator. She tells me that 90 percent of the parents came last year to parent-teachers' night. I comment how different CBHS would be if we had the same statistic. I also tell her about the problems I'm having at CBHS. Later, it occurs to me that griping about my current circumstances probably isn't the greatest sales technique.

MONDAY, MAY 31—TUESDAY, JUNE 1

Tests Up the Wazoo

Even though we have finals next week, the math department still has to give more tests this week. Nobody knows why. Mr. T. expresses his unhappiness over my impending meeting with Linda. I again offer to call the whole thing off, but he says it's too late for that.

Later, I've forgotten today's staff meeting but luck out by accidentally walking by while it's in progress. I offer some feeble excuse why I'm late. I can tell by Glenn's expression that he doesn't buy it and knows that I'm just absent-minded. The themes center on "our shocking truancy," "the school's breaking up," and how the combo of downsizing and the new schools' taking over the building have caused the math staff to be "scattered to the wind." *Sic transit gloria.* Mr. T. asks us to stay. CBHS isn't reducing the enrollment by all that much. Because so many teachers are leaving on their own accord, he might need to hire instead of fire math faculty. Can he guarantee me I won't get freshmen next year? I ask. No. I think but don't say, "Then I'm outta here."

WEDNESDAY, JUNE 2

Intervisitation #4

In the words of SNL's Roseanna Roseannadanna, "It's always something." And the myriad of somethings everyday at CBHS made me forget to visit other teachers' classes. Now I've got to scramble to meet Mr. T.'s three outings per semester quota. Today, I plop myself down in Bill Kojac's advanced algebra class for juniors and seniors. He also teaches calculus to the few upperclassmen qualified to take it at CBHS. Bill, mustachioed and about 5'8" with graying brown hair and horned-rim glasses, looks like he's come right out of Central Casting to play the part of a high school math teacher. He's served here since 1984. Back then, the neighborhood was Italian-Jewish and they taught Italian in the school. Even Hebrew. Discipline was not an issue, though there were more kids in the school. Some 5,000 he says. Then the neighborhood began to change. The Italians and Jews moved out and blacks and Latinos took their place. The sturdy-looking housing stock still looks fine on the outside. But instead of single families on the inside, there probably are multiple families crowding in there now. The project housing in back of the school was already there, but didn't dominate the feeling of the area.

Says Bill, "CBHS used to be a creampuff school where everybody in the Bronx wanted to go." Then about ten years ago, things started to change and the downward slide accelerated in the last five years. No longer did the school have a roster of bright kids. He feels programming changes brought about lower standards. The better students migrated to other schools.

As I sit down in this class, it takes me exactly three seconds to realize that none of the kids resemble my own teens. They are sitting quietly(!), doing the Do-Now, taking notes, being students for cris-sakes. They're the proven survivors. It occurs to me that Bill's been teaching upperclassmen trig and calculus for so long that he's never had the problems the teachers of today's freshmen face. No wonder he's always so calm. This is what teaching life is like when all the trouble-makers have dropped out of school and the struggling, under-qualified kids have stopped taking any more math. He teaches the maybe 5 per-cent or less of the kids headed for college.

But Bill isn't just taking advantage of the quality kids in the seats in front of him, he's engaging them in a question on the board using ran-dom numbers. The kids generate their own data on a T-83 scientific calculator. Bill posts their numbers one-by-one on the board. Computing their own results and its relevancy to the question draws them in. They're interested. Other math teachers tell me they make a point to sit in on his classes. I'm sorry that I didn't see more of his instruction. All of the new math teachers aspire to have a chance with the better students. And I'm one of them.

No Exit

Later, Kris and five others walk in late for my exam. One girl wants to study first. Everyone has a pencil!

Ahmed shows up, grabs an exam paper from the bottom of the pile, spilling the rest. He demands a calculator. When I ask for his ID, he refuses and tosses the calc back in the box. "You're a real get-along guy, Ahmed," I tell him.

"What's that?" he queries. I shake my head, too preoccupied with getting on with the test to go in for more of his shenanigans.

I decide to try one more time to understand Ahmed. "Tell me the truth, if you can, Ahmed. Why are you failing? I know you could do this math if you tried."

"Personal problems, *Mister Klass*." No sarcasm this time. Just despair. "If my mother came into school, she would tell you to fail me."

He stops talking and just looks helplessly around the room as if he wants to escape. I can't find anything to say, either. We both know he's going to fail my class and we don't want to talk about it. I tried, but I never could find his home number. Nevertheless, I feel I have let him down.

Rod Bonano announces he's coming back next year, although he had planned to go to another school. He wants to spend the year sitting in on Bill Kojac's calculus class. He feels it's not *de rigueur* to ask for Bill's notes, but maybe he'll ask for the syllabus. I decide to ask Bill for one, too. Bill kindly consents. I remind him a few times thereafter. I never do get it.

I go to look for Daniel Marsh in his office. It's time for our appointment with Linda. By coincidence, Linda's secretary is there and tells me the time slot has been changed again.[4]

THURSDAY, JUNE 3

"School Stinks"

emblazoned on Dalia's T-shirt provides my only laugh of the day. Later, for my ongoing outreach program, I call Daphne Buono's home. She's been absent a lot. I'm told her dad died. I feel sick. These kids can't get a Goddamn break. A tide of helplessness and hopelessness rushes over me.

FRIDAY, JUNE 4

Can't Take A Joke

I ask Perry to please sit down in my class. Why? he wants to know. And start taking notes. Why? again. After more of this juvenile "why" routine, I go over-the-top mad and hustle him out. I'm trying to prepare the kids for final exams, and I don't want to put up with nonsense. Also,

---

[4]This kabuki ritual play finally does come to an end. Linda, barely masking a smirk, informs Daniel and me that under the UFT contract rules the clock has run out and she can take no corrective action on my part. Sweeter tears have never been shed by a principal.

maybe my anger management self-improvement program isn't perfected yet. I really didn't want Perry to go. I still have a very small, but finite, hope he can pass. I've been giving him pep talks for weeks now not to quit. This is his third go-around at trying to make it through this course. You can do it, I've been telling him. Now he has an excuse to fail. Crap.

Later in the session, I go over the same algebra problem for maybe the twenty-third time. "You never taught us this," one boy says. I laugh for minutes. The silliness of his remark hits me squarely on the funny bone.

In the T-L, I find I've been frozen out of the copier. Over my limit for the term. Now I can't make sample tests for my sections. I plead my case to Juanquier, the chief copier magistrate, who luckily swings by. Oh, it's for finals? He punches up a few buttons on the giant Rube Goldberg device and I'm in business.

Several teachers warm up to a bull session on educational theory. "Can teachers motivate?" No, we concur. Only sometimes, for a day or two. Marisa says she has to repeat a topic ten times for the kids to get it. They don't know what a square foot is. Her students can only understand if she teaches them one-on-one. Ms. Tottle volunteers that she assigned drawing a portrait for the final exam, but her kids didn't know what "portrait" meant.

"You can only be happy as a teacher if you try to reach the 20 percent," she tells the crowd of teachers. I find it interesting that my 20 percent rule seems to hold for so many of us.

In my UFT professional development group, Jean aches from being kicked by a 6'2" female student. It wasn't intentional. The chorine was just fooling around, kicking her legs up high in the air, and struck Jean by accident. But Rockette routines don't belong in class. Jean has high blood pressure and goes to the nurse. The doctor there won't take her blood pressure. Regulations forbid it and the nurse won't use his instrument. Also against the regs. *Catch-22* was written for life at CBHS.

SATURDAY, JUNE 5

I grade papers all day. Almost no one passes. I'm furious and discouraged. Have I helped anyone this term?

Monday, June 7
Letter from a student to Victor:

Dear Mr. Gallo
You are one of the best teacher I've had. I would like to see you tech for years to come. You've gave me confidence to stand up to people and say, "Your damn right I'm smart." The only thing I'll ask you is why does it smell evertime I've been in you room. There was a few times it smell o.k.

Thank you
Sign Anonymous

It's the start of finals week. Amber says only two kids passed her test. I thank her for letting me know I'm not the lone ranger on this desolate mesa.

Casey spies a cartoon of a plane crashing into the Empire State Building drawn by one of his students. He tells Mr. T. about it, who in turn tells him to go to Room 135 where he expected to find school counselors. Instead, he finds police detectives who come into his classroom and uncover fireworks on the illustrator. Last Friday afternoon, firecrackers had gone off in the classroom next door to him. A coincidence? Nothing was done to the boy, as far as Casey knows.

Ms. Tottle, whom I call Helen by now, tells me that the teacher she respects the most teaches at Lehman College. He told her last night that we can only teach 20 percent of the kids in city schools. There it is once more. The 20 percent rule.

TUESDAY, JUNE 8

Intervisitation #5

I take a seat in the back of Dr. Rod Bonano's second semester algebra class for freshman. Rod has a Ph.D. in pharmacology. He worked on computer-aided drug design at the New Jersey Institute of Technology before changing careers. It's his third year teaching.

Rob's a focused and soft-spoken sort. He doesn't even use notes for putting the problems and solutions on the board. He's also learned to write sort of backwards on the blackboard so that he's always facing his students. I can learn a lot from him. These kids are enrolled in one of the special programs called College Now. I notice two of my better-behaved students from last semester in the room. One of them waves at me. It's Brandi, who gave me a tie for Christmas. Later, Rod tells me that if kids aren't quite passing, but close, they will pass his course, but will have to go to after-school tutoring next year. That's what all my kids should be doing right now.

In my own classes, I give sample problems for the final that are identical to the test. I don't care whether I'm making it too easy or not. I'm hungry for some success. When I tell Elton he never works in class, he puts his arm around me and says affectionately, "You're my nigger from way back." I could definitely stay here at CBHS if more of the children were like him.

A Final Moment

In my 4th period, at first Ahmed looks calm then worried. "I have personal problems," he admits again to me privately, as if I didn't know that already. We don't speak to each other again. He doesn't even show up for the second day of final exams.

Back in the T-L, my whining about my failure this year inspires Rob Simmons to console me. "We should view teaching as a collective effort and not measure ourselves by our own inconclusive results." Very sound reasoning. But he's had a few successful years logged in. Eating lunch here, I'm sitting next to Rob, Victor, and Joel Farmer. For me, the wheel has come full circle since meeting them at the faculty outing last summer. I consider once more the practical beat-the-system advice of Victor, the cynical hopelessness of Joel, and the enduring we-can-do-better thoughtfulness of Rob.

WEDNESDAY, JUNE 9

Intervisitation #6

Regular classes are ending soon and I squeak in my last required visit. I decide to sit in on Glenn's class, even though he's not feeling up to par. He's just going over the final exam. Glenn's ailing—gout, a cold, and some kind of metabolic disorder have got him down. It's a fourth semester algebra class for sophomores, but it seems more like the playground of last semester. Same old thing with kids diddling around in their usual transgressions. Nevertheless, Glenn knows his material and plows dutifully through it, including the administration-required and also ineffective cooperative learning groups.

Glenn reacts to the kids the same way I do, or used to anyhow—a combination of scowls and stern rejoinders. This potion doesn't have any better magic effect in his class than in mine. Some kids read magazines, even though I'm sitting near them. I'm angry just watching them. I want to shout, "Don't you know he's put the exam on a silver platter?" Glenn's effort at preparing them a sample test is wasted on almost all of them. A few girls diligently working together provide the only exceptions.

Overall, it's a useful session for me. The experienced teachers I observed before never indulged themselves with lofty witticisms for their own amusement. I make a silent pledge: "From now on, I'm going to try to keep my not-too *bon mots* to myself." Glenn's sarcasm sails over their heads in content, but the kids catch the drift of the negativity. I realize how guilty I am of the same mistake. Witty cheap shots just maintain a confrontational atmosphere. Naturally, only compliments appear in my written comments. I know Glenn will improve with experience. I hope I do, too.

THURSDAY, JUNE 10

It's Finals Day

and teachers cram into the air-conditioned T-L. Overall, the mood is joyful. But I'm having an anxiety attack. I should have taught more to the final. I expect Kris, pain in the rear though she is, to pass the test. During the exam, she asks for hints on how to do a problem I was sure she understood. Now I'm scared.

When I arrive early to my last class, Helen stands there, shaking her head in disgust. "This is the hardest job in the world. The kids are abusive. I wouldn't call them animals because animals don't behave that way." I don't ask for an explanation as she abruptly wheels her cart of art supplies out the door.

FRIDAY, JUNE 11

A Saving Grace

In my SPED class, Tristan comes to me with a question while I'm working with another kid at the blackboard! This is perhaps my singular triumph of the year. He's a smart boy, but won't say much. Throughout the term, he's refused to go to the board or answer questions. I remember he whispered to me that he has emotional problems. Still, I feel we have developed a rapport.

In the T-L, I strike up a conversation with Jesu Fiore, a history teacher who's spent the last twenty-eight years teaching, twelve of them at CBHS. We talk about the newly arrived English-as-a-Second-Language students. "ESL kids start out as good students, but become corrupted by the other kids. I can tell because by the end of their third year, they have become failures, too."

MONDAY, JUNE 14

One Last Kiss

My last finals today. Several kids sashay in late. In the SPED class, Carlton wants to know how to use his calculator. Great, now he wants to learn.

After waiting patiently to hear back from the parochial school about the position I applied for, I finally call first and leave a message for the headmistress. In return she leaves a message on my answering machine, "Larry (the accountant) is not retiring. Thank you." Click. Teaching is more of a hardball game than I thought. I had expected more courtesy from a charitable parochial girls' school where I had two interviews. And it took forever to drive there into the city. Too bad. The thought of having my own classroom was tantalizing.

TUESDAY, JUNE 15

Get Serious

Linda shows her face at a UFT meeting. She stands erect and immobile, her arms folded across her chest. Her frowns aren't all that inspiring, either. As a troop leader, she makes Jimmy Carter look like Napoleon. She discusses new school hiring issues. And from now on, there will be thirty-four students in a room. Nice to see her.

With finals over, we the math mavens now proctor Regents exams. Amber, my morning companion in the T-L, trots in during an exam and passes out lollipops. But only to her kids. I'm irritated by this blatant display of favoritism. Testing is the only time when I see the kids intent and serious. If only they would bring some of this focus to class, they could transform their lives—and the teachers'.

In the T-L, I talk to Lana Martano, my SPED paraprofessional. "What could I have done?"

She's sweet and reassuring, "You did everything you could."

We both thought more kids would pass. For a short time, everyone was clicking—even Sabrina. But the effort and concentration faded with the springtime sun. Knowledge flowed out of their minds, like flour through a sieve—not a clump left. We sigh over Jason and Carlton.

"They could have done it—especially Carlton," Lana muses. But his efforts evanesced as he jived and wiggled his shoulders daily to a beat and rhythm heard only in his head. The kids wanted to do better, but not sincerely. "How about Dalia? You passed her, right?"

"Didn't quite make it." Now I'm squirming. Dalia was borderline and I could have given her a 65 without a thought.

"You should pass her, Ric. She worked hard and did homework."

I don't know what I was thinking. Here I'm looking to save kids and Dalia really tried. After all the school she missed during her suspension, she still scored better than most. Lana, Dalia's guardian angel, saves the day for her. I change the grade to passing. I'm mad at myself for almost missing the opportunity.

The SPEDs now have the highest average scores of all my classes. I talk to the woman in the SPED office who met with Sabrina before. My passing students want out of the program. They're superior to my "normal" kids. Can they get out? Maybe. She'll see about it.

WEDNESDAY, JUNE 16

A Remarkable Prognostication

I tally my finals' grades. In my fourth semester class, only a quarter of the students scored over 50 on day two of the exam. The other teachers don't have much better results. In the T-L, as Victor grades papers, he tells me he failed all the kids in his repeater class. It's never happened to him before. The one kid that came close had nineteen absences. Victor knew he would have to defend a passing grade so he failed him.

Tenure headlines as today's topic in the T-L. In the new schools, teachers can be hired by committees instead of by tenure. A scary proposition for some of the teachers. They don't like the rules being changed on them at this late date.

I proctor a Math A Regents exam. Most prior ones had a multipoint trajectory problem. A few days ago, Juanquier told me he's certain that the test will require constructing a geometric figure instead. He's dead right. Was it just a lucky guess?

THURSDAY, JUNE 17

Keeping Cool

The math department gathers for the semiannual ritual of grading the New York math Regents exams in a hot room without A/C. "Why can't we get the air-conditioned room across the hall?" echoes through the humid air. Victor, with his New York can-do bent, promptly secures a key to the locked igloo facing our furnace. Several heat prostration deserters duck out with him. The exodus triggers consternation and veiled threats from Sueann, the department's dominatrix and acknowledged boffo Regents examiner.

"We could be cited by the New York Regents Board for moving papers from room to room," she protests to the growing number of teachers assembling in the nascent Hall of Revolutionaries. Keeping my head down, I have already quietly taken a seat directly under the A/C vent in the rear of the platformed room.

Since multiple looks are required, as part of the grading process each examiner is supposed to initial the scores. When Keith and others forget to put down their John Hancock, a steady stream of irritability flows from Sueann. Her petulance keeps the day offkilter.

A student's response on one test lightens the mood. "I don't know much 'bout math but whatever my teacher Mr. Amigas says is right, is right cause he's the man." Cortez enjoys the rest of the day as the graders' official "The Man" man.

Hail to the Chief

Later that afternoon, I attend a rally for the UFT president, Randi Weingarten. Daniel Marsh takes the podium. Dressed to the nines, he introduces our union leader.

Randi warms up the crowd with, "We're working a six-hour, forty-minute day next year. Considering who we are dealing with, nothing is going to be perfect." I already work so many hours voluntarily I've never paid attention to this detail, but the other teachers seem to know the significance. She wants us to approve the new agreement on scheduling. Weingarten is dynamic—alternatively crouching and gesturing. Overall, a crowd pleaser for the union set.

She rallies her constituency: Mayor Michael Bloomberg is cooking the books by holding back third graders this year so that next year's citywide fourth grade tests will look better. "He's a guy who gets a little ditty in his head about something he thinks is about education." She describes Joel Klein and Bloomberg as men who combine arrogance and ignorance. Because they were successful in their careers, they think they know something about educating, she continues. They garnered $50 million in grants from the Gates Foundation but "they know shit about running schools. They're total creeps and we hate them." So much for niceties. She goes on: "Why make them look good by cooperating? We could fight and try to get them defeated in November." I'm shocked by her raw language, but overall pleased getting treated to a real union foot-thumping speech. She successfully piques the crowd's blood thirst for administrative meat.[5]

She also proclaims that CBHS will pass from this veil of tears, unless . . . unless SHE, our president, takes up the holy grail to fight for CBHS, despite the ever-growing new schools within its perimeter.

Now the bad news. There's no parental involvement in CBHS. The parents no longer hold monthly meetings in this Bronx school because no one comes. "Ten parents showed up at the last one." Brooklyn community support and political support capped overcrowding in that borough. She has her own ditty, it seems. "I've been singing to myself the Mick Jagger song. 'If you can't get what you want, get what you need.'" It's good to know you can count on Mick when you need him.

Daniel Marsh terminates the meeting suddenly and pushes forward a rushed vote to support Randi's efforts to keep CBHS alive. I was the solitary nay vote. CBHS will just become a dumping ground for the losers, making the new schools seem better than they are. Then the administration will use the certain disaster to prove the union's incompetence. I decide to explain my vote to a few of the lingering teachers gathering their things in the T-L.

FRIDAY, JUNE 18

Vip Him

I don't believe in corporal punishment. I've never struck my own two kids, even though they ask for it plenty sometimes. I was spanked three times and remember each vividly.

---

[5] The UFT finally ended their two and a half year contract dispute in October '05, coincidently just before Mayor Bloomberg's reelection.

*Once by my mom, when I was three and crossed a busy street
alone. She cried bitterly afterwards. Once by my dad, when I
was four and turned the sprinkler on him and his new silk suit.
I never knew he could run so fast. And the last time, when I was
five and created a rocket out of match heads and aluminum foil.
Dad didn't appreciate my setting the launch pad (my train table
in the basement) on fire. The worst part of the episode was that
the device just exploded and didn't go anywhere. Working on
Apollo finally satisfied my rocketry yen.*

*My grandfathers weren't confrontational either. Except—
when Dad was a boy, a teacher sent a note home asking that
he bring his father to school for a talk. Walking back to school
together at the appointed time, my dad exhorted my Russian-
born grandfather in Yiddish, "My teacher is an anti-Semite.
Don't let him get away with anything. Tell him off good,
Pop." My grandfather just listened, saying nothing. When
they arrived in the classroom, my grandfather pointed to my
father and said only these words to the teacher, "Vip him, vip
him, vip him."*

*I wouldn't dream of hitting these kids at CBHS or even
putting a finger on them. I won't even touch a female student
on the arm. In the faculty meeting today, they repeat the rule
that yelling at or even raising one's voice to the kids is legally
considered corporal punishment. Wait a second! Isn't that
going a bit too far? Here's the problem. We can't give deten-
tions at CBHS. I've asked around and no one seems to know
why. Some speculate that there's no money to provide for
oversight by the teachers (they must be paid for that by union
contract) or for a detention room. Others speculate that many
kids have jobs after school and their families depend on the
money.*

If, au contraire, we boot les enfants out of class for mis-behavior, they're recycled back in a flash by Security—faster than I can inhale a croissant. In a 3,000+-enrollment school, keeping all the disrupters in a penalty pen would require an Alcatraz. Even if the kids are suspended, they'll probably come and hang out anyway. Many of them already cut classes and hide in the varied passageways. The wise guy kids know that teachers are powerless, with the result that discipline in this school always borders at a dangerous level. Our rules and laws meant to protect children seem to have gone haywire. In my opinion, these kids have a right to be disciplined. A right for their own good.

MONDAY, JUNE 21

Getting Pumped

We have to re-grade the tests examined by two of the math teachers. Bibulous O'Malley, soon to leave for Ireland and, judging from his breath, already celebrating his return to the land of leprechauns, and Farmer, an endless administration critic, made multiple mistakes. True to form, Mr. T. casts no blame and only quietly mentions why to the teachers who had found the errors.

I've noticed that Juanquier's students had gotten higher marks than they deserved on the tests and were graded by Juanquier himself. I internally debate if I should say something to Mr. T. when Mr. T. announces that Juanquier will no longer mark his own students' tests. Simmons then complains to Mr. T. about his own findings on the matter and I gingerly join in, saying that Juanquier's test results are inflated.

During the recount, Will Gerard reveals that he had caught the soon-to-retire Toni-screamer re-marking exams to make the school look better. And something else. Toni Harmony is a close buddy of

Juanquier's and she's on the New York State committee that designs the Regents tests. I remember how Juanquier sure guessed right about the multipoint question on geometric constructions instead of the usual trajectory problem.

I later sneak out to have a job interview with Nina Rueno downstairs. Nina had been running the night school and now she's being given an opportunity to run her own show as principal of Corona Academy High School, a new experimental high school funded by the Gates Foundation. Nina, a late 50-ish, no-nonsense type, combines a motherly attitude with a cleric's air of propriety. During the interview, kids come in and out, treating her like she was their mom. "They're all babies," she tells me.

Nina recast her career in her thirties to become a teacher. She was the first president of her community college alumni association. I'm excited by the prospect of creating a new environment with no freshmen—and my own classroom! It doesn't matter to me that the entire school will be assembled this summer, entirely out of trailers. Darwin comes in the door during our conversation, obviously to interview, too, and not too happy to see me there. I want to tell her that even if you don't take me, don't take him. Darwin's openly negative and hateful of the kids—I certainly know how that could happen. Still, I don't think he's cut out for dealing with Bronx kids—even less so than I. Nevertheless, I keep my own counsel on the subject.

I end the day by giving gifts of jam to Katherine and Mr. T. I point out to Mr. T. that I avoided selections prepared with liqueurs, knowing that he's a devout Muslim. I think he was genuinely touched by the consideration. He surprises me by suddenly rising from his chair and giving me a hug.

TUESDAY, JUNE 22

Un-Surplussed

The end is near, and winding down in the teacher's lounge I read a note from Mr. T.:

> Please be advised that you're tentatively scheduled to teach the following math classes for Fall 2004 Term.
>
> Classes:
>
> ME3
>
> M$1
>
> Regents - prep
>
> Your tentative session is: period 3 to period 10.

I'm surprised, considering that a couple of months ago I assumed I was getting canned. The proposed scheduled isn't really that grim. Regents prep is more of the same. I'm sure I could do a better job of it next time. ME3 means teaching a new course for me, intermediate algebra. At least I wouldn't be bored teaching the same thing over and over again. M$1 is the killer, the nefarious code for a freshman course. Mr. T. knows my aversion to the freshmen. Maybe he thinks that teaching just one of the villains' courses sandwiched between two others would appease me. Or maybe he just didn't care—someone's got to teach the *Lord of the Flies* ruffians, and I'm still at the bottom of the tenure totem pole.

Victor amuses a small crowd with anecdotes, including one about when he used up all his sick days to go to Atlantic City. He ran into a CBHS female math teacher at the dice table. Incredible, according to Victor. Women don't even play craps!

Mr. T. intentionally introduces me to three teaching interns, including one poor sucker from Bangladesh. Mr. T. knows I won't sugar-coat the environment here, but that I want to make a difference.

Bangladesh Sucker: "They (the little darlings) do show respect to the teacher, don't they?"

Former Sucker (me): "Absolutely not. It's infuriating." What fun registering the shocked look on his face. He isn't sure whether to believe me until we adjourn to the library, sit down, and I read them the riot act about teaching kids in the Bronx.

Serena Hindar and her guidance counselor hunt me down in the library. I'm in no mood to see one of my flunkees. I'm told she's headed for Long Island University with only mean Mr. Klass standing in her way. She scored a 62 on my final and handed in squat homework. I put on my no-way, tough-guy stance with both of them but quickly cave in and change her grade to passing. "She did do pretty well the second marking period," I tell myself mentally, licking the wounds of my lowered standards.

I mosey over to Mr. T.'s office to nose around about the other teachers' final grades. We're each supposed to give an overall pass/fail accounting of our classes. It seems Juanquier has cornered all the scholars in the school and passed 100 percent of his seraphs. He helped his stats along a bit. His tests are identical to prior Regents exams and he uses the same raw score of 37 out of 84 points (a 44 percent score) to pass them. In other words, he feels that since the official Regents exams scale up the scores, he can do the same thing! Who can blame him?

I head back to the T-L and find Glenn filling out certificates of honor for the brighter dummies in his sections. Supposedly, a student has to get a 90 or better average for the cert—that rules out all my kids.

"Don't be such a tight ass," Glenn yaps at me. "These kids need a little encouragement." I feel sufficiently shamed to ink a paper medal for Stephanie Whitby and Jocelyn Cortero. In the burbs, Stephanie would be on the honors bench—not a real player. But here in the Bronx, she's one of the few bright stars. Jocelyn, I must say, tried hard as all get out to do well—struggled isn't too strong a word. Hardly an honors candidate, but what the hay?

WEDNESDAY, JUNE 23

More Backsliding

Results of the Regents grades are printed. I'm surprised that several students of mine whom I failed actually passed the Regents test. On second thought, I'm not so surprised. While the actual score is out of a potential of 87 points, the reported scores are "scaled" so that barely a 40 percent score is now considered 55 percent, which already should be a failing grade. The politics of the entire system could not be more transparent. Obviously, New York can't fail the majority of its New York City high school students, thereby setting itself up for claims of racism, incompetence, educational terrorism—just for starters.

Mr. T. has never interfered in the grading but does indicate that if teachers want to reverse a failing grade to a D, mindful of a student passing the Regents exam, it's OK with him. In light of this policy, I backslide and change Zaire Rijak's borderline F to a D. Zaire was one of the few quiet, respectful kids—so why not?

Now comes Dais Sulvado, all drenched in tears, charging down the halls after me in hot pursuit. "My father is coming from Santo Domingo with an illegal passport just for my graduation. If he finds out I'm not graduating, he'll kill me. I want to go to Berkeley College (essentially a secretarial school not remotely to be confused with the Berkeley in danger of plunging into the ocean with the rest of the Bay Area) and study accounting."

This bit of news about Dais' college aspirations hits me like Jean Harlow's revelation, "I read a book the other day," struck Marie Dressler in *Dinner At Eight*—I nearly fall over. I enlist the help of Glenn. She's also enrolled in his math class and must convince us both, since he also failed her. I decide to play this one politically correct, so I tell Dais that I must confer on the matter. Here go I to her guidance counselor.

I'm only one degree of separation from Dais' dad ducking into the U.S. illegally. Am I an accomplice? As I wend my way to the guidance office, my objective is clear—swindle the counselor into begging me to change the grade, leaving me with a clear conscience and no responsibility.

"I'm glad to defer the decision to the guidance counselor's office. I certainly don't want to stand in the way of my student's progress," says me, the demure and understanding math teacher.

But the counselor was too cagey. No way will she even gently twist my arm. "The decision is entirely yours, Mr. Klass," comes forth her steely reply. Clearly, she's heard plenty of appeals by the time I drop in. CBHS is definitively a CYA institution. No bloody way was she going to let me off the hook and hang on it herself.

Dejectedly, I head back to tell Glenn the bad news—we have to make the decision ourselves. Using very bad judgment, we debate the matter—to fail or not to fail—openly in the T-L, to the amusement of the senior staff hiding from their own failed delinquents. Victor in particular takes delight in our dilemma. "What a bunch of wimps. Can't stand the pressure, huh?"

Glenn and I take our predicament outside to the hall. "She failed. She never did homework," I seize the verbal offensive.

"Not for me, either," Glenn sighs agreeably.

With Talmudic logic, I now take the other side. "But she does want to go to college. Who are we to say no?"

"You've got a point there," Glenn nods again in agreement. "So what do we do?"

What we do is follow the noble tradition of CBHS—cave in and let tear-soaked Dais go on with her life at Berkeley College. I hope she graduates there without having to beg for it. Later in the T-L, Glenn and I pay the consequences by running the gauntlet of cackles from the veterans for folding our cards.

Nina R. wants me in the new school. Hooray! No more freshmen! I reach my goal—flee the moronic, infantile, uncivilized, and barbaric wildlings. Later in the day, I drive by the still-undeveloped site. The muddy field sits sandwiched between a South Bronx post office wrapped in barbed wire and South Bronx High School. Overall, the neighborhood's dismal but could be worse with some new housing construction underway nearby.

The Great Escape

I bump into Elton. He's being mainstreamed and is escaping the SPED program. The same for Cory, Jerry, and Dalia. *Cuckoo's Nest* comes to mind again. Randall Patrick Murphy, the ex-con in the movie, frees the other inmates. I've done the same (including losing my mind in the process?). The year hasn't been for nothing.

Before lunch, I run into Collin Hardy. I'm forever wearing my hair coat. Today's self-flagellation is no exception.

"I just didn't reach many kids this year," I complain, fishing for a little sympathy.

"If I reach one child a year, I'm a success," he confides.

A rush of envy sweeps through me. All his kids passed the Regents exams. He teaches in one of the small new schools upstairs—a shepherd for a superior flock. Still, he strikes me as a perfect role model to teach here. He stands out with his braided hair and elegant English Guinea accent. In short, a cool guy. I don't have enough hair for cornrows like his. On the other hand, maybe these boys and girls in the Bronx will need to get along with all of society. Maybe it's good for them to be acquainted with a mix of styles and colors. It's the end of the year and I've come to no conclusion on this subject.

Goodbye and Good Luck

The end of year luncheon starts out on a sour note. An announcement is made: After twenty-one years at CBHS, Bill Kojac is scrambling aboard one of the new schools. Another death knell.

A chord of similar notes rings out. Toni, everybody's favorite incubus, is leaving our choir as well. Several of her retired pals come for fond farewells. Still others, including me, aren't unhappy to see her go. Victor tells the whole congregation a revealing story about how she demanded one of the lockers in her classroom for herself. Glenn comments that in complimenting her, her friends sprinkle in stories about how competitive and combative she is. Even Santino offers, "I often had to restrain her." "Good riddance" is my own thought.

Since no one else thinks of it, I decide to offer a few words of thanks to Mr. T. He was an electrical engineer, taught school for five years, plus spent the last two years as an assistant principal in mathematics. I go a little bit out on a limb and liken his excellence to being comparable to the head of General Motors. Rob Simmons meets this remark with an especially unsupportive glance. He later tells me that in his Wall Street days he personally knew the chairman of GM—Mr. T. is *no* head of General Motors. In my conclusion, I repeat what Mr. T. says frequently to us, "We think about one thing only—what is best for the students."

FRIDAY, JUNE 25

A Change for the Better?

In all, I changed five grades from failing to a passing 65 as a result of their Regents' marks. One element the passing students all had in common is that they hadn't devoted their lives to making mine miserable. I'm not a complete wuss, however, and fill out a form entitled SUBJECT

FAILURE FOR CANDIDATES FOR GRADUATION for four kids to justify failing graduating seniors. I really like one of them, Norton. But he failed all his tests, did nearly zed homework, and didn't even show up for the final exams. What can I do?

One other grade I didn't change was Blaze's. She got a 72 on the Regents but was borderline pass/fail in my class. I even filled out the form to change her grade, but started discussing the change with Glenn seated next to me in the T-L. We're surrounded by other teachers doing the same thing—caving in.

So Glenn asks, "How was her homework?"

"Not much."

"Attendance?"

I look in my log, "Thirty-one absences."

"What? Are you kidding? Change *her* grade?"

So much for my passing Blaze.

MONDAY, JUNE 28

Linda's Last Love Letter

In my mailbox, a message from our leader greets me. Besides thanking the staff for our efforts, she writes,

> As we look towards next year, I know that I can count on your support in our continuing efforts to make Central Bronx High School the School of Choice for the Bronx!"

I start to tear up this sad joke but stick it in my clipboard instead. I might want to save it in case I ever write a book.

Also a note from Amber.

> Ric –
>
> Thanks for hanging out with me in the teachers' lounge at ungodly hours of the day. Hope to see you as much next year.
>
> ♥
>
> Amber

The teachers meet for final goodbyes and a last-day conference. The Math A Regents results are out—76 percent achieved a score of 55 or more compared with 77 percent last January. Fifty percent of the kids scored a 65 or better on the Math B test. The scores and percentages of the Math A test are almost entirely bogus since the grades are adjusted up from a completely failing score. The Math B results, on the other hand, might be more realistic. When one takes into account that only the better kids even take Math B, the fact that 50 percent of them could get a passing score probably makes sense. Mr. Rhoda laughs when telling us they admitted a new student just two weeks ago. Over-the-counter kids with minutes to go on the clock!

With my insides feeling hollowed out, the school year ends with both a bang and a whimper. What have I learned this year?

Ric's Rules of Teaching Urban High School Underclassmen

Rule #1: Most of the kids have the intellectual firepower to learn—they just can't/won't.

Rule #2: Math teachers of freshmen (including failed older kids) spend most of their time waiting/hoping for the kids to grow up. They're *de facto* social workers without the proper training and (often) lack the proper disposition.

Rule #3: Teachers can reach 20 percent of the kids—80 percent won't/can't listen, even for a few minutes.

Rule #4: The 80 percent who won't/can't learn should be classified special education kids with corresponding educational resources afforded them. They suffer from a number of maladies: ADD/ADHD, no responsible adult at home, missing parents, drug abuse (their own or their parents'), no place to study, sleep deprivation from after-school jobs, and/or too much TV. They should be treated with care.

Rule #5: Small schools are a nice luxury, but what we really need are small classes. Fallout: The economies of scale lacking in small schools will eventually force us to phase them out.

Rule #6: It's not the school administrators or teachers' union—it's the home life and environment of the kids, stupid.

Rule #7: Kids have the right to be educated to live a productive life. That may not mean going to college. It does mean knowing how to write a check, do a home budget, shop intelligently, and learn job skills. It doesn't necessarily mean knowing how to solve an exponential equation.

Rule #8: Kids have a right to be disciplined.

Rule #9: Kids have a right to have their parents/legal guardian be legally responsible to make them act decently—maybe even make them do their homework.

Rule #10: Fundamentally, urban education is social work with the imparting of knowledge only a desirable byproduct. What is required is an entire infrastructure addressing behavior modification, family dynamics, socialization into a civil society, and anger management. We need teams of experienced social workers to help these kids adjust to the inevitable process of growing up and facing the world. We all desperately need kids to buy in. When they do, they will learn, gladly.

On the Way Out

of the building for the last time, I stop at my mailbox. In it, I find this letter,

> From Ketchum Saunders
> Dear Mr. Klass,
>
> this is to an old teacher who bin in Central for as long as thirteen years teaching boring ass math, and the way he is teaching is easy to me. He is funny too so I never really sleep in his class. He teaches real slow too so I can understand it. When students dont cooperate he runs quickly out the room screaming for security like someone got killed. he kicks them out so others can learn and he is never absent.

I needed this note. Now I'm eager for next fall. It will be nirvana teaching at Corona Academy High School—just kids determined to start over. And I'm just the right man for the job.

Aren't I?